TABLE ◆ OF ◆ CONTENTS

DOWNLOAD YOUR FILES

Downloading your files is simple. To access your digital files, please go to the last page of this book and follow the instructions.

For technical assistance, please email: info@vaulteditions.com

Copyright
Copyright © Vault Editions Ltd 2025.

Bibliographical Note

This book is a new work created by Vault Editions Ltd.

ISBN: 978-1-922966-69-8

MUTANT RAT

Pro tip: Emphasise the arched back to create tension

Draw a strong curved line running from the nose over the back and down to the tail to define the creature's silhouette. This arched line gives the mutant rat an aggressive posture and helps you align the limbs around a clear, dynamic flow. It's an easy way to unify the pose and communicate its threatening presence.

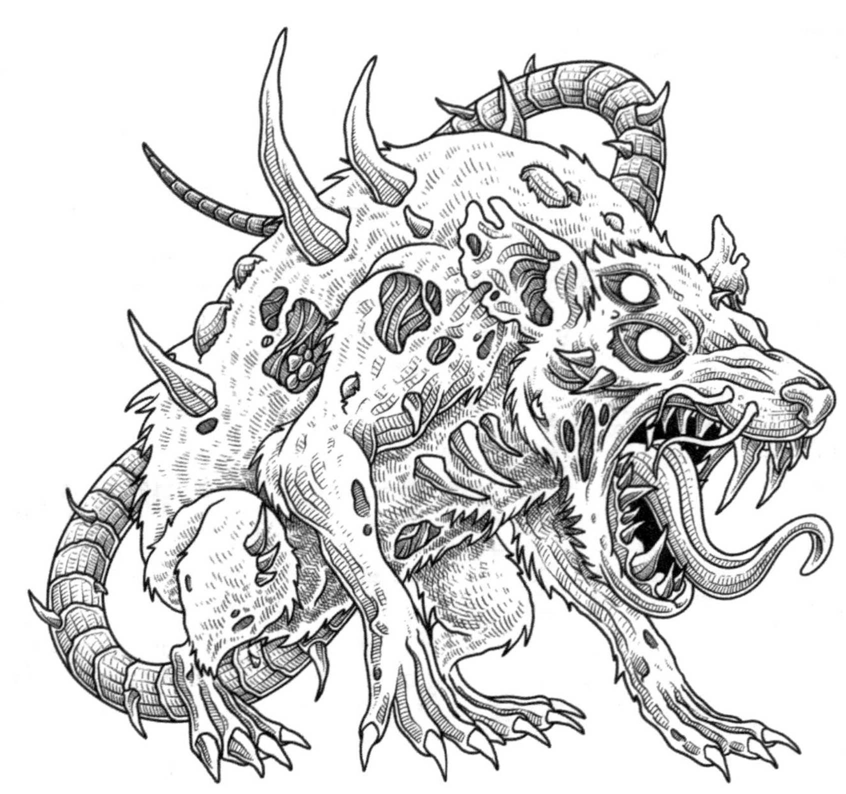

01

02

03

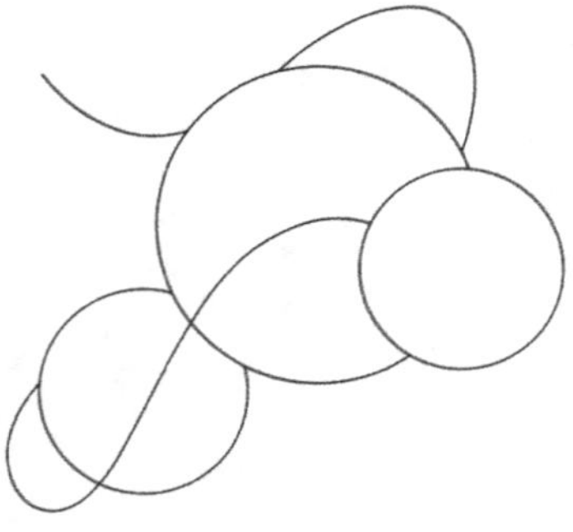

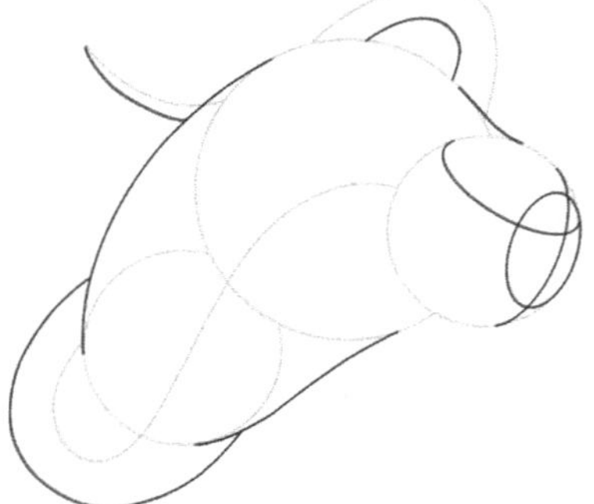

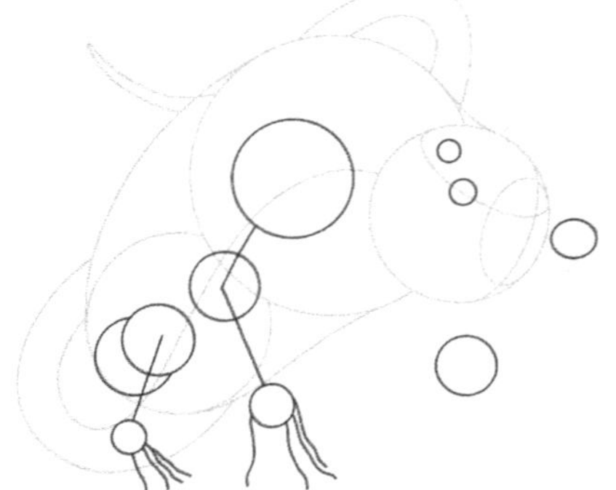

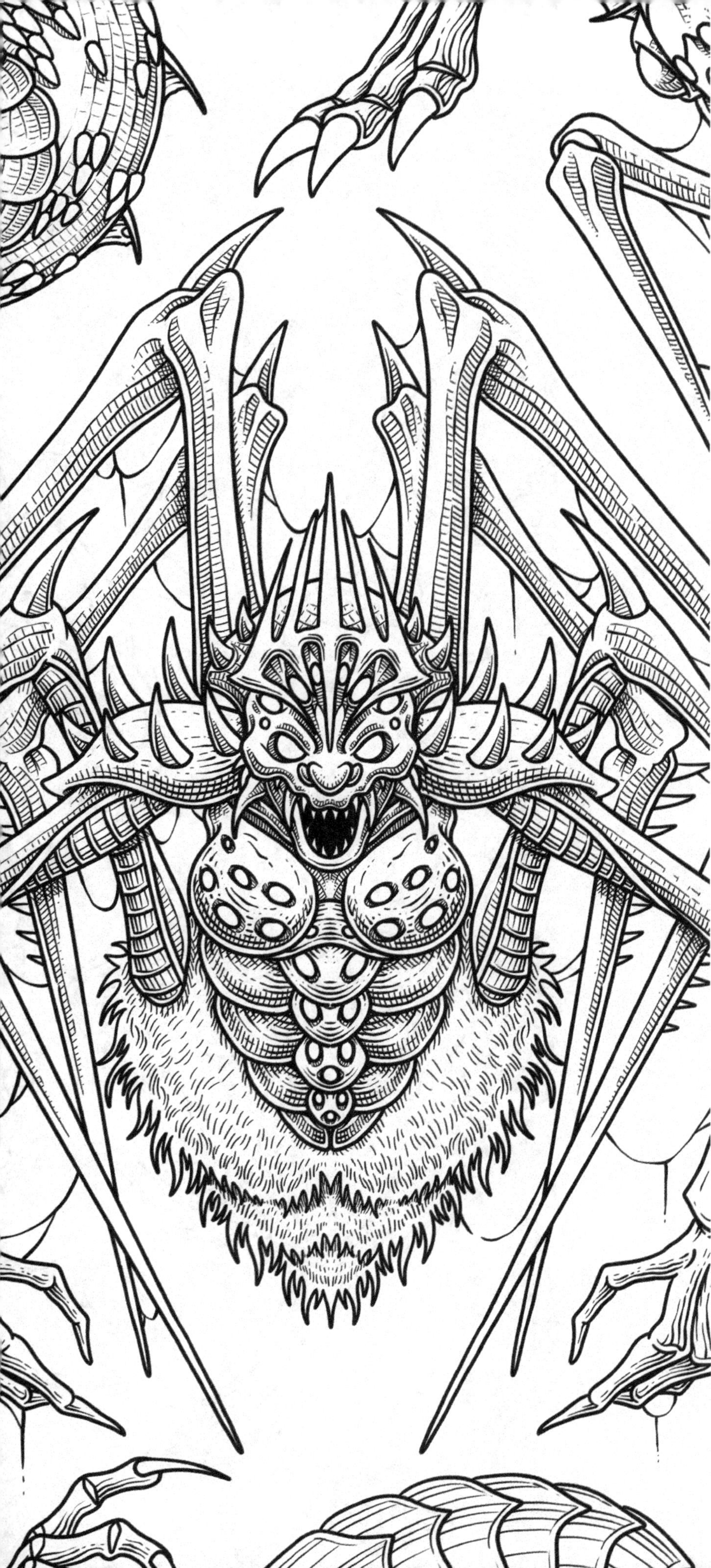

HOW TO DRAW
MONSTERS & BEASTS

A HELPFUL MANUAL FOR
ARTISTS AND DESIGNERS

STEP BY STEP

HAND DRAWN
UNIQUE 40 DESIGNS
BEST QUALITY

EDITIONS
Vault

INTRODUCTION

Monsters and beasts have fascinated artists and storytellers for thousands of years. From ancient myths to modern fantasy, these creatures embody power, imagination, and the unknown. *How to Draw Monsters & Beasts* is your ultimate step-by-step guide to creating 40 extraordinary designs inspired by legends, folklore, and pure invention.

Discover how to draw iconic figures like the centaur, griffin, and phoenix, alongside contemporary creatures such as zombies, swamp dwelling monsters, mutant rats, aliens, and more. Using the Vault Editions 12-step drawing process, this book breaks complex designs into simple, achievable stages that help you build confidence, refine technique, and unleash your creativity.

Each creature offers a new challenge, teaching anatomy, movement, and expression through dynamic forms and detailed features. You'll learn how to use texture, silhouette, and gesture to give your monsters life and personality, and gain the skills and confidence to invent your own original designs.

Whether you're a tattoo artist, illustrator, concept artist, or fantasy enthusiast, *How to Draw Monsters & Beasts* is both a practical guide and a source of creative inspiration. Explore your imagination, push your drawing skills further, and bring your own world of monsters to life.

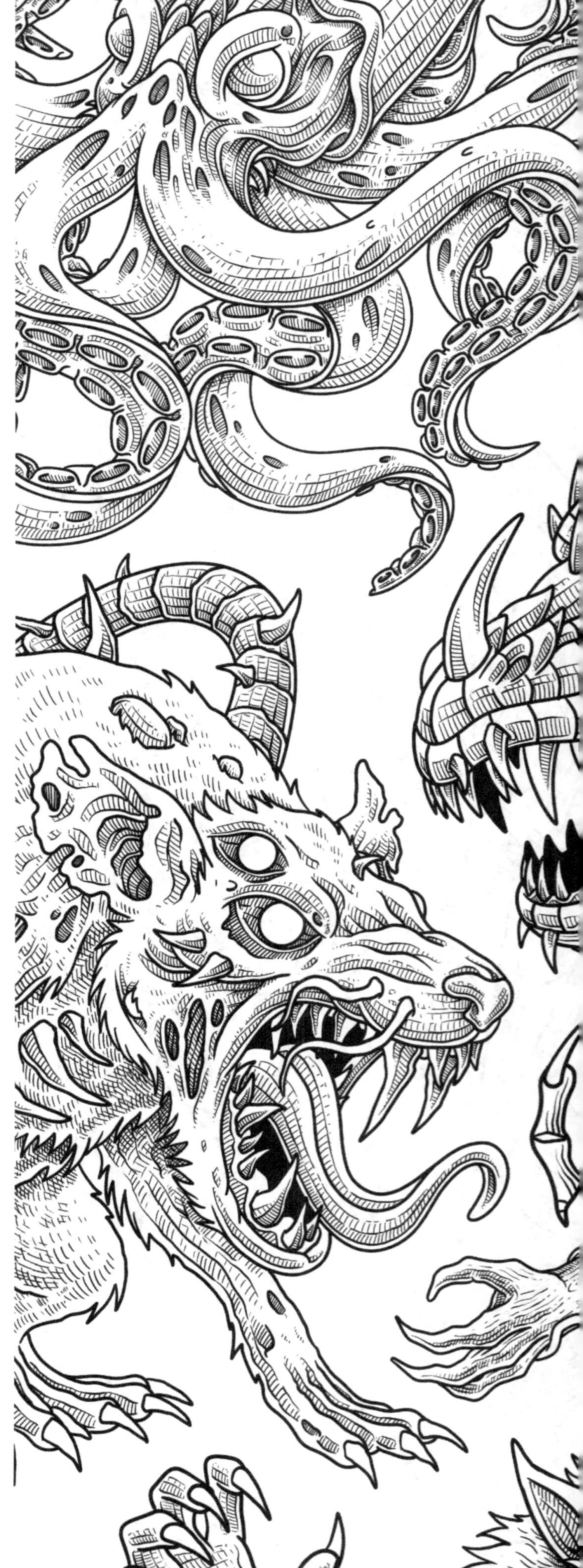

04

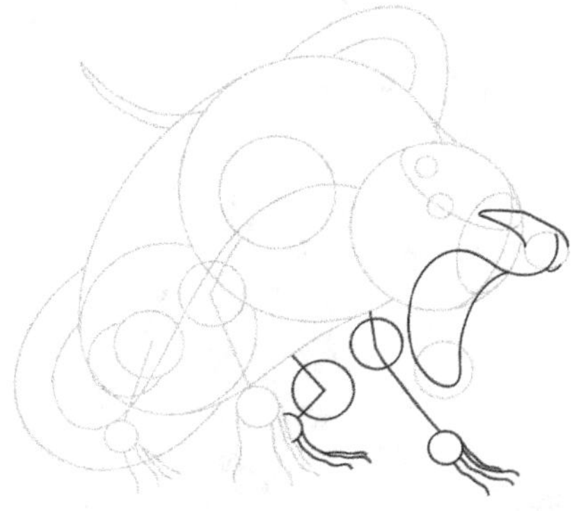

05

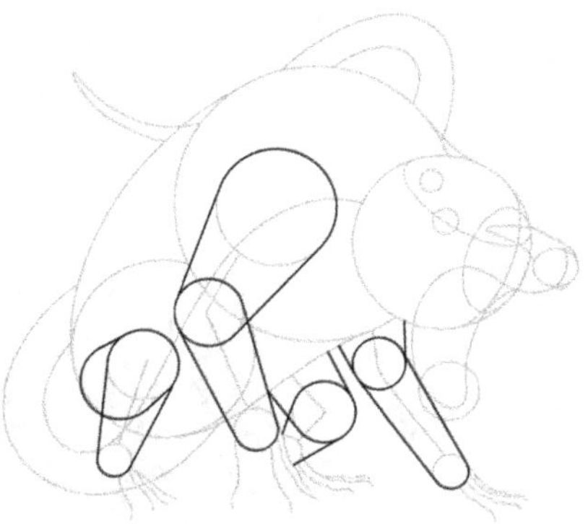

06

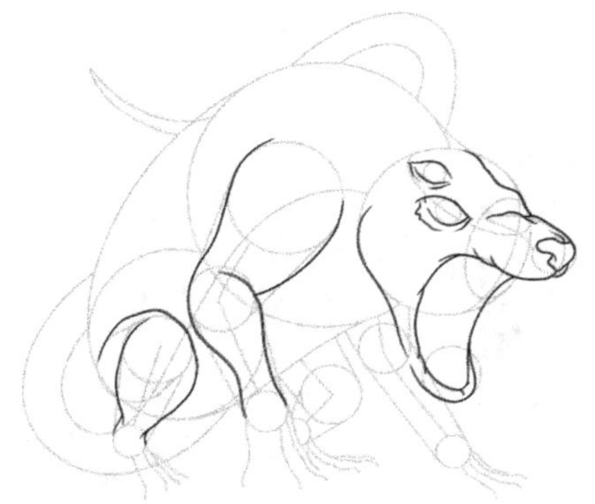

07

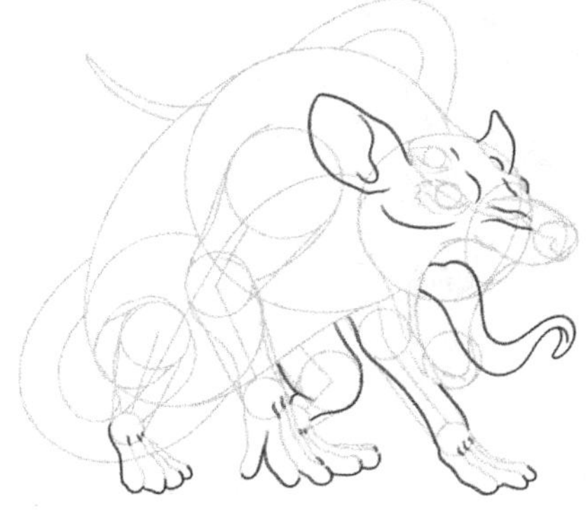

08

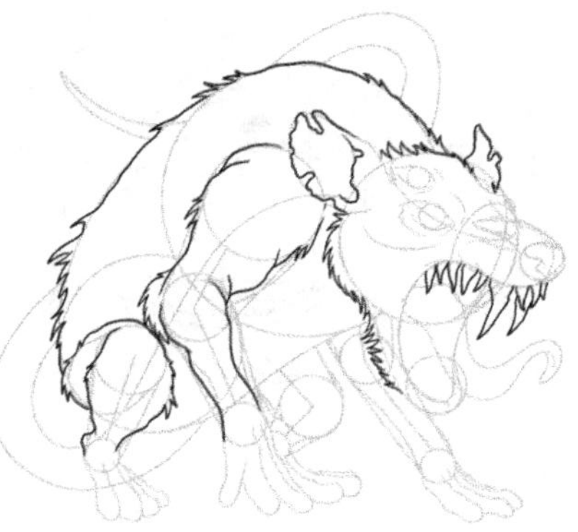

09

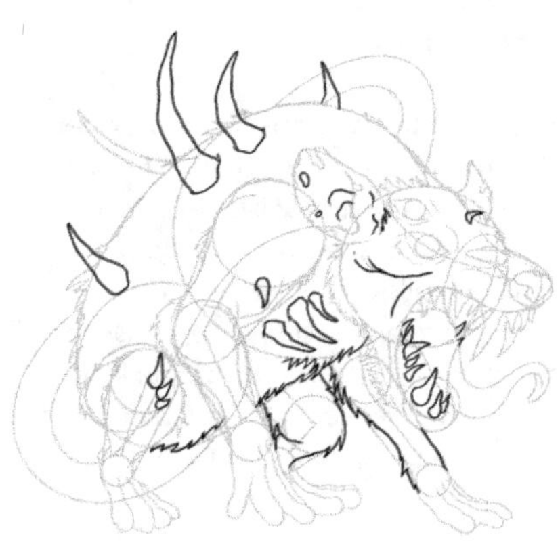

10

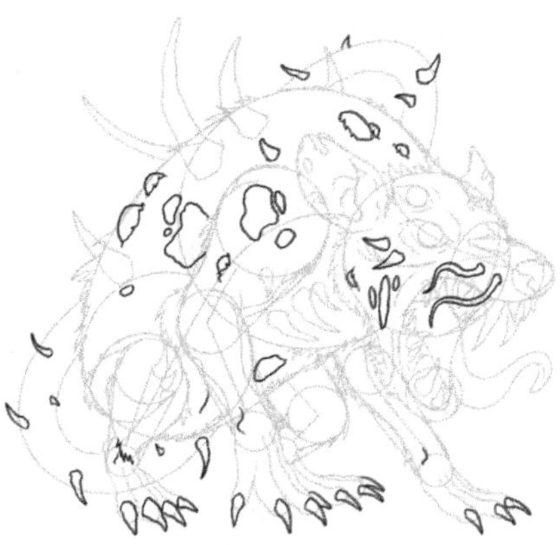

11

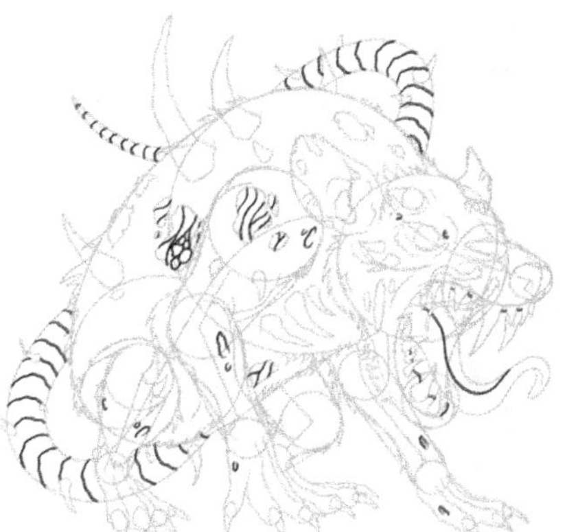

12

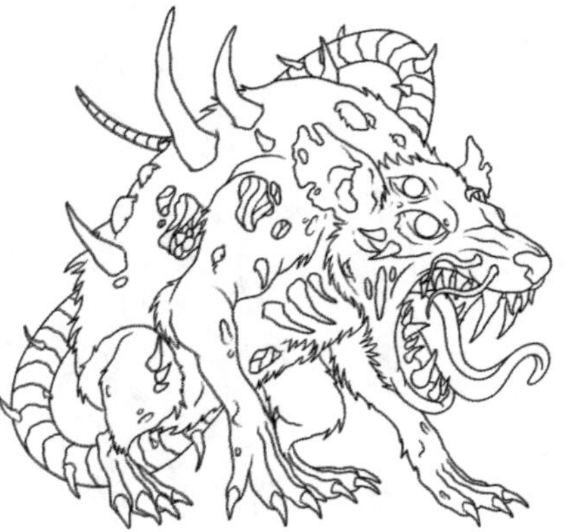

HOW TO DRAW MONSTERS & BEASTS

KRAKEN

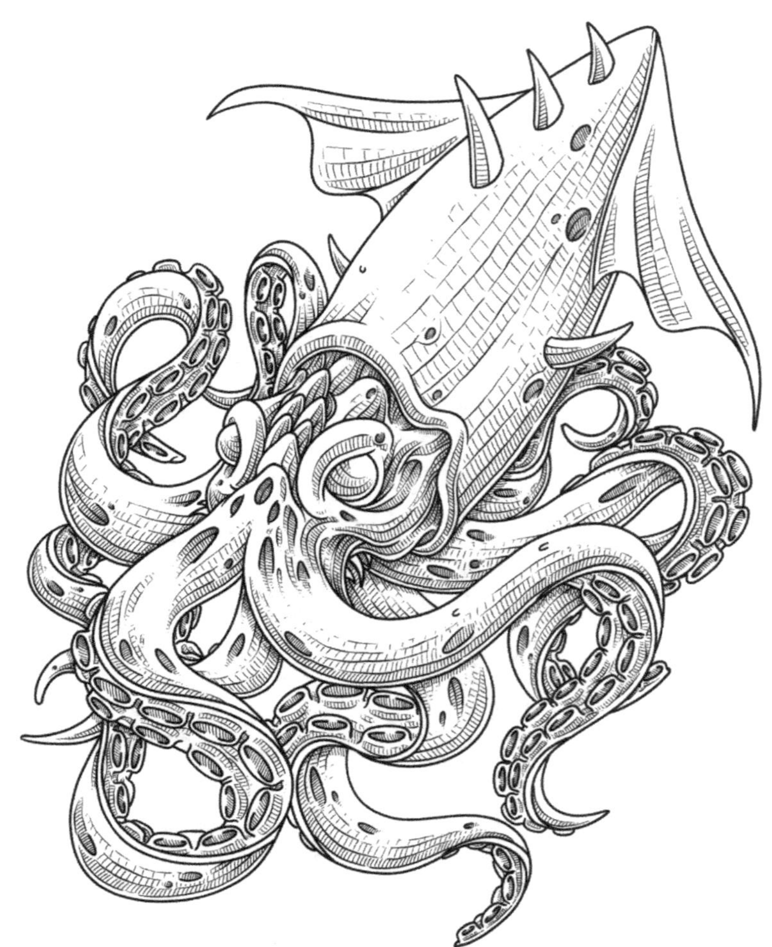

Pro tip: At step 6, establish a clear tentacle flow

Lay in the tentacles using long, sweeping S-curves that radiate outward from the head. Keep their bases evenly spaced around the central form, and let each tentacle follow a different path to create a sense of movement and depth. Defining this flow early gives the composition energy and prevents the tentacles from overlapping awkwardly later on.

01

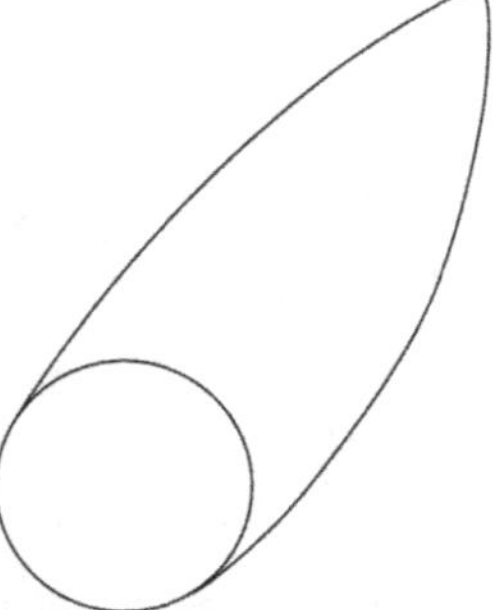

02

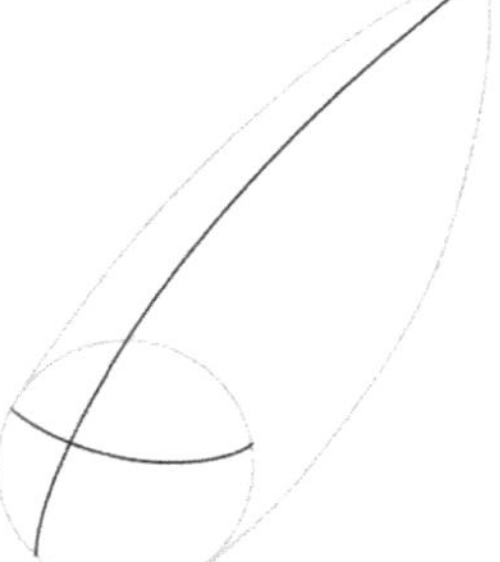

03

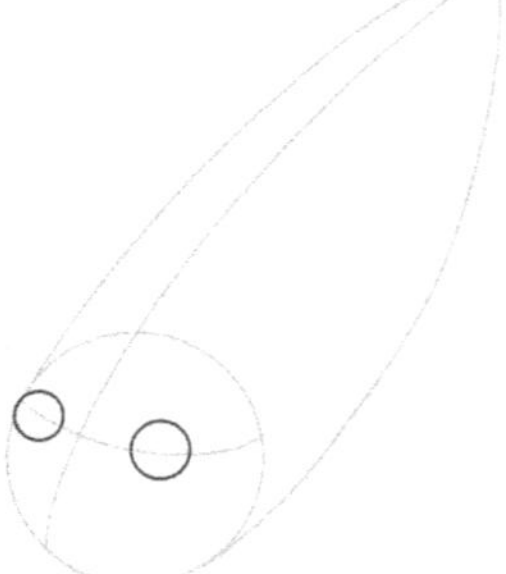

04

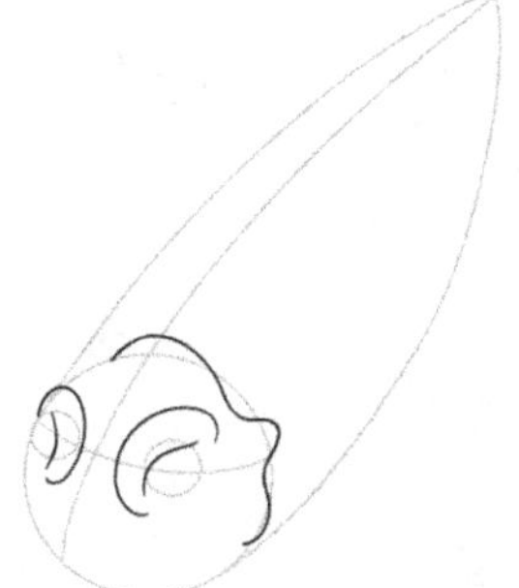

05

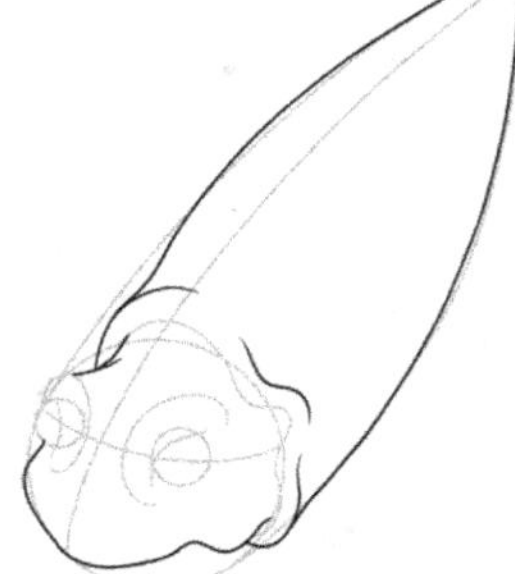

06

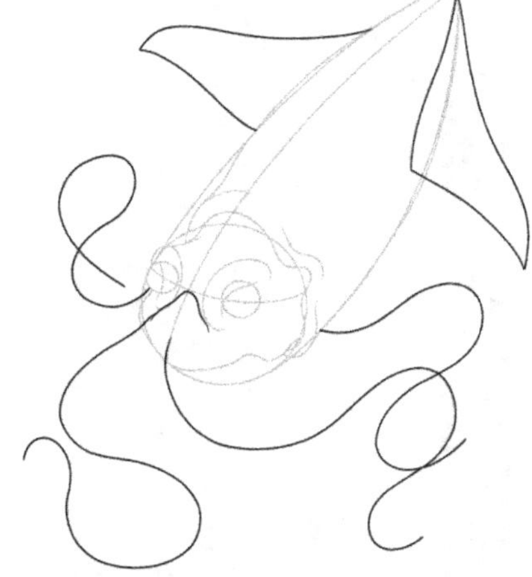

07

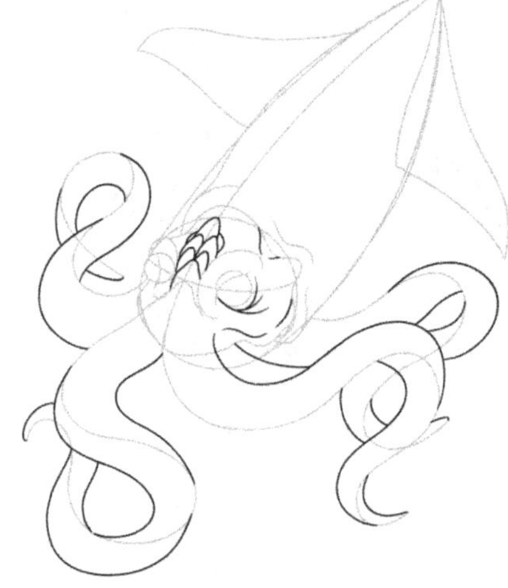

08

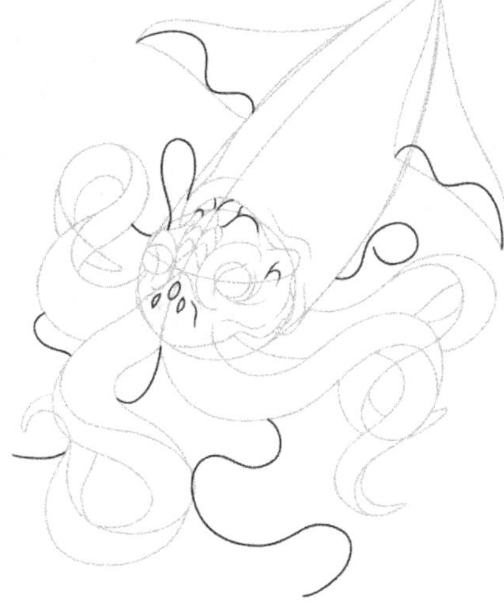

09

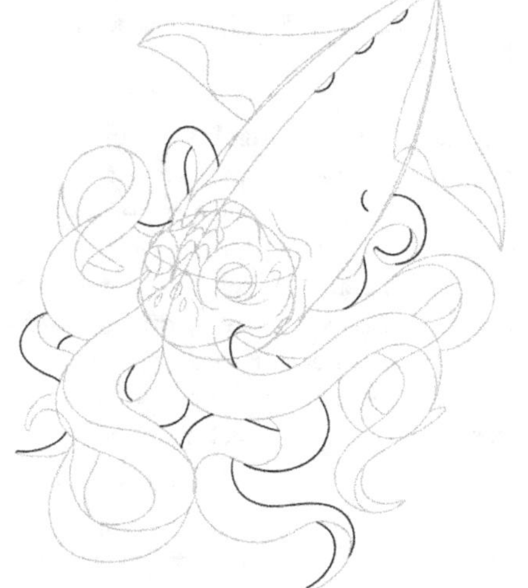

10

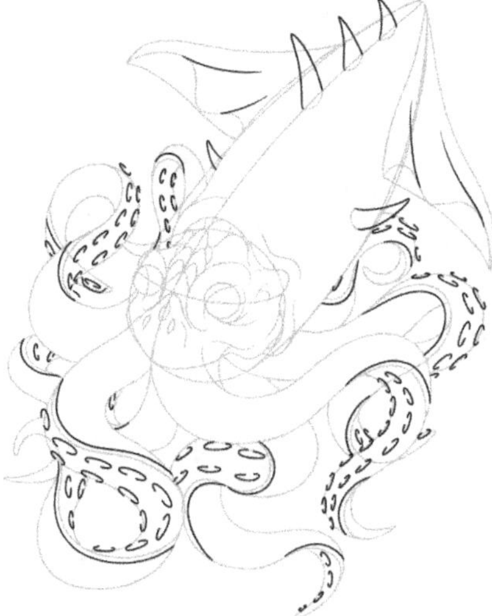

11

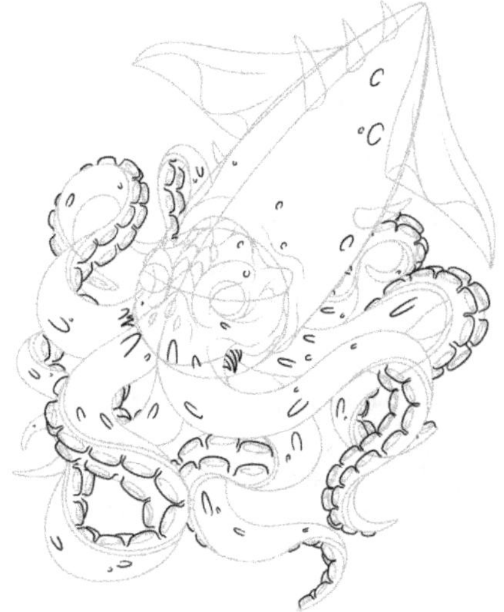

12

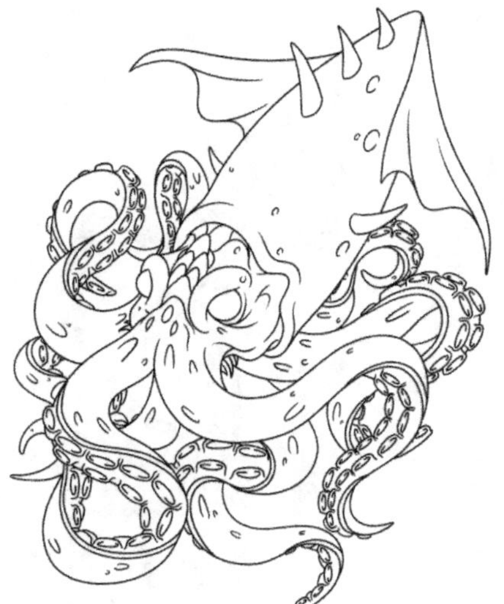

INSECTOID BEAST

Pro tip: At step 06, angle the legs out from the body

For insect-style creatures, the legs should attach high on the sides of the thorax and angle outward before bending down. This wide, splayed base gives the creature stability and a more convincing insect stance. Keep the upper leg segments nearly horizontal and let the lower segments curve or angle downward to create a natural, silhouette.

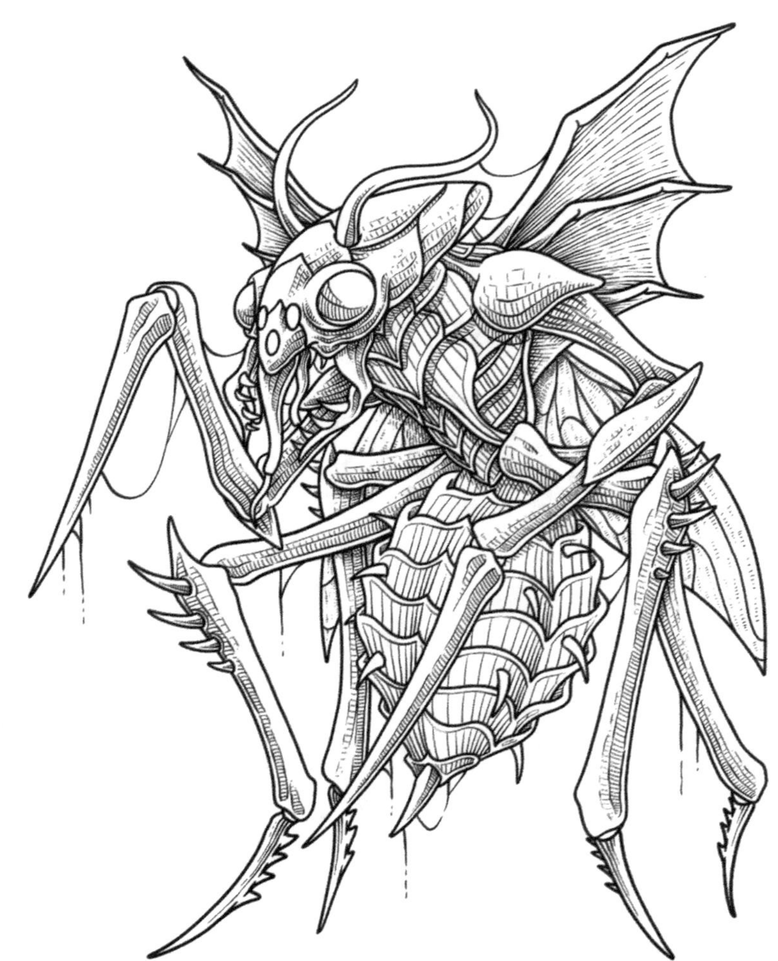

01

02

03

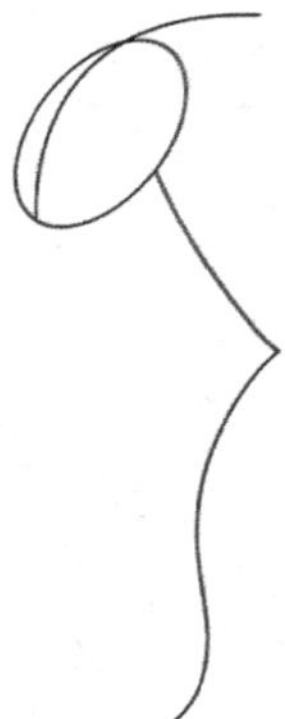

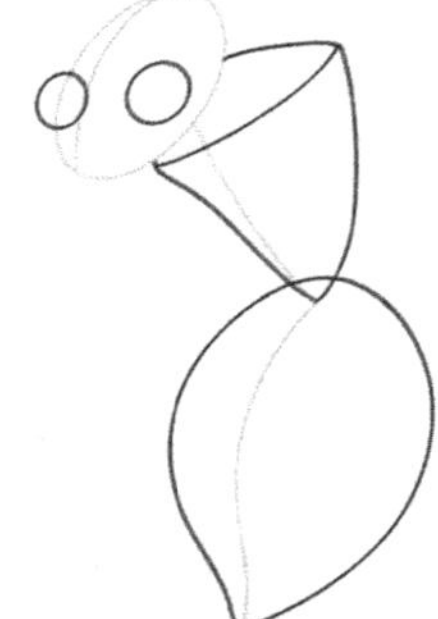

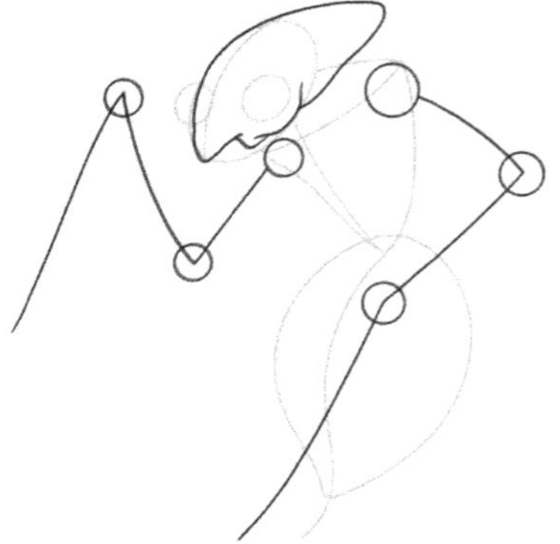

04

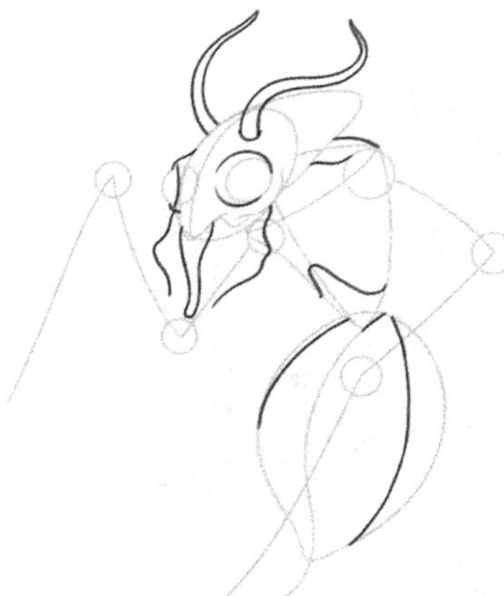

05

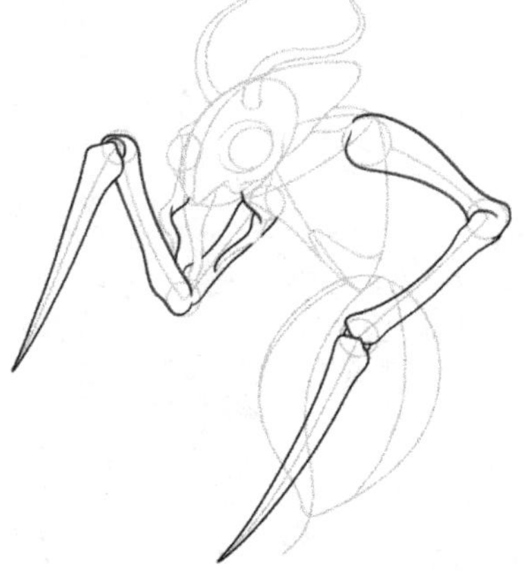

06

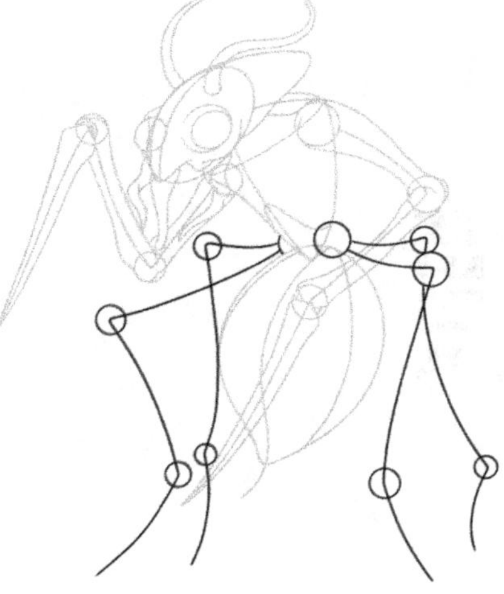

07

08

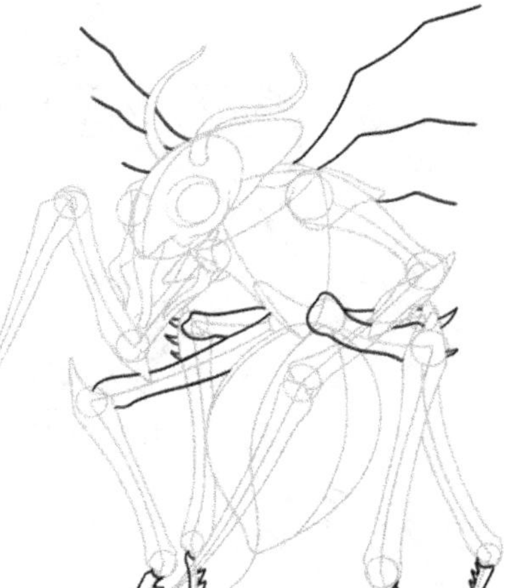

09

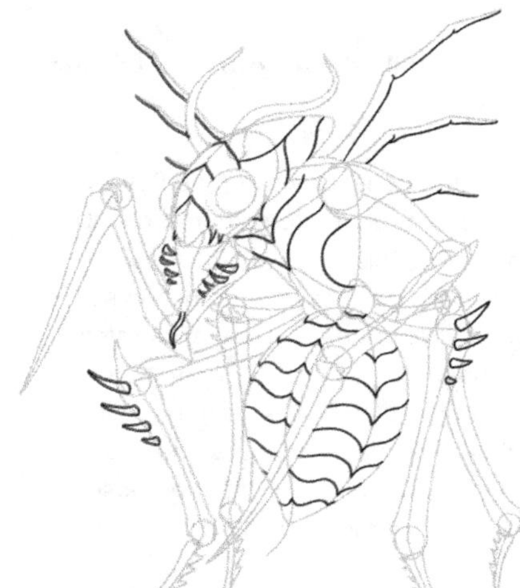

10

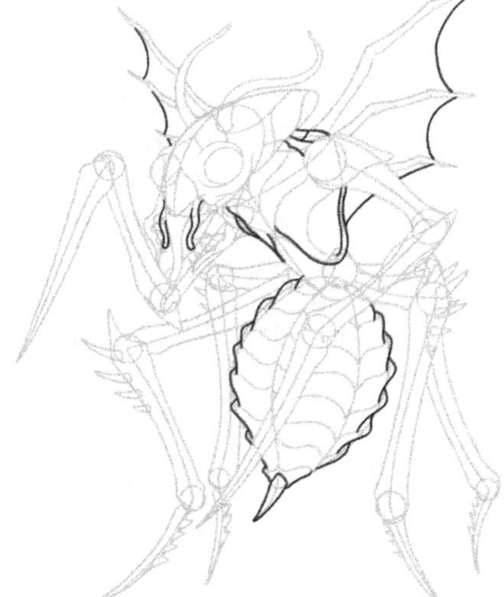

11

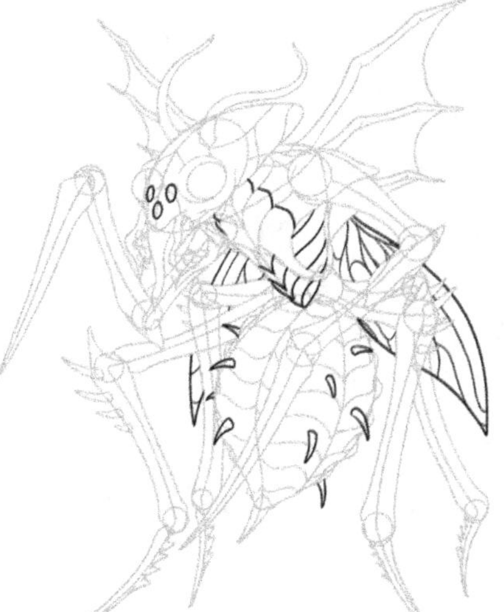

12

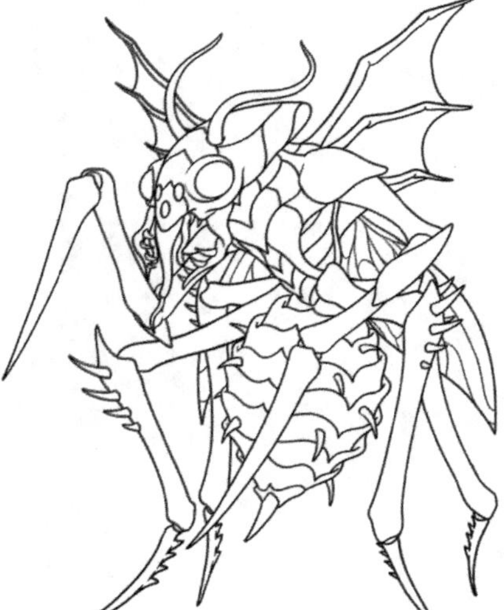

HOW TO DRAW MONSTERS & BEASTS

ALIEN

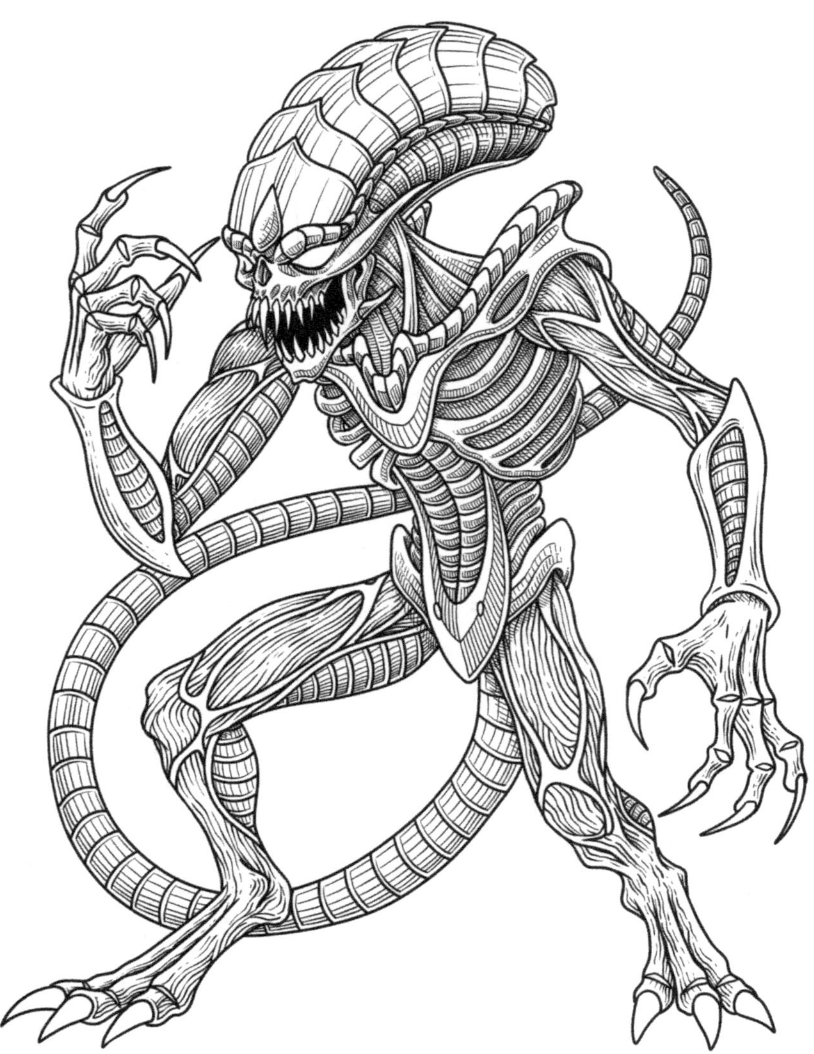

Pro tip: Build the pose around the spine curve

From the head, draw a single flowing curve through the torso to represent the spine. This curve establishes the creature's balance, direction, and sense of motion. Once it's in place, use simple cylinder and sphere shapes to block in the limbs, always checking that they follow the energy of that spine line. This keeps even complex, inhuman poses feeling dynamic and grounded.

01

02

03

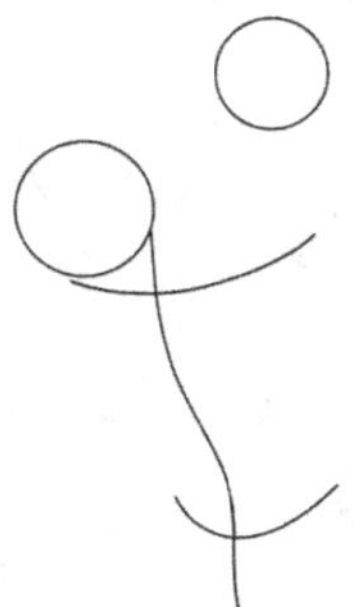

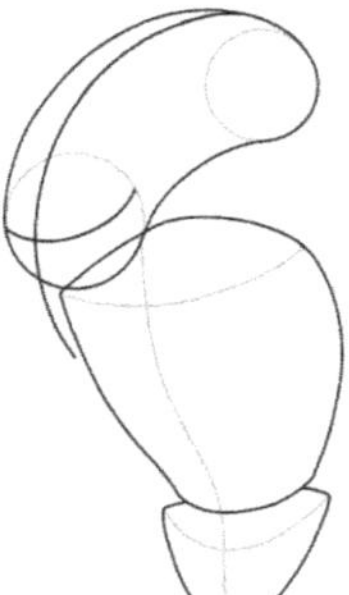

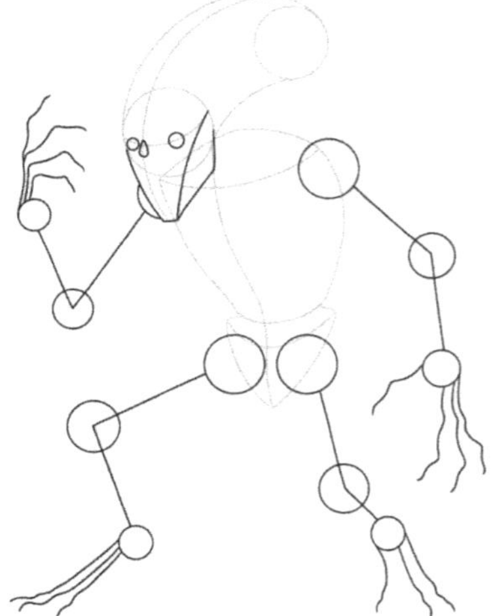

04 05 06

07 08 09

10 11 12

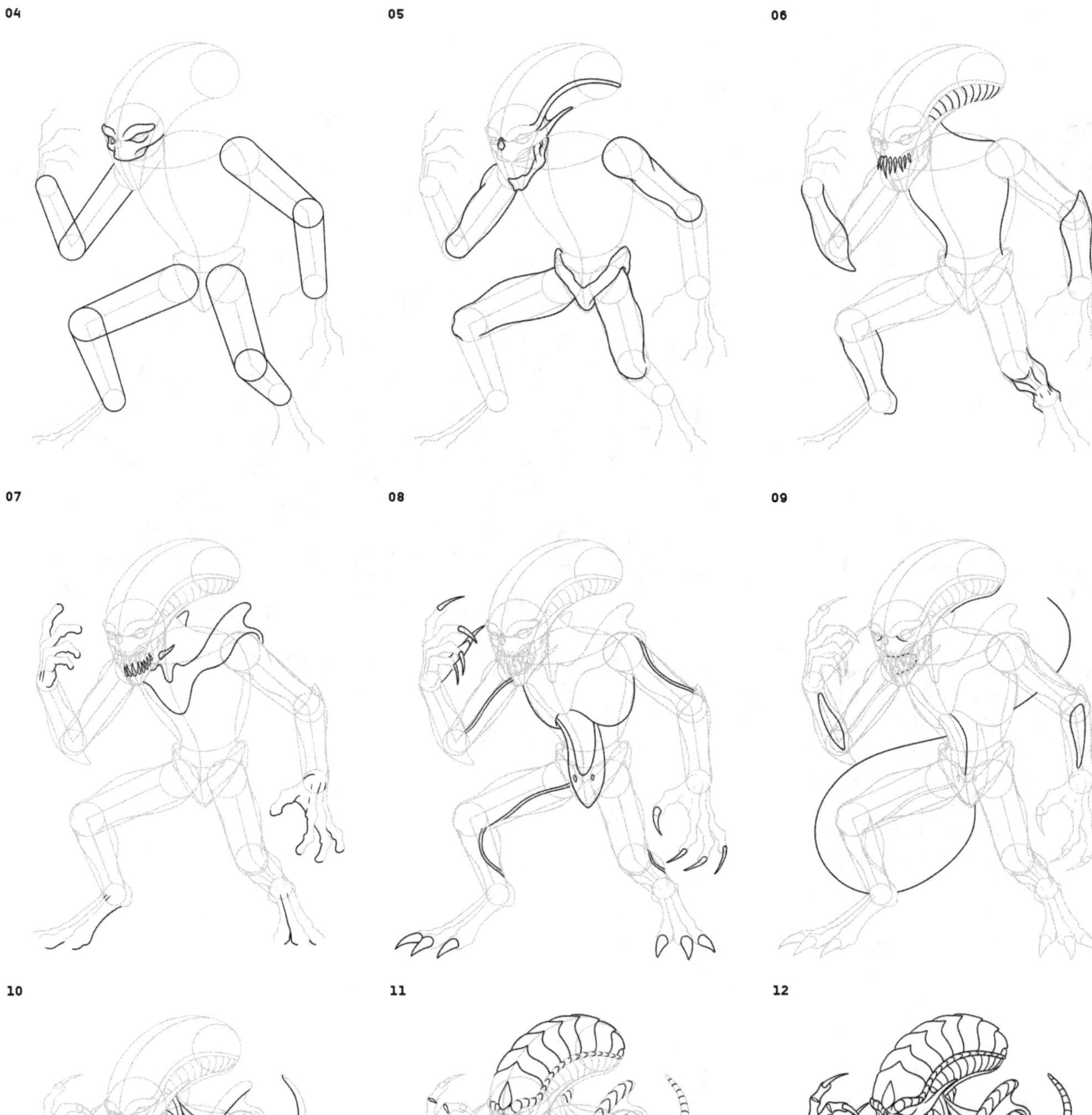

SPIDER QUEEN

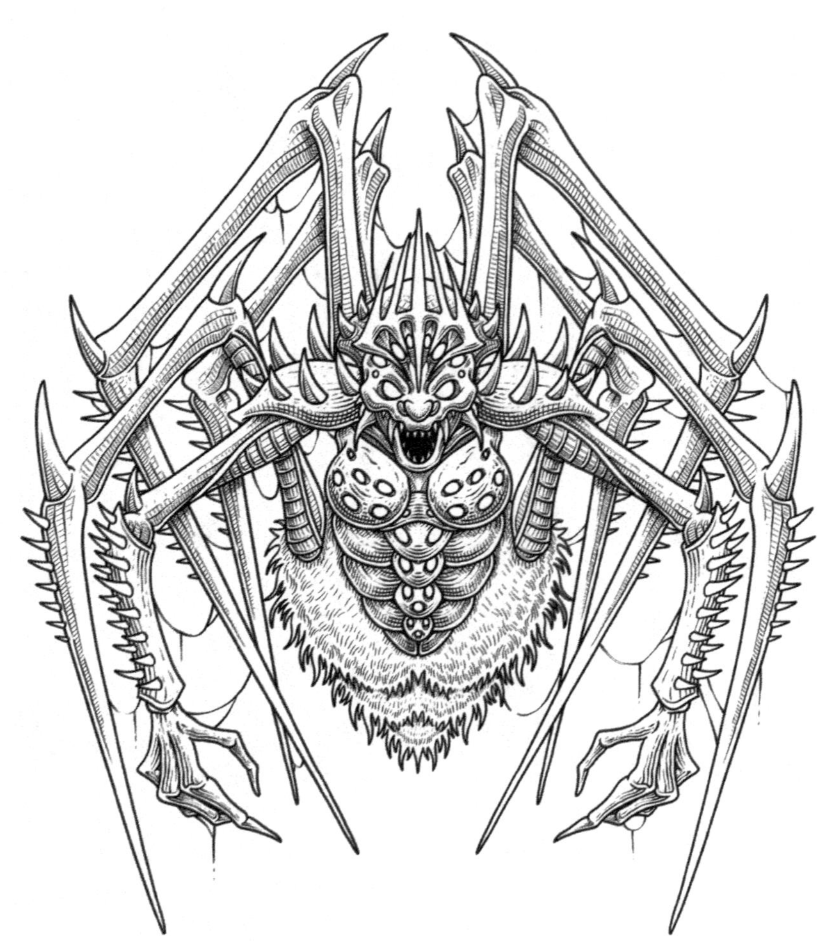

Pro tip: Anchor the legs around the thorax

Use the central thorax (mid-body) as your primary anchor point for all the legs. Start each leg from an evenly spaced position along the thorax's sides, imagining them radiating out like spokes on a wheel. This ensures the legs feel structurally integrated with the body rather than floating or misaligned, giving the creature a more convincing and balanced design.

01   02   03

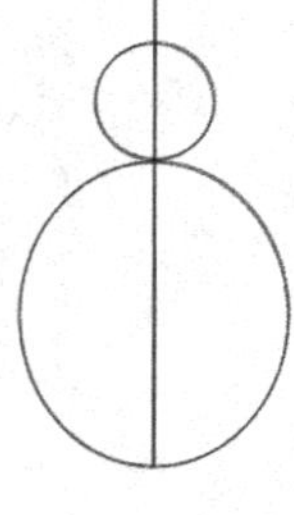

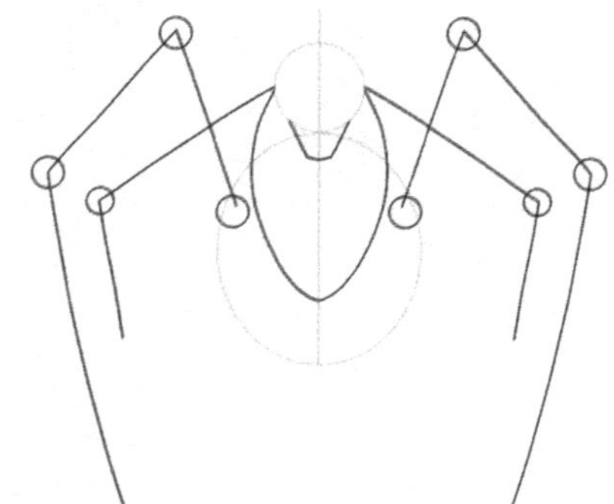

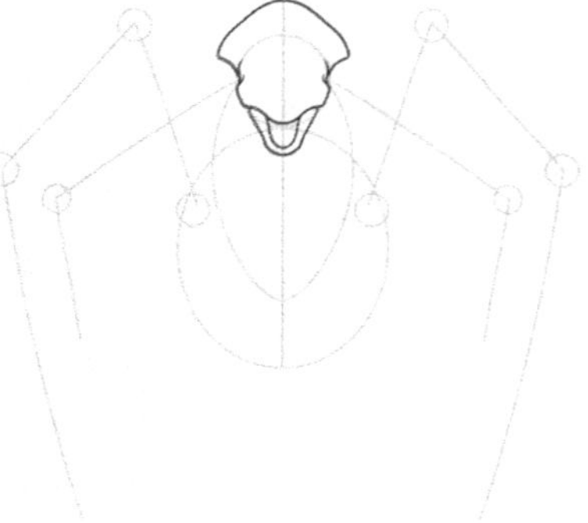

04

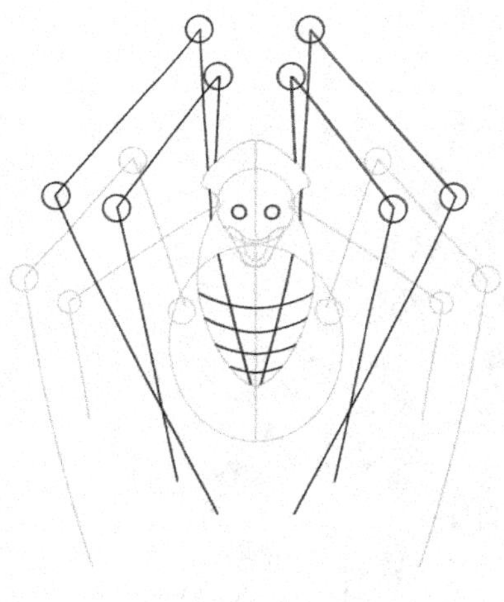

05

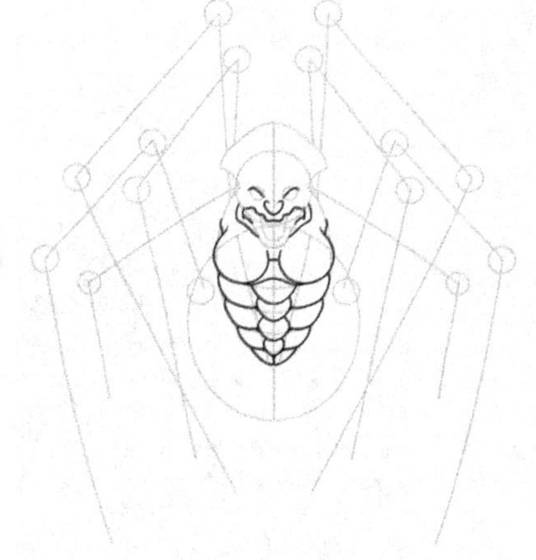

06

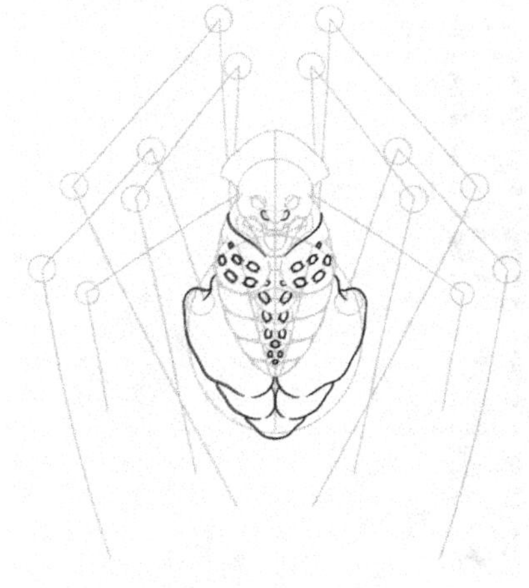

07

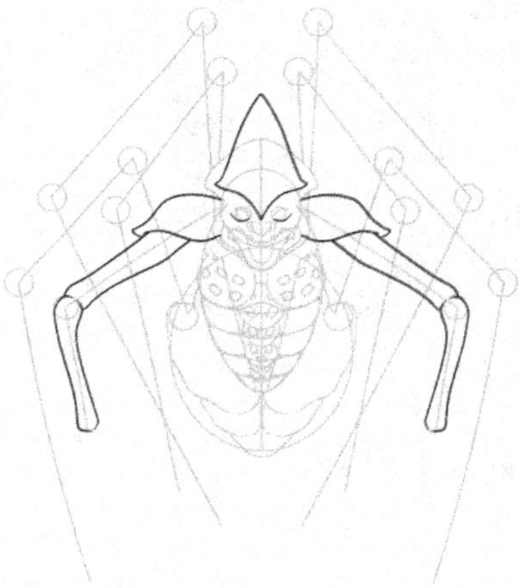

08

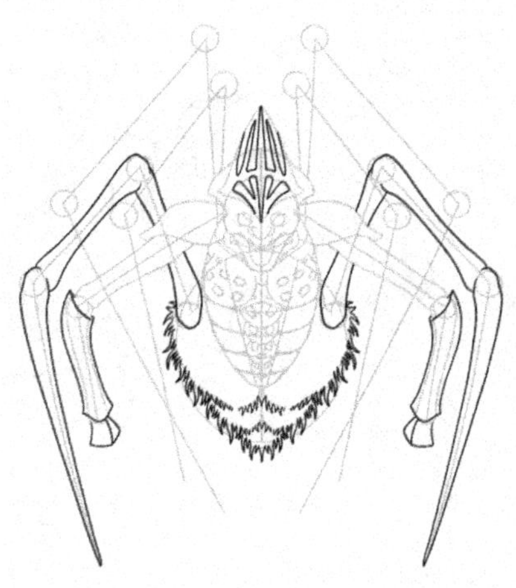

09

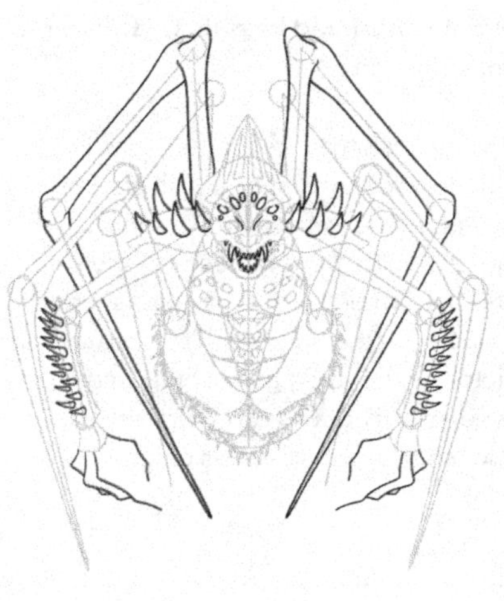

10

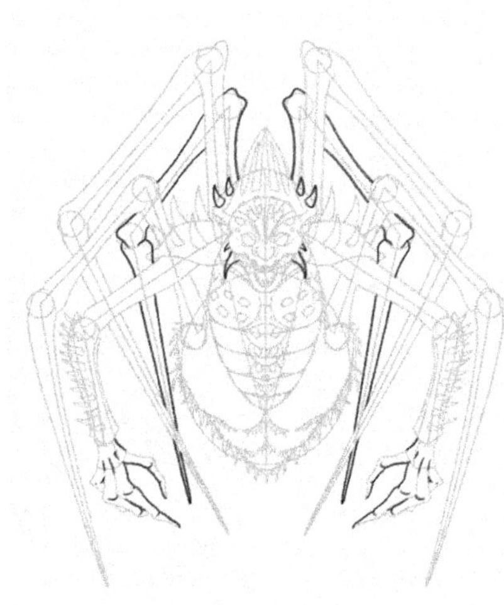

11

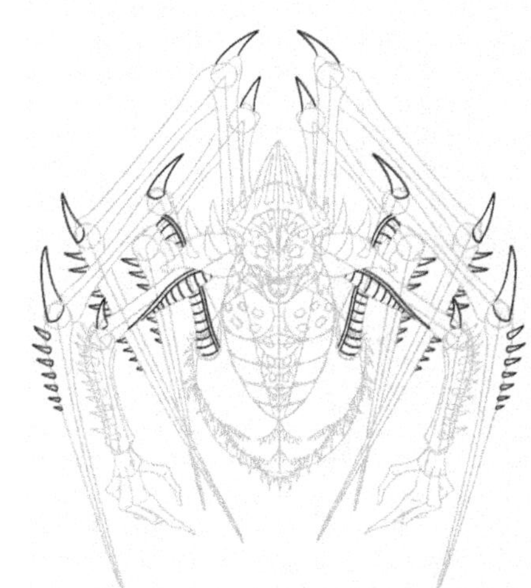

12

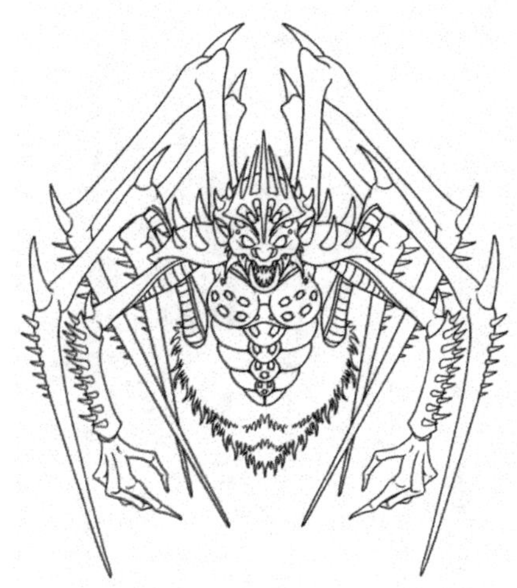

SWAMP MONSTER

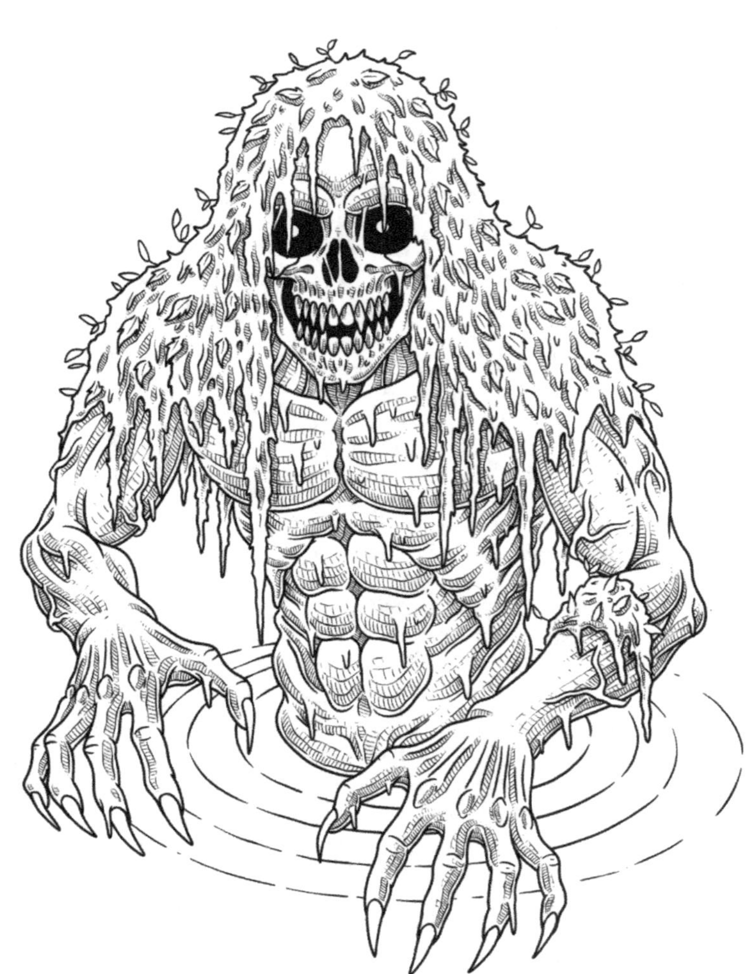

Pro tip: Use head heights to determine torso length

To establish the torso length, use the head as your measuring unit. For this creature, the torso spans roughly 2½ head heights from the base of the skull to the bottom of the ribcage. Measuring this way keeps the proportions consistent and helps anchor the figure's bulk, especially when working with exaggerated or monstrous forms like this one.

01

02

03

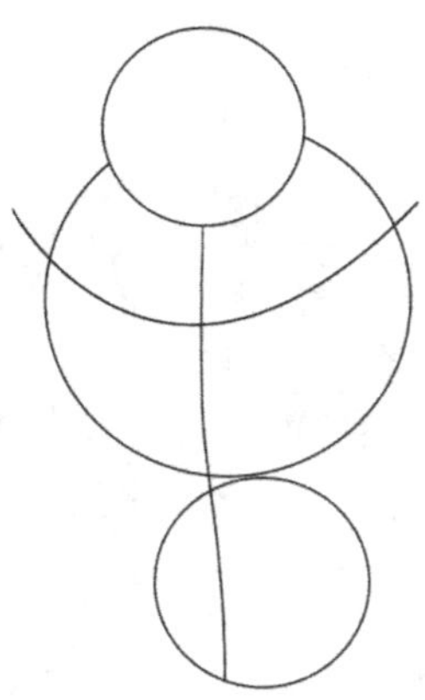

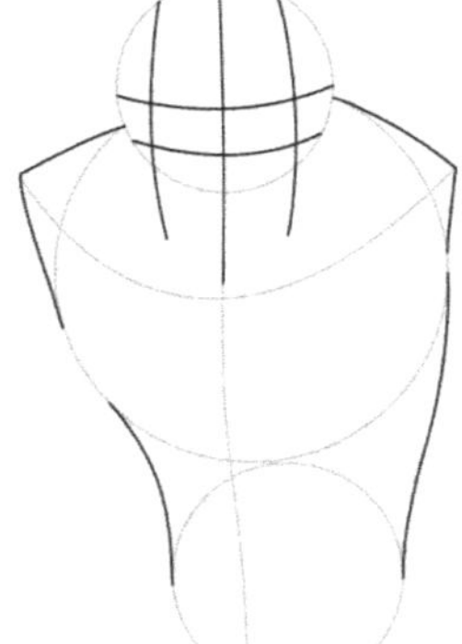

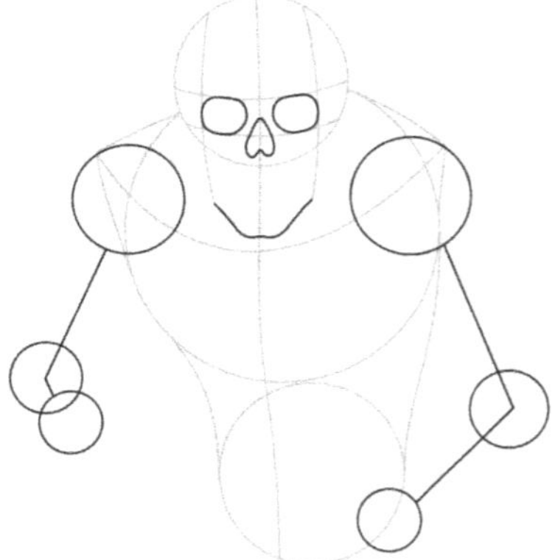

04

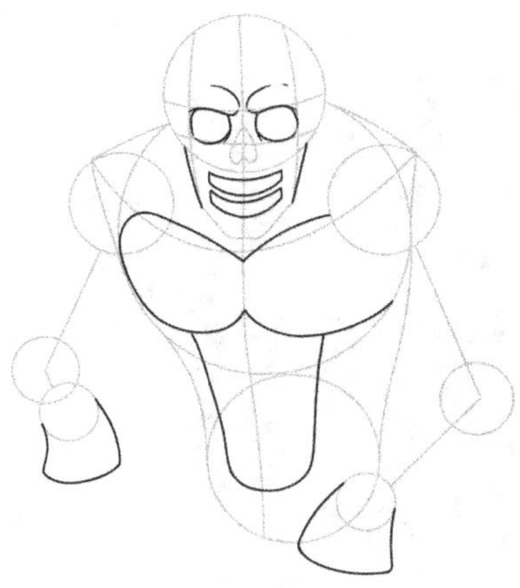

05

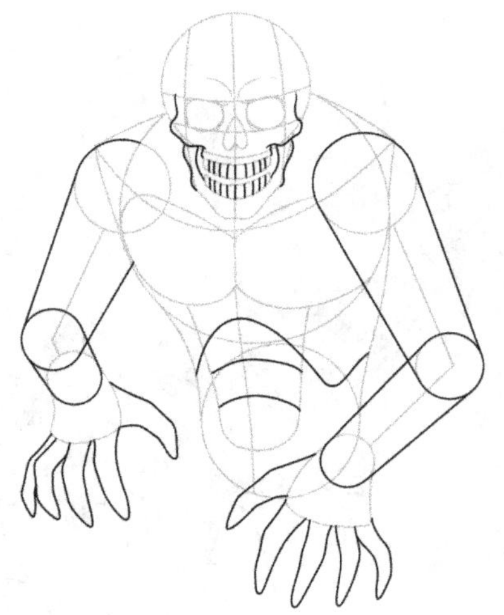

06

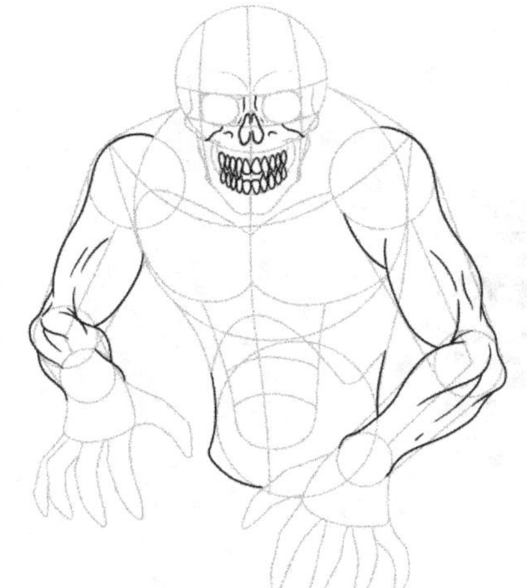

07

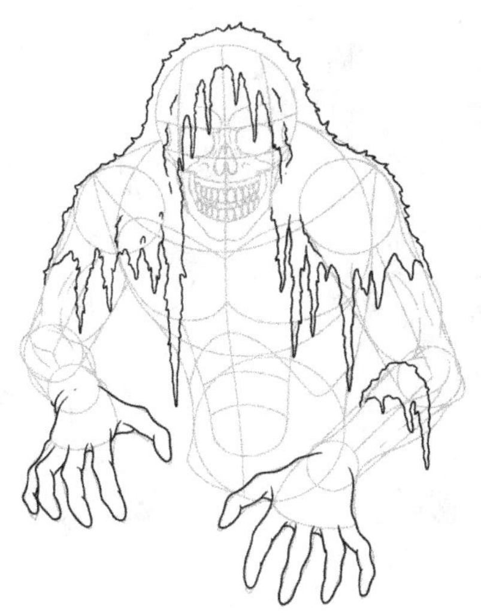

08

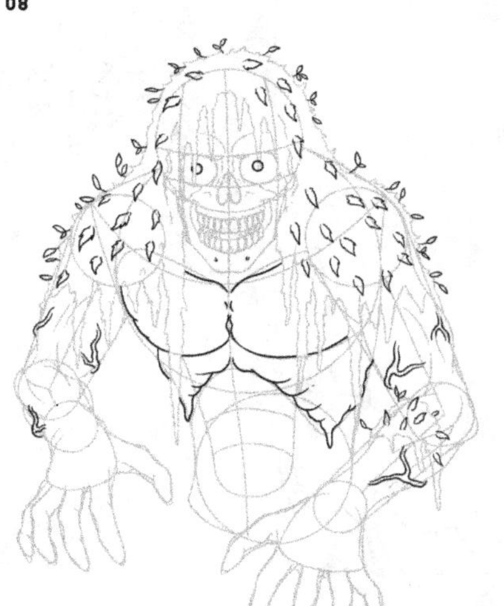

09

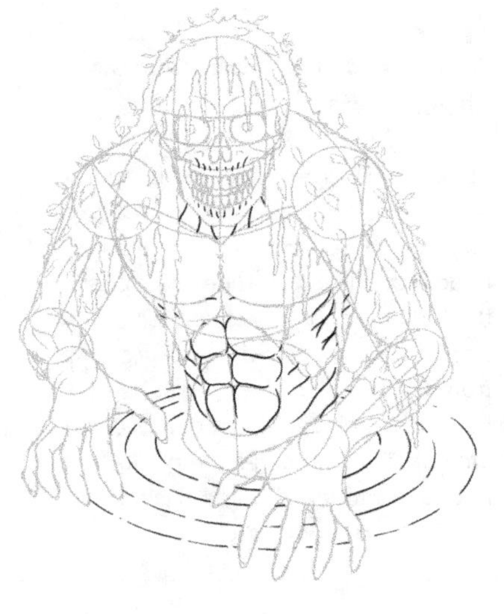

10

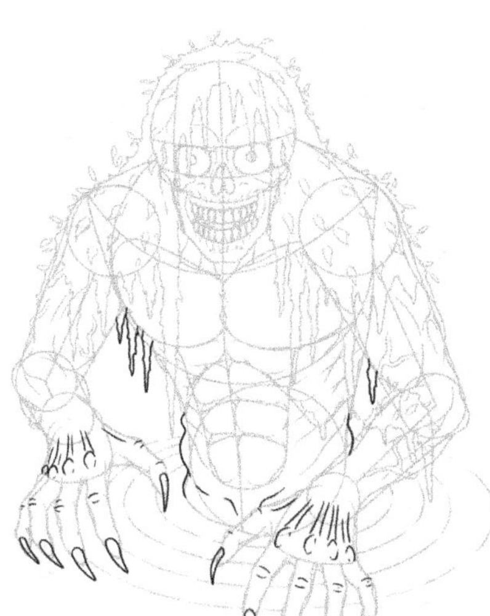

11

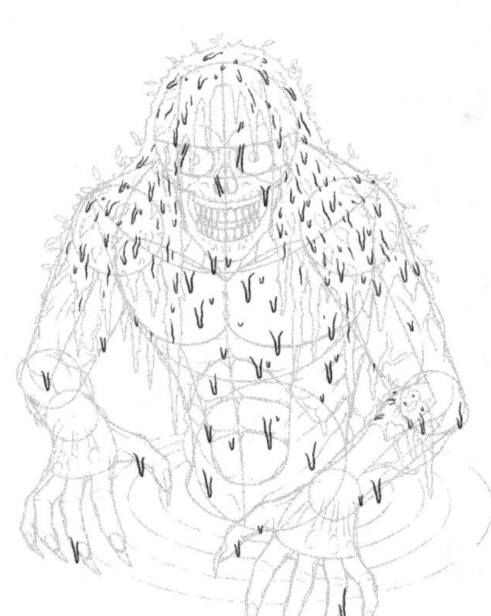

12

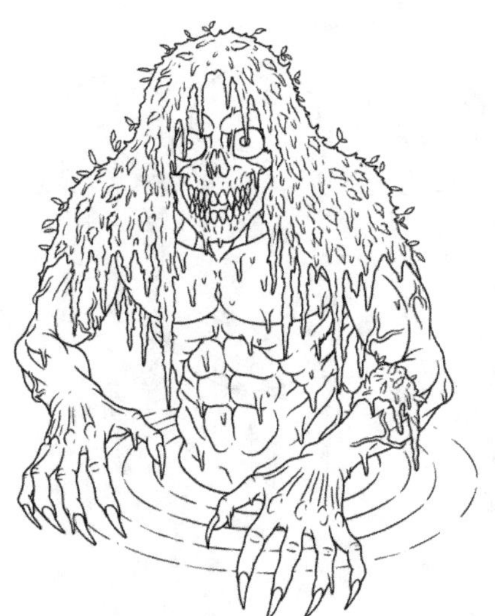

CEREBUS

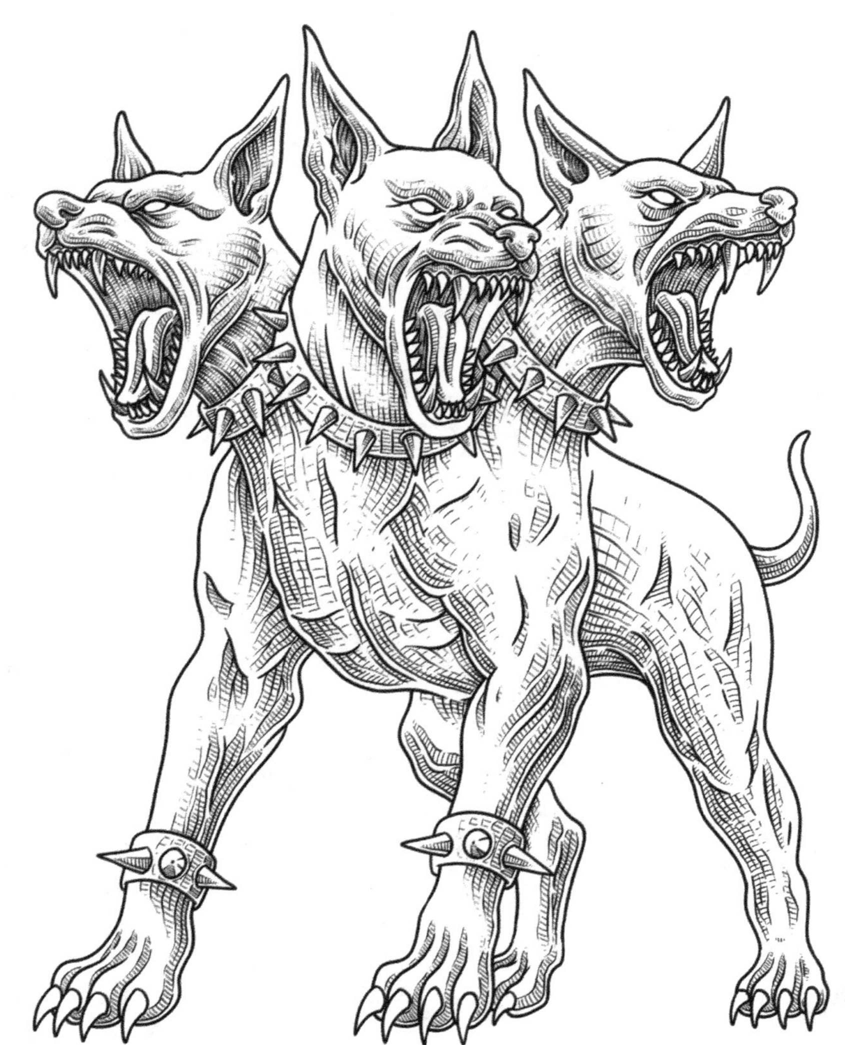

Pro tip: space the heads using the ribcage width

To position Cerberus's three heads evenly, use the width of the ribcage circle as your measuring unit. Place the central head along the spine line, then position the left and right heads so their centre lines sit roughly one ribcage-width apart from the centre of the middle head. This keeps the heads balanced, prevents crowding, and ensures the necks flow naturally into the shoulders without overlapping awkwardly.

01

02

03

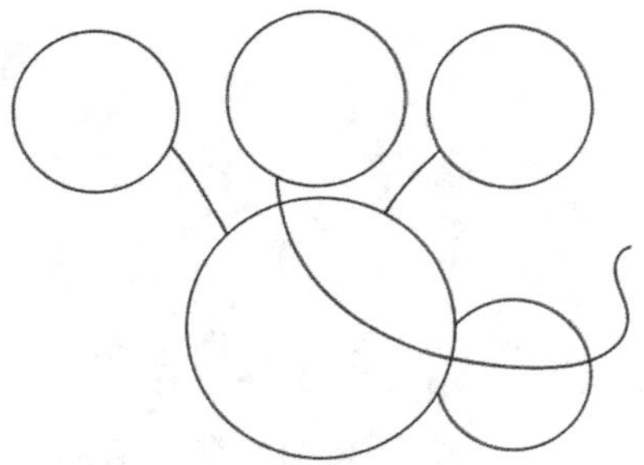

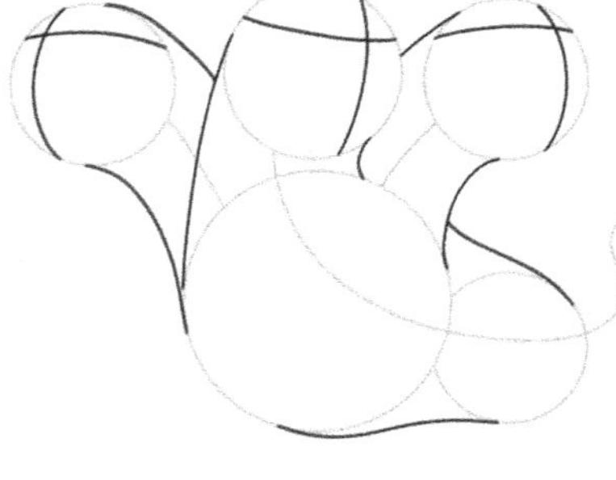

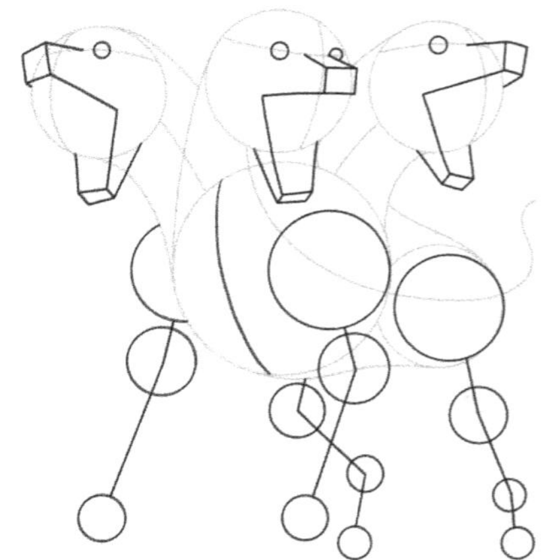

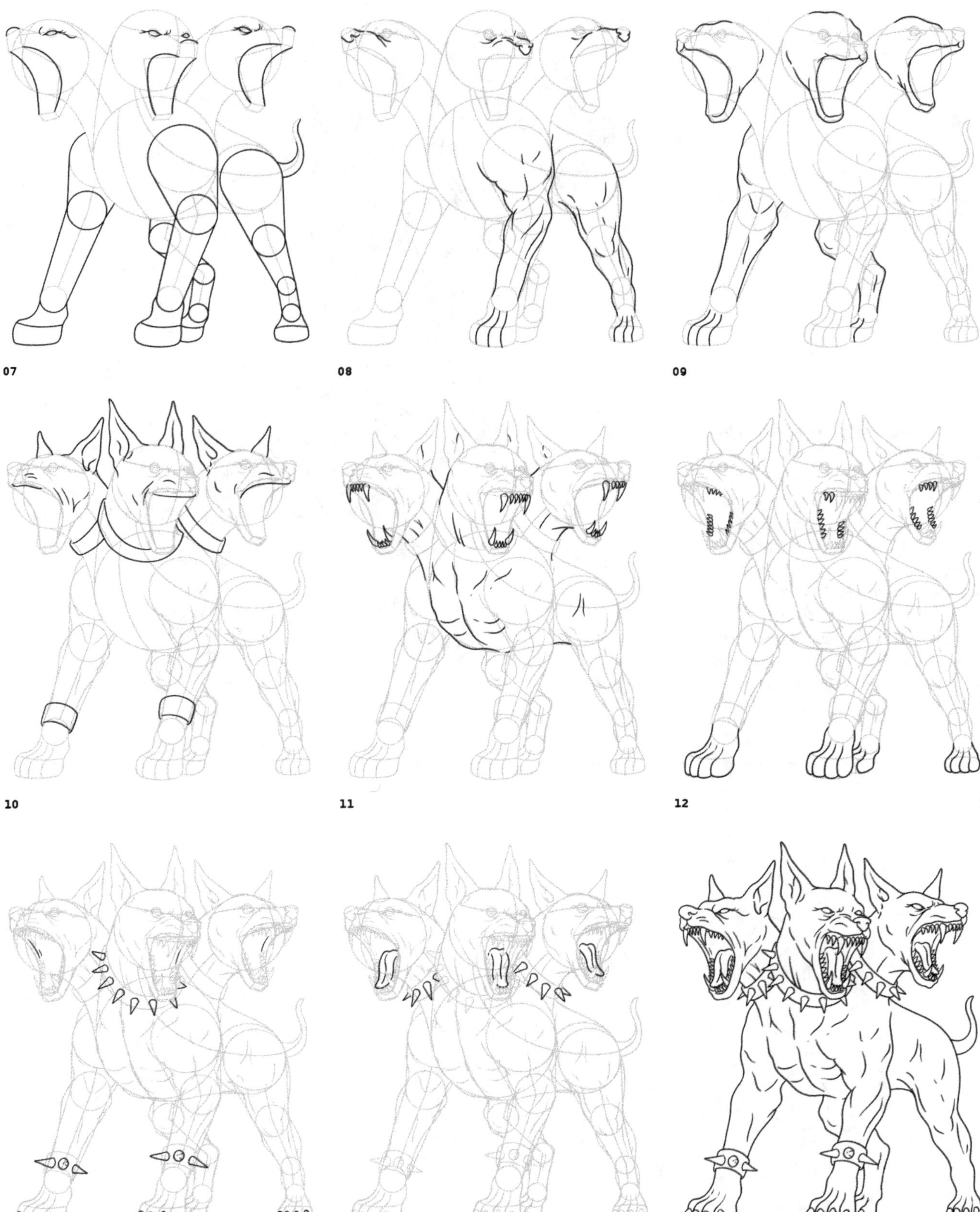

04
05
06
07
08
09
10
11
12
HOW TO DRAW MONSTERS & BEASTS

HYDRA

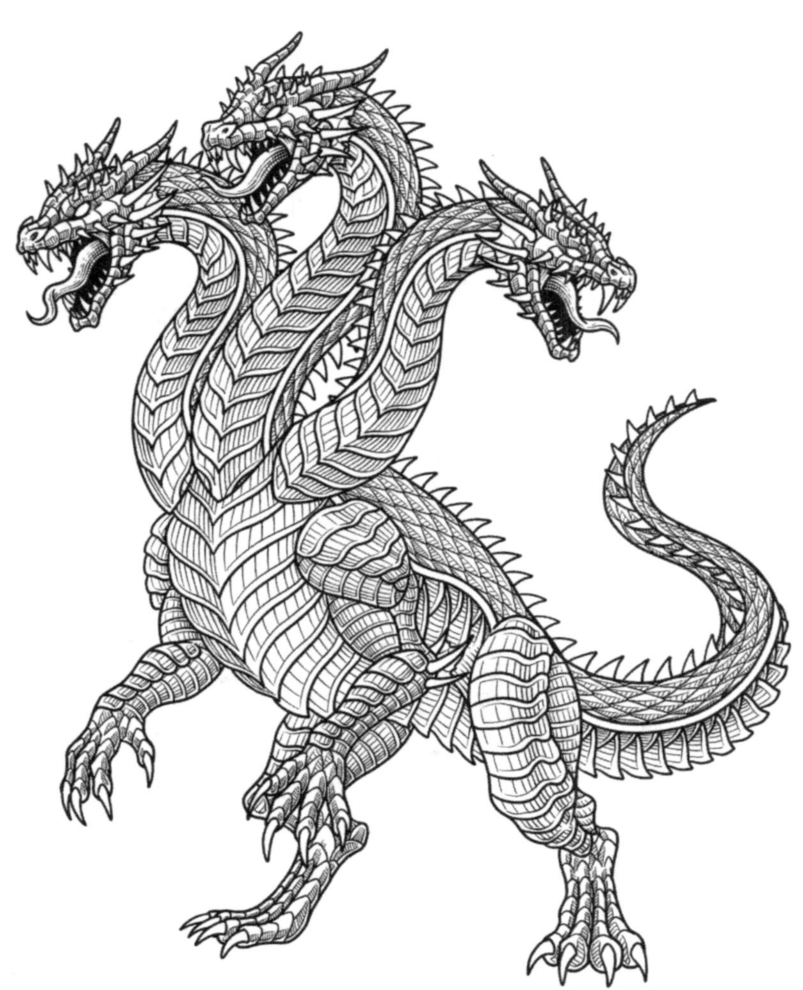

Pro tip: Stagger the necks along the hydra's spine

To keep the Hydra's multiple heads clear and readable, position each neck so it emerges from a different point along the spine, rather than clustering them together. Space them evenly, angling the outer necks outward and the central one upright. This creates a strong rhythm through the composition and prevents the necks from tangling visually as you refine the forms.

01

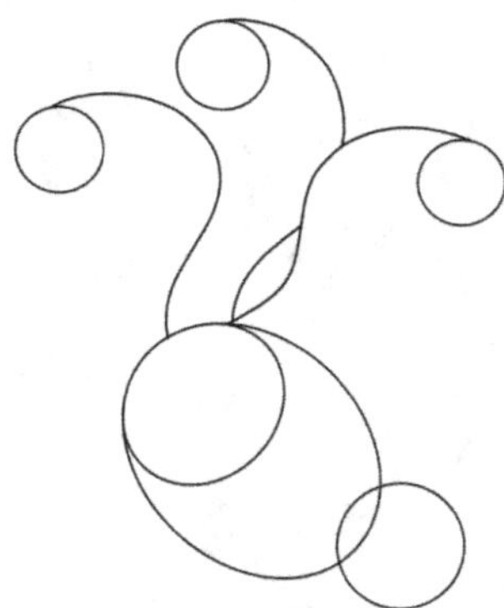

02

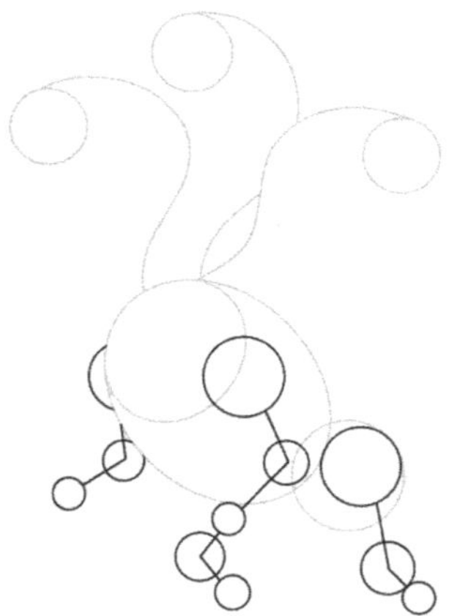

03

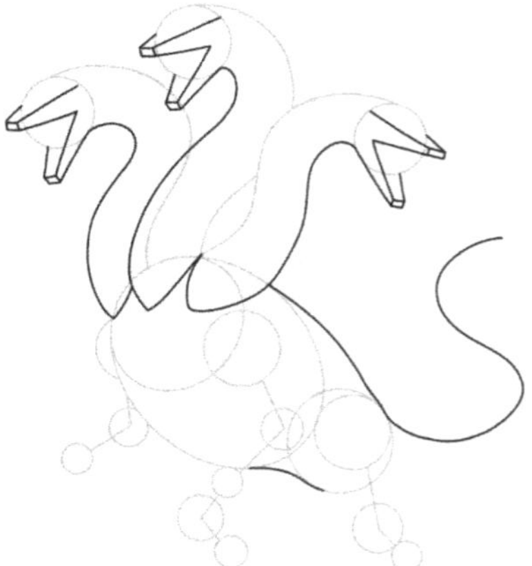

04

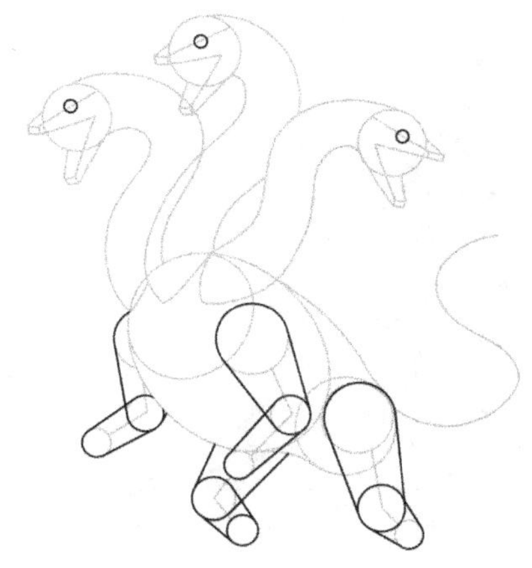

05

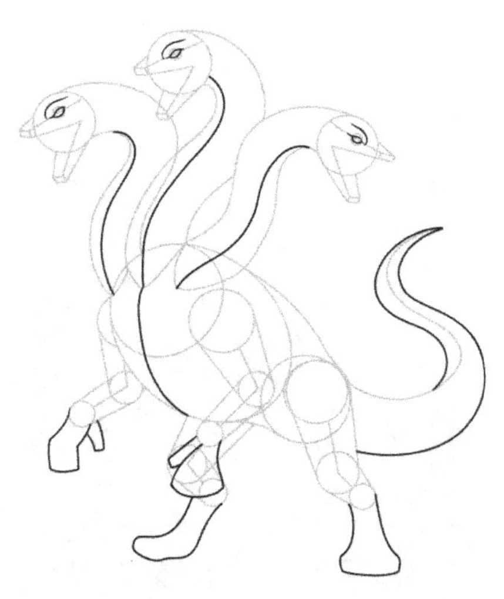

06

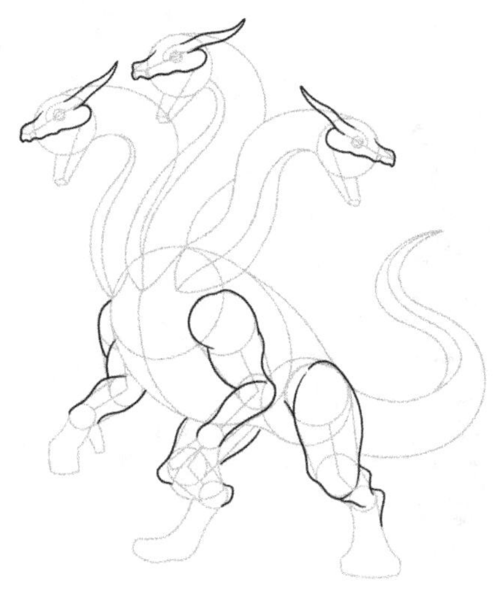

07

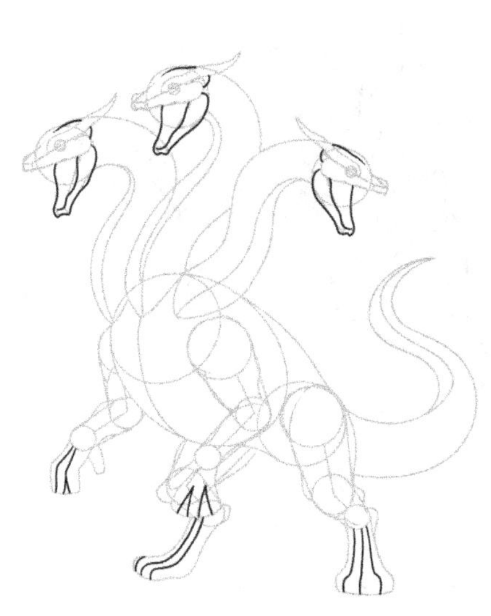

08

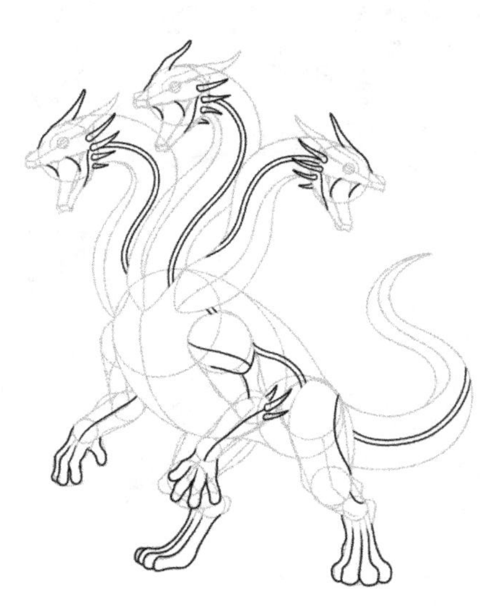

09

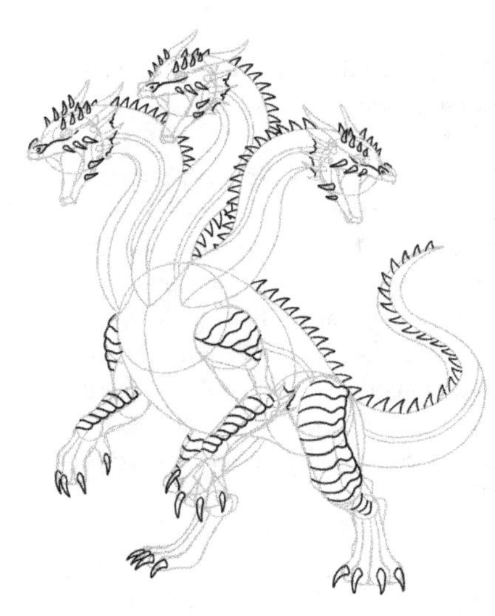

10

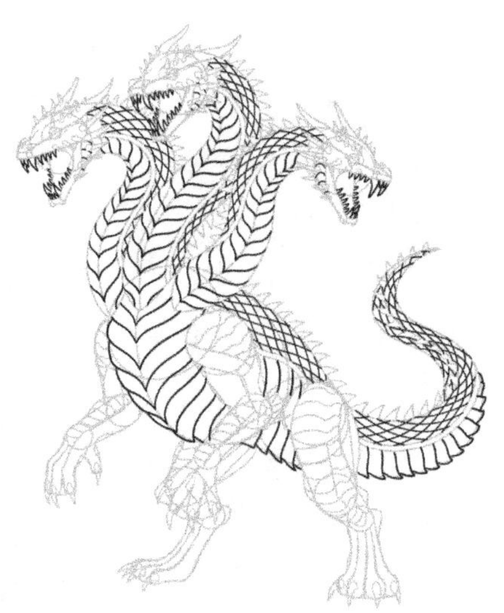

11

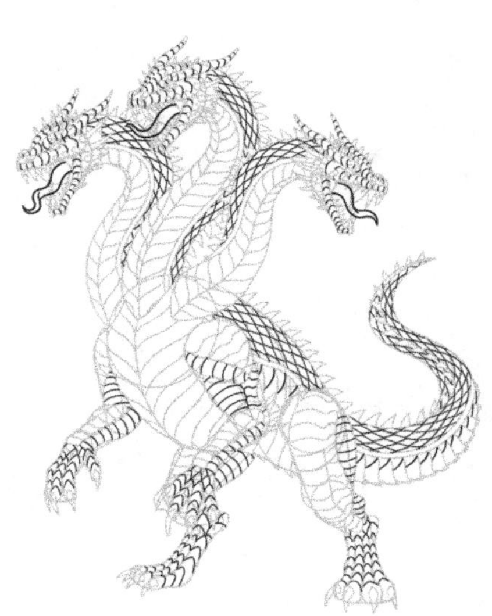

12

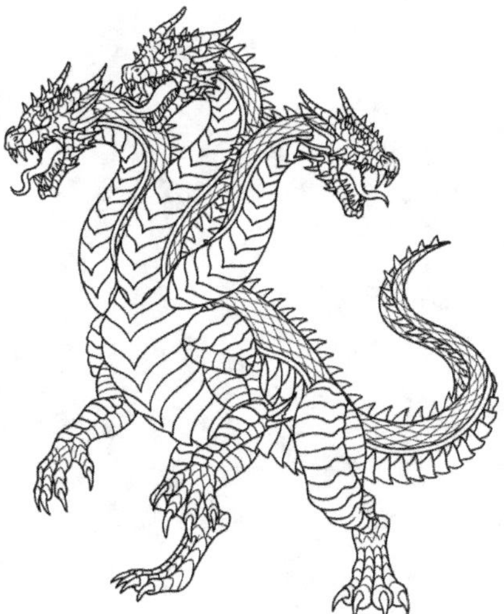

HOW TO DRAW MONSTERS & BEASTS

DRAGON HEAD

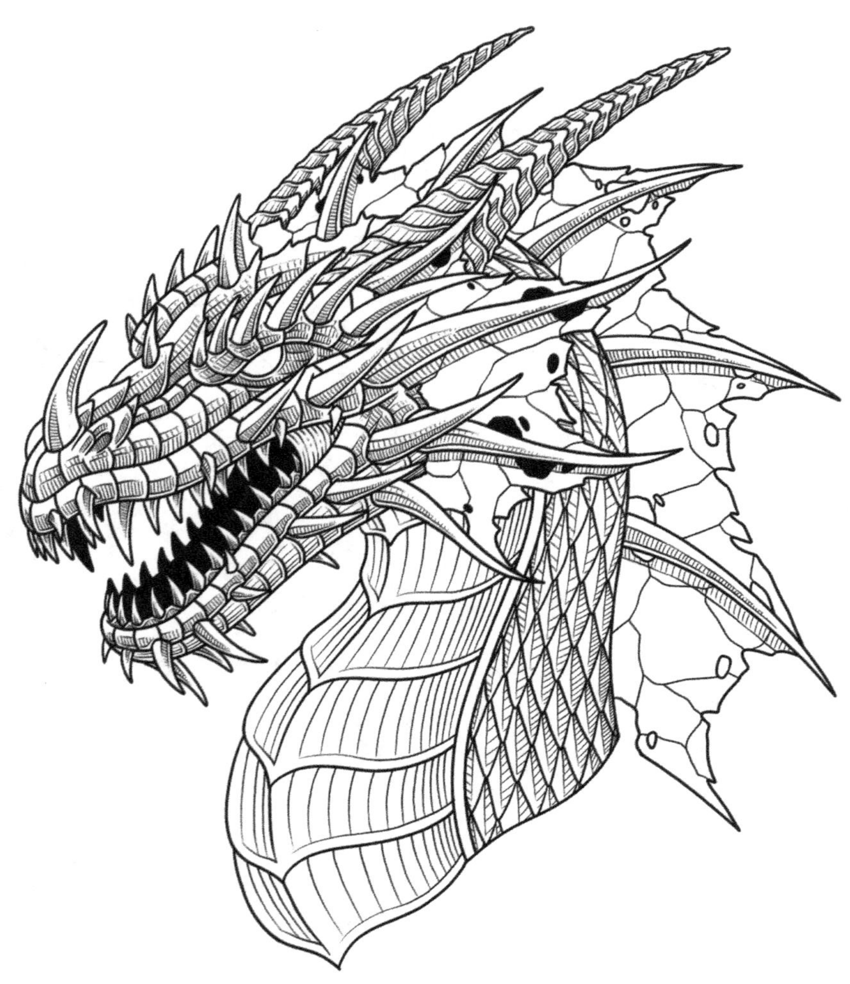

Pro tip: Use the snout boxes to anchor perspective

At step 02, start by blocking in the dragon's snout with two stacked rectangular boxes extending from the front of the head. These boxes define the angle and depth of the muzzle, making it easier to place nostrils, teeth, and other details in proper perspective. Once these are locked in, wrap the organic forms of the face around them to keep the structure solid and believable.

01   02   03

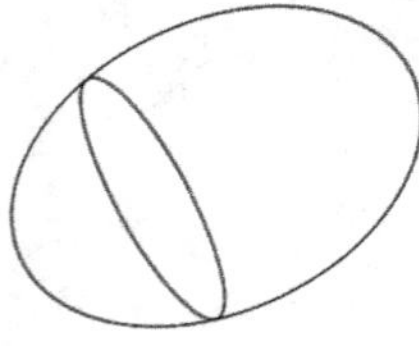

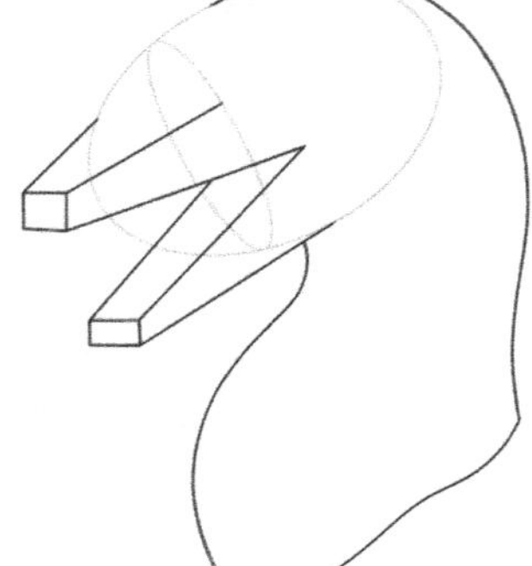

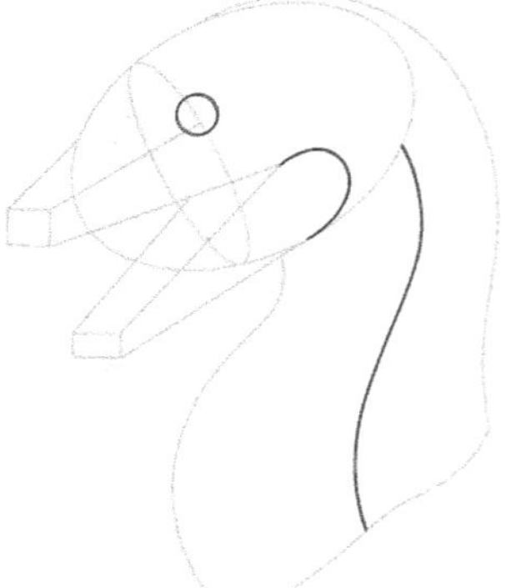

04

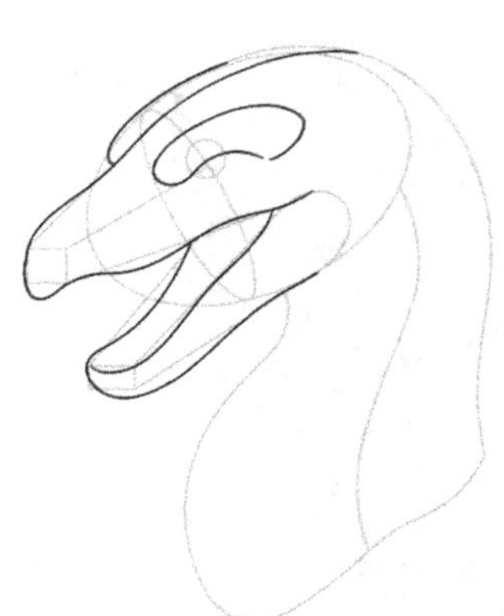

05

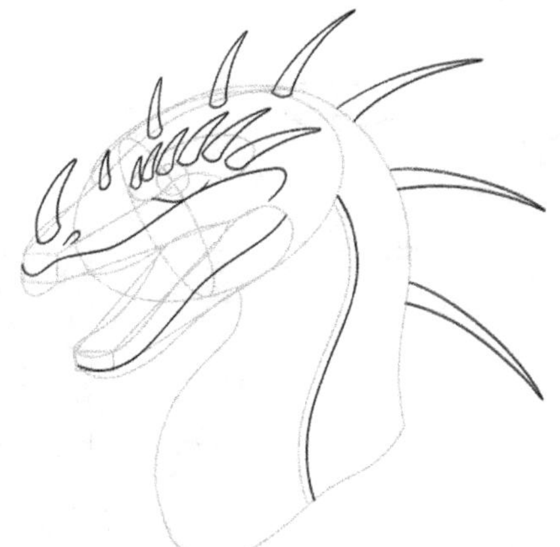

06

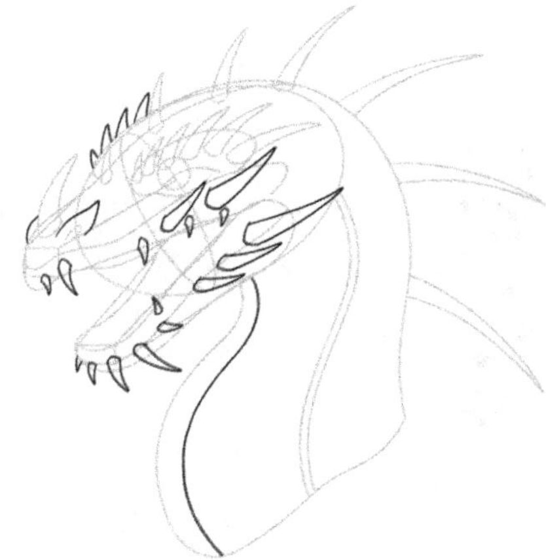

07

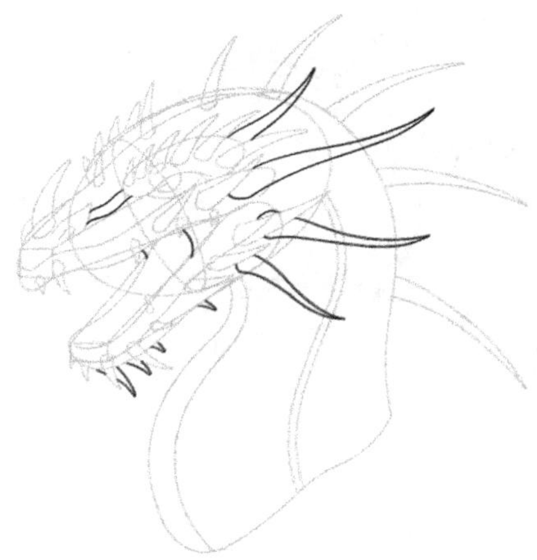

08

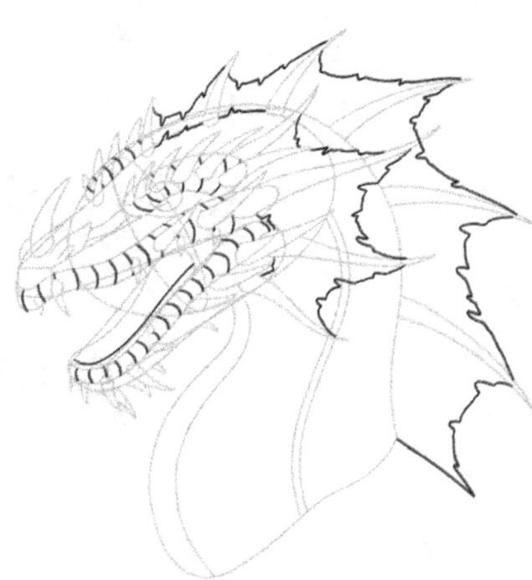

09

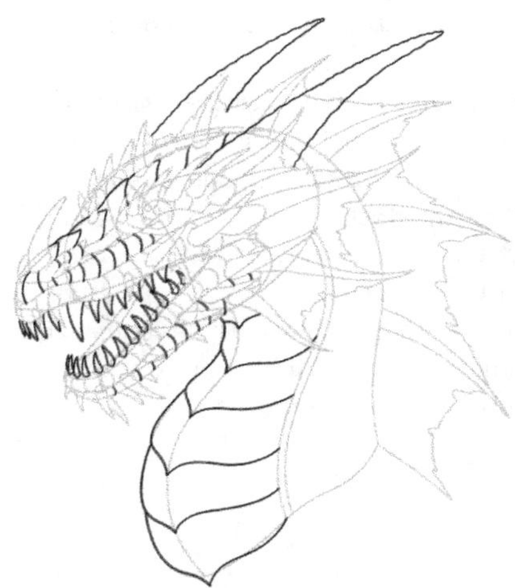

10

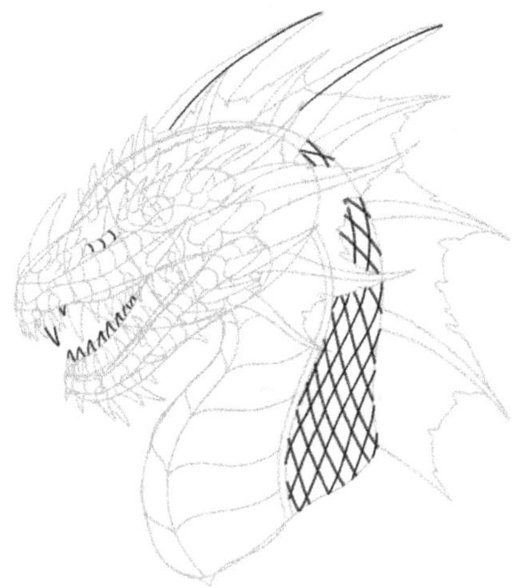

11

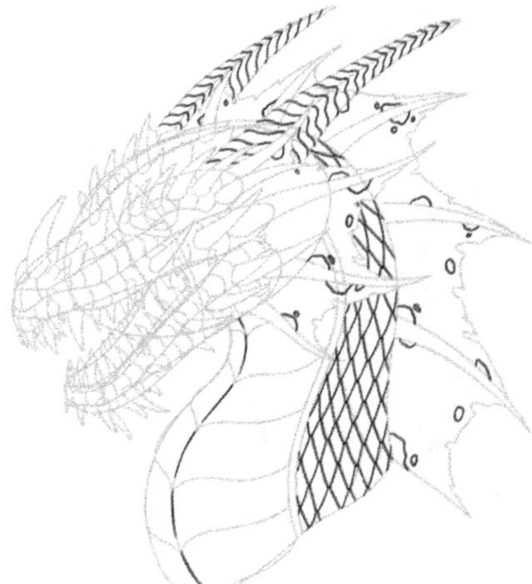

12

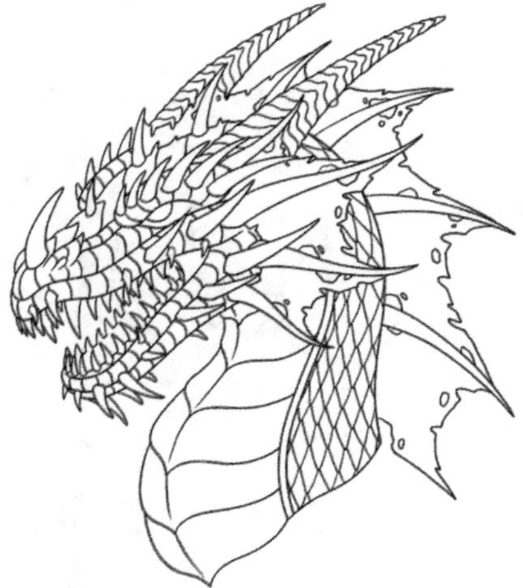

BASILISK

Pro tip: start with a flowing spine line

Begin by sketching a single, sweeping line to represent the creature's spine, then build the body around it using three interlocking circles for the head, chest, and hips. This spine-first approach instantly defines the Basilisk's posture and movement, making it easier to place limbs, wings, and the tail in a way that feels fluid and balanced.

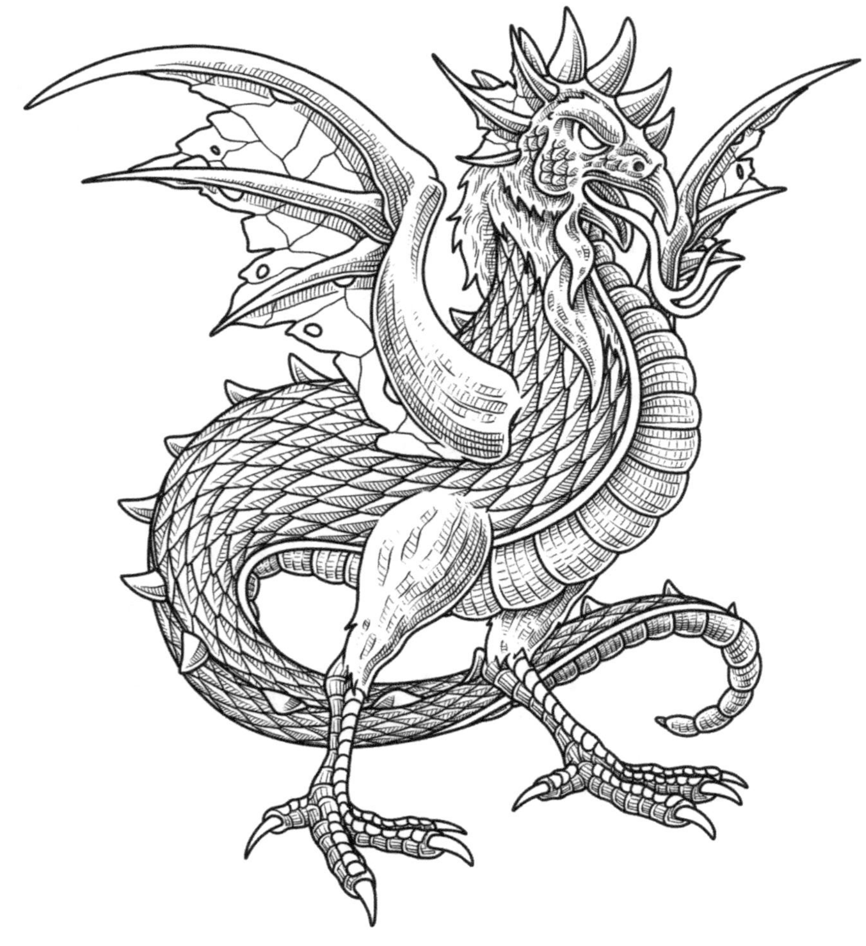

01

02

03

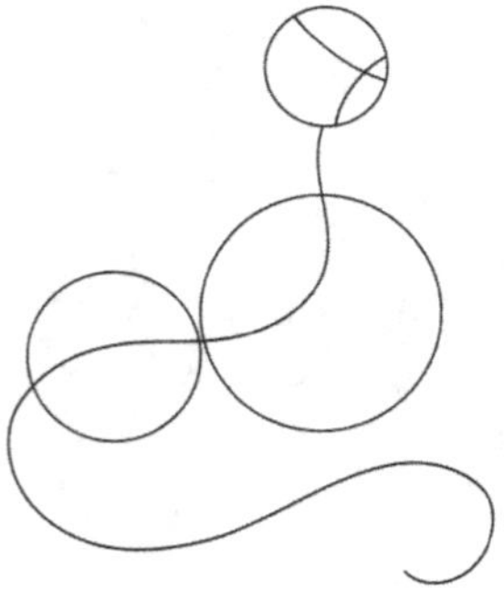

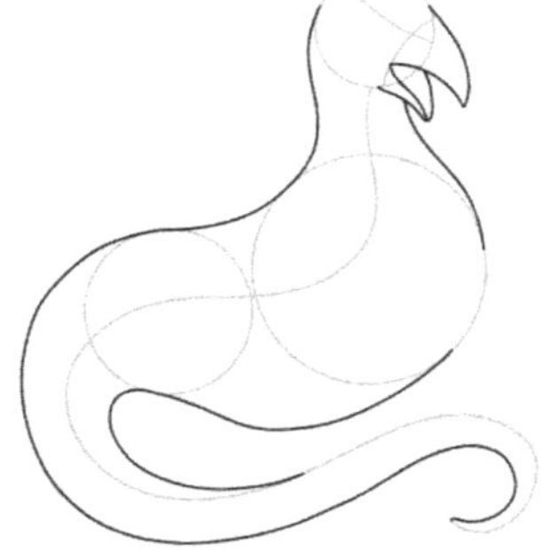

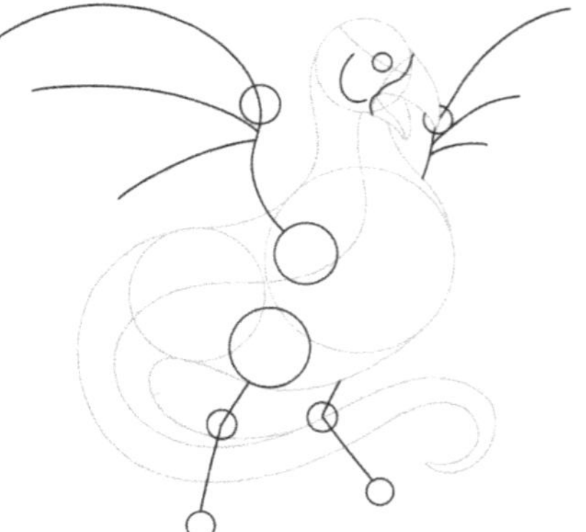

04

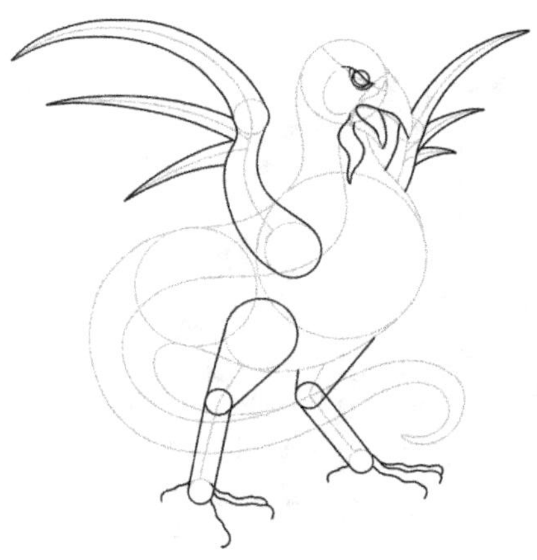

05

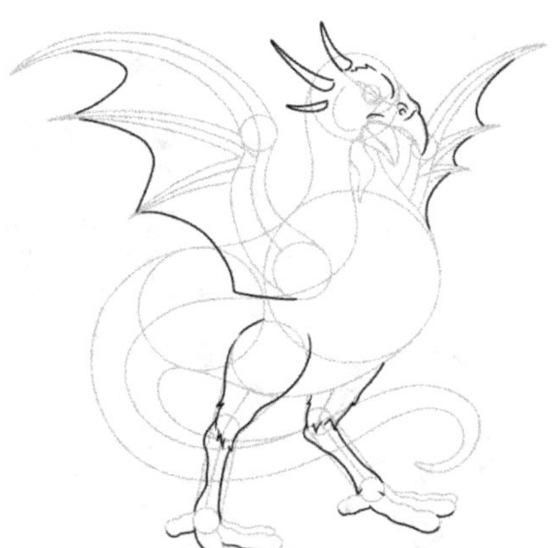

06

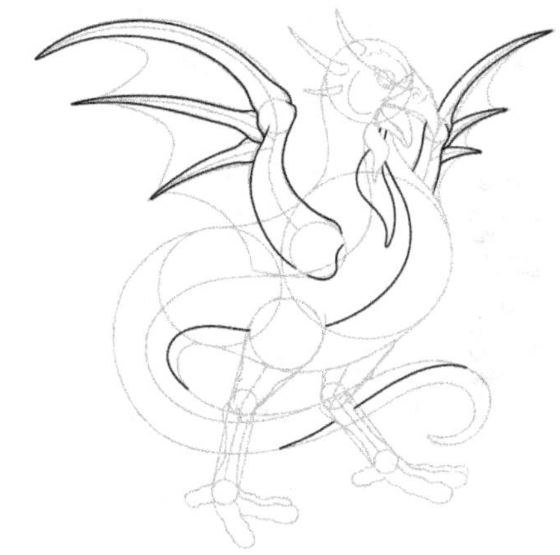

07

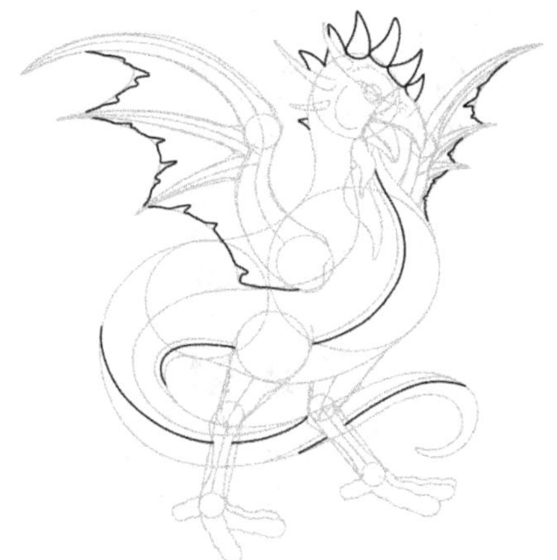

08

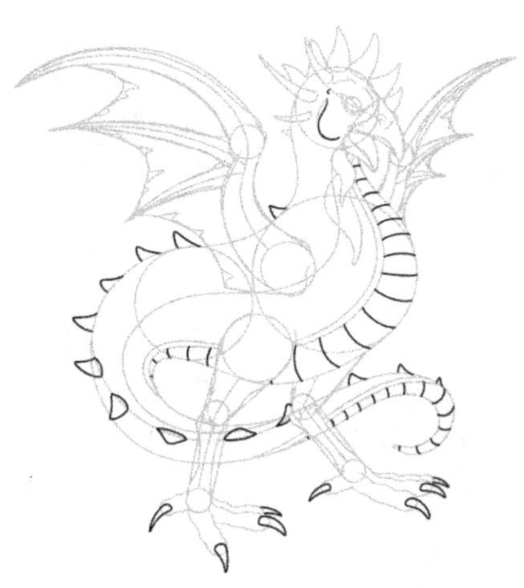

09

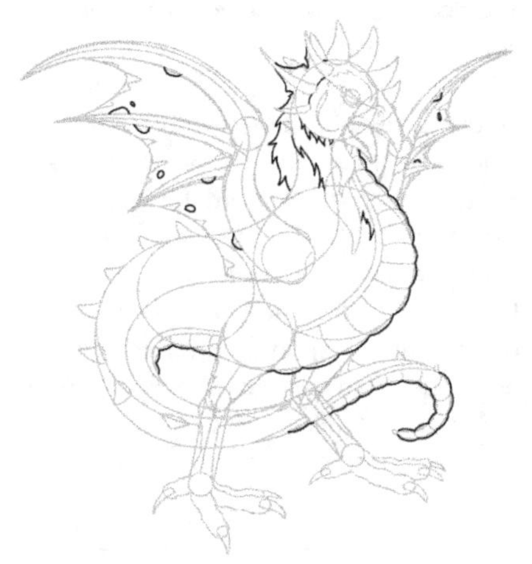

10

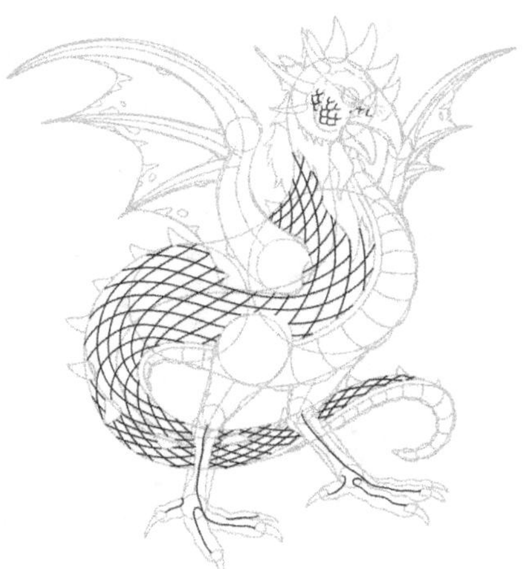

11

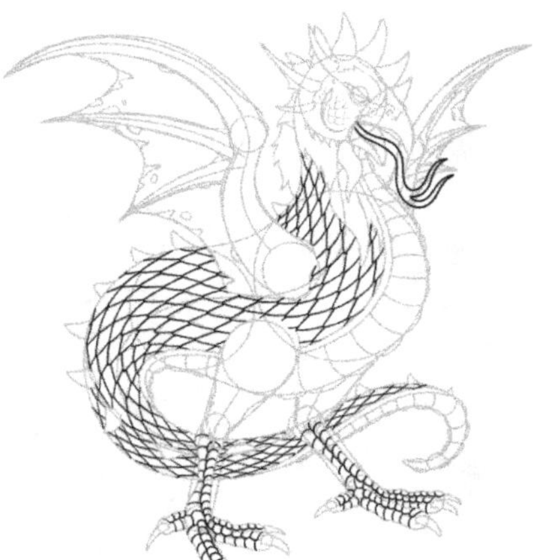

12

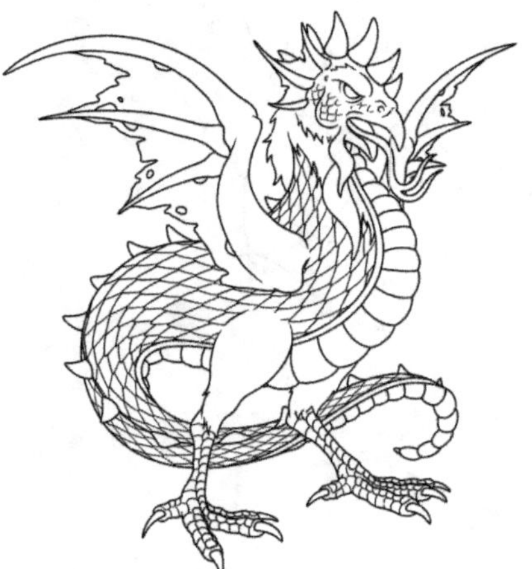

BIGFOOT

Pro tip: emphasise the weight through the torso tilt

To give BigFoot a powerful, grounded stance, angle the torso forward along a central axis that runs from the base of the skull through the pelvis. This forward tilt shifts the centre of gravity over the bent legs, creating a sense of heavy mass and momentum. Keep the shoulders broad and squared to reinforce the creature's strength and bulk.

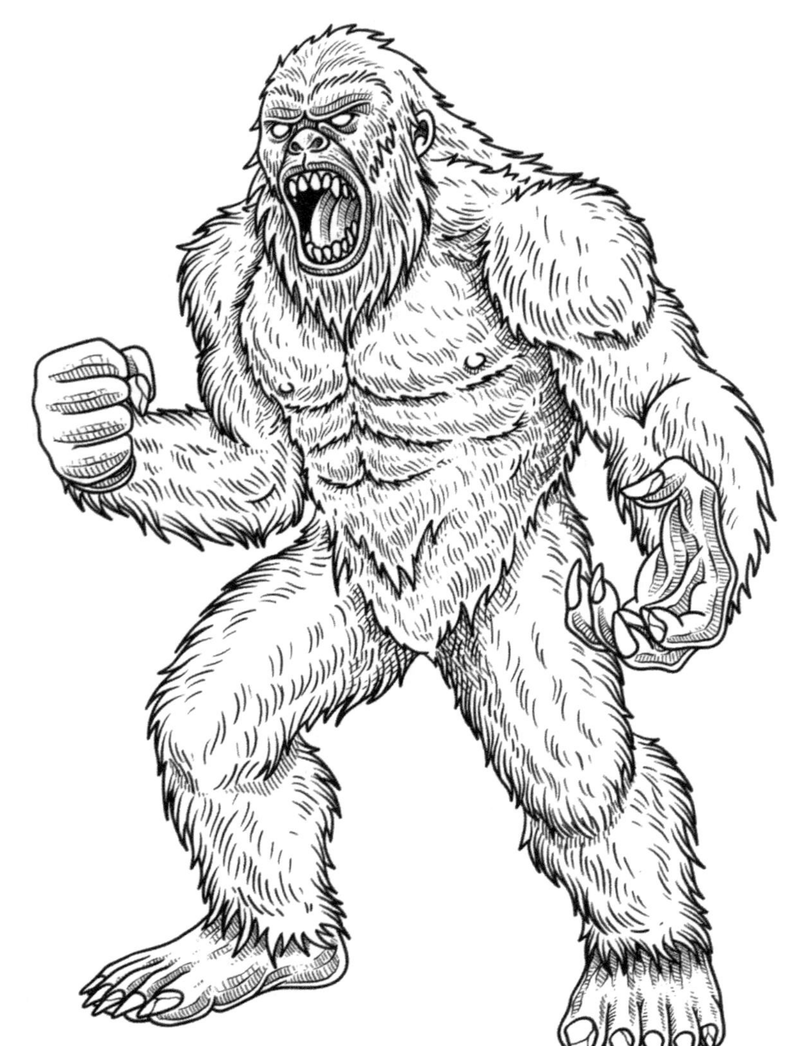

01

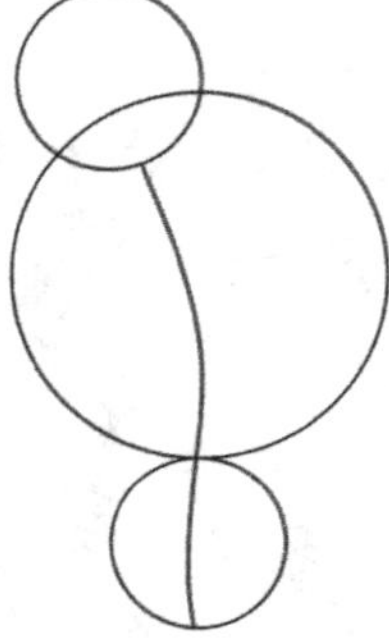

02

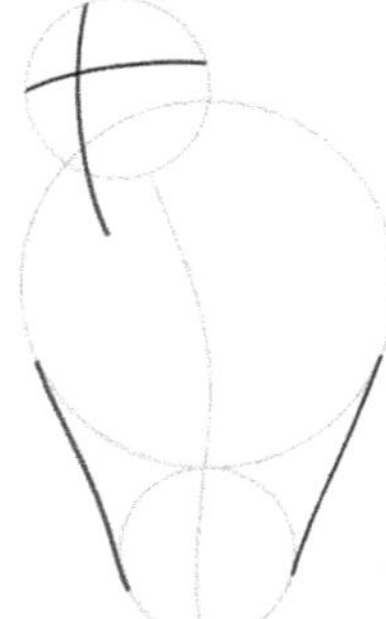

03

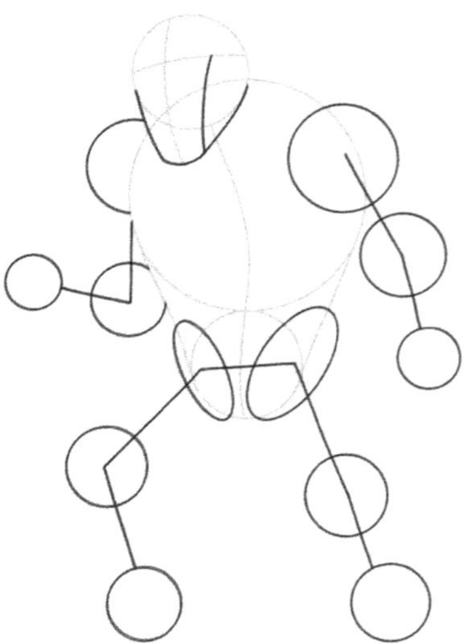

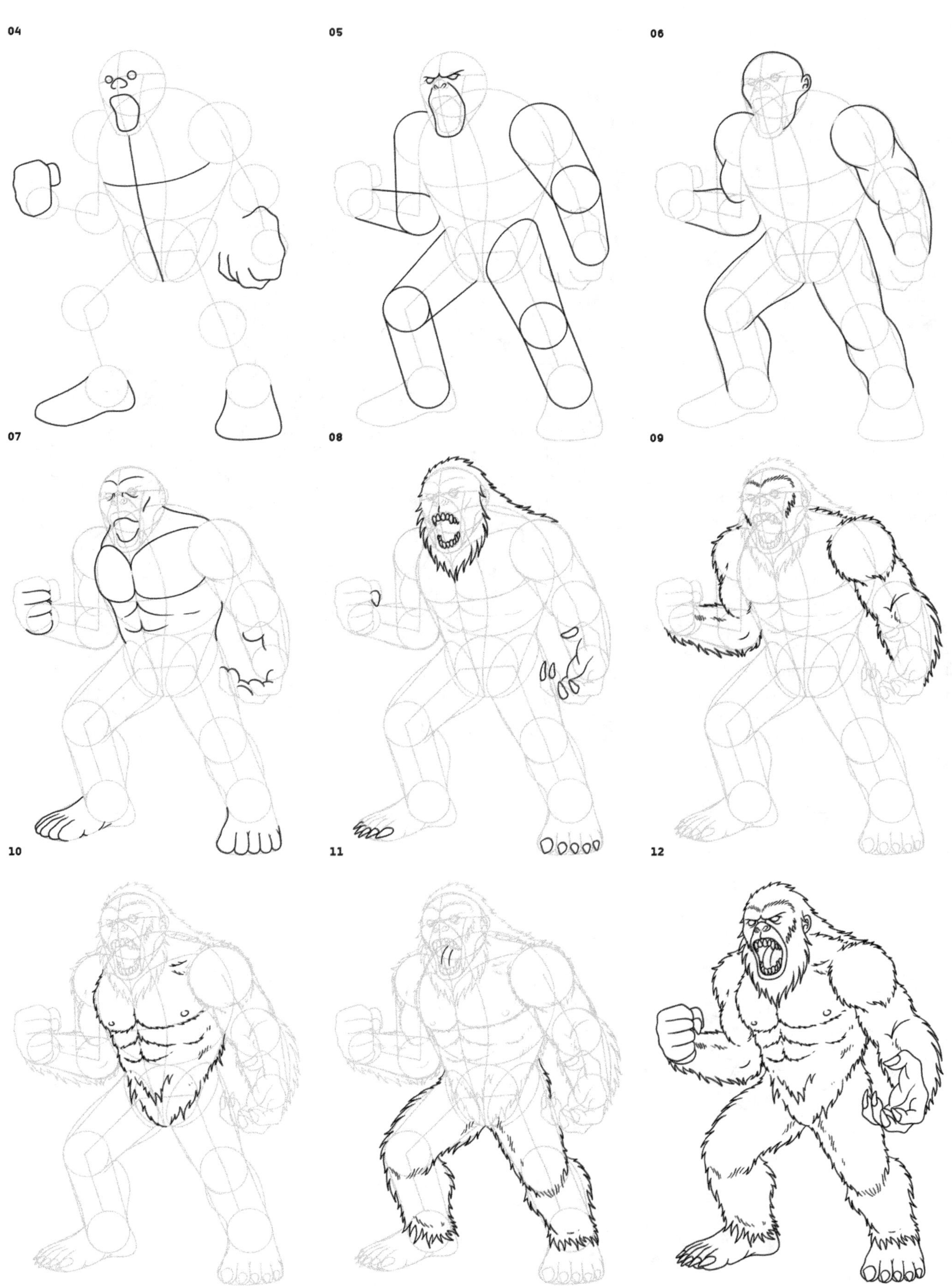

04
05
06
07
08
09
10
11
12
HOW TO DRAW MONSTERS & BEASTS

CHIMERA

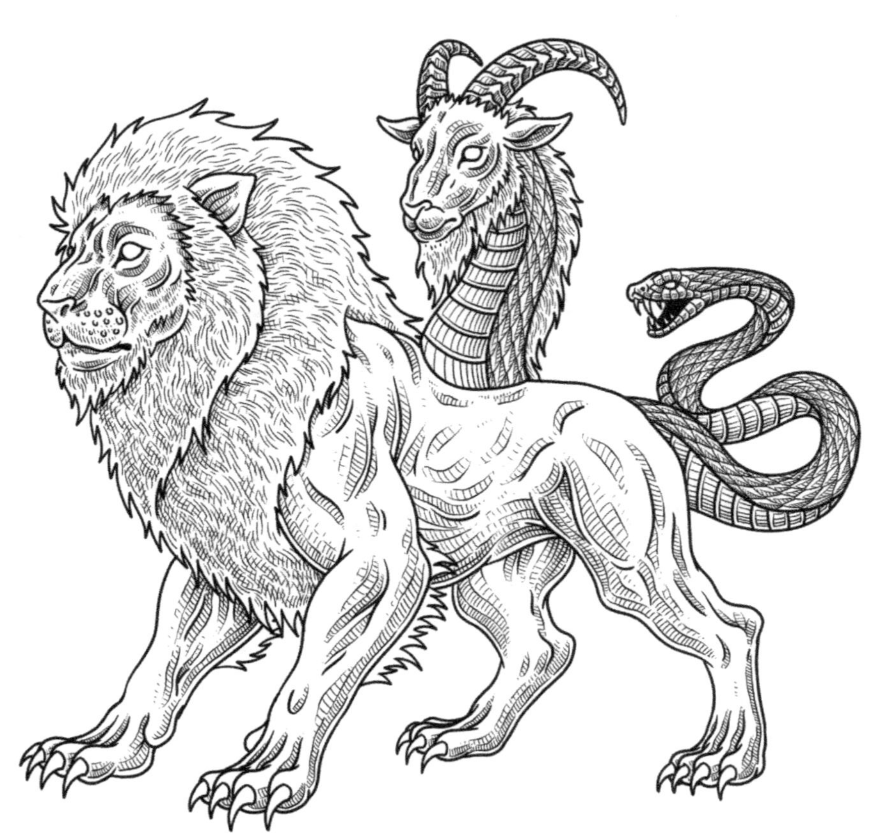

Pro tip: stagger the necks along the spine line

To position the Chimera's three heads clearly, place the lion's head at the front of the ribcage, the goat's head emerging from the top of the spine near the shoulders, and the serpent's head extending from the end of the tail. Aligning each neck along different points of the spine prevents visual clutter, ensures each head has space to read clearly, and reinforces the creature's hybrid anatomy.

01

02

03

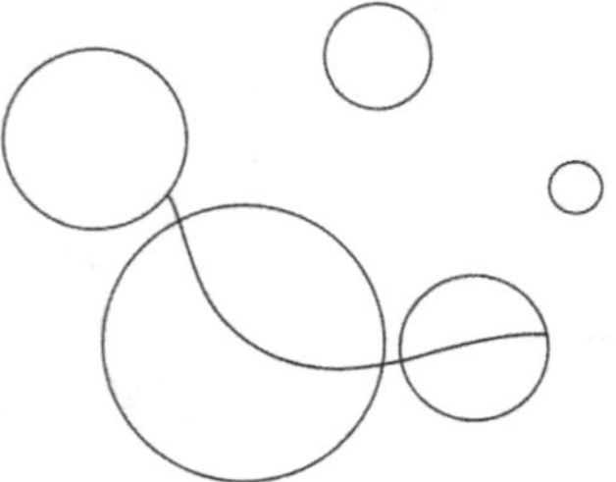

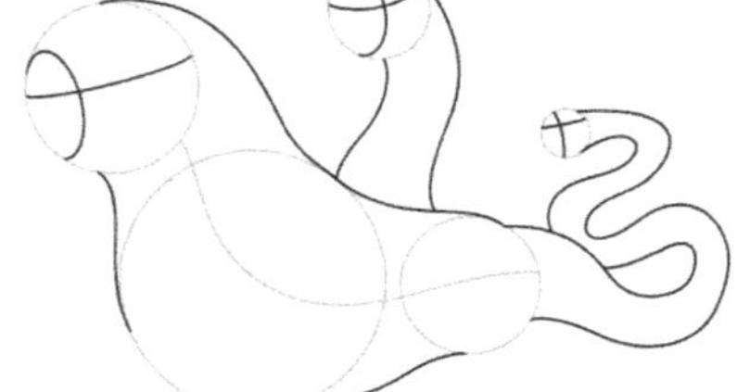

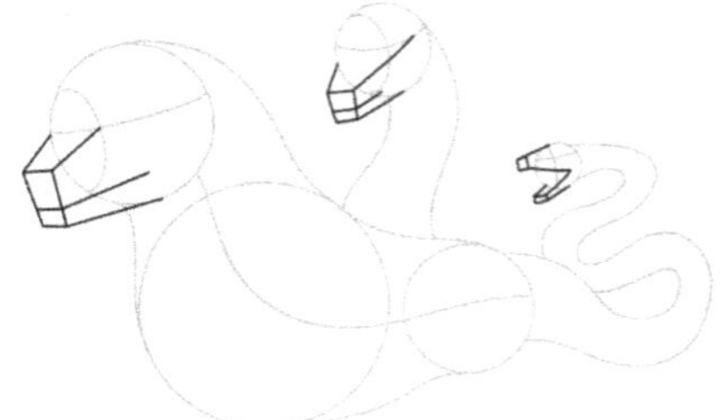

04

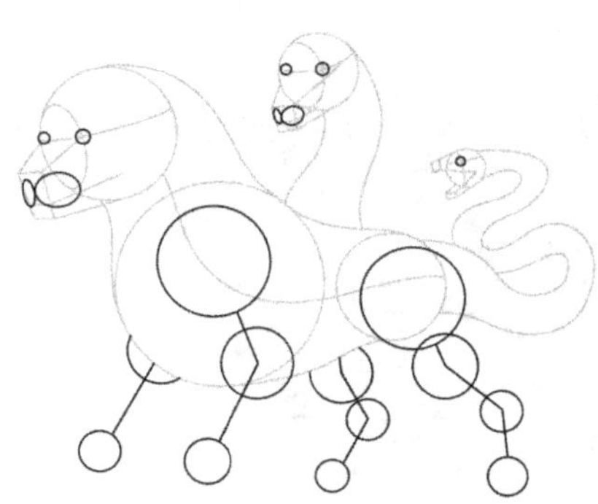

05

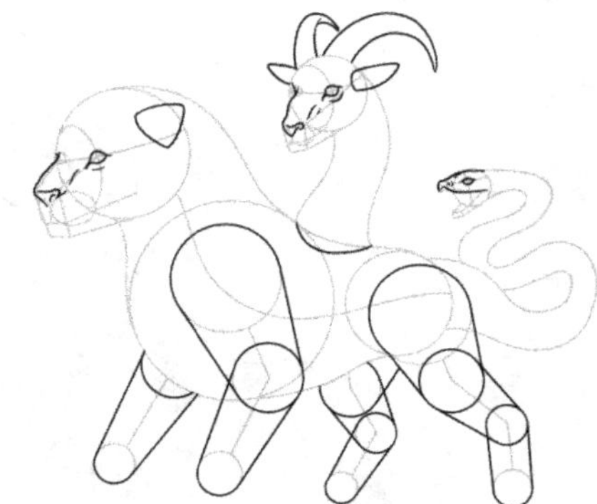

06

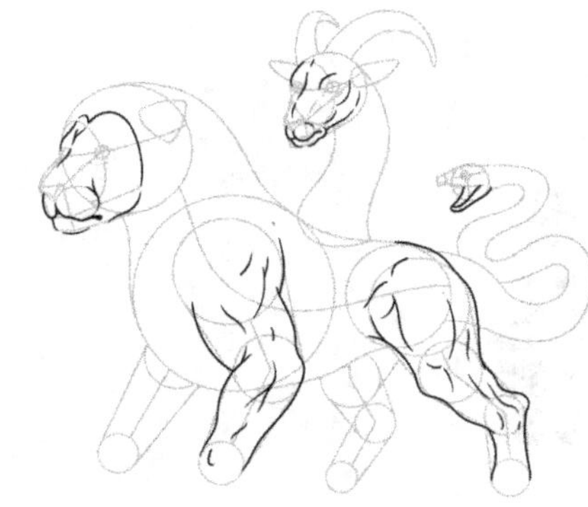

07

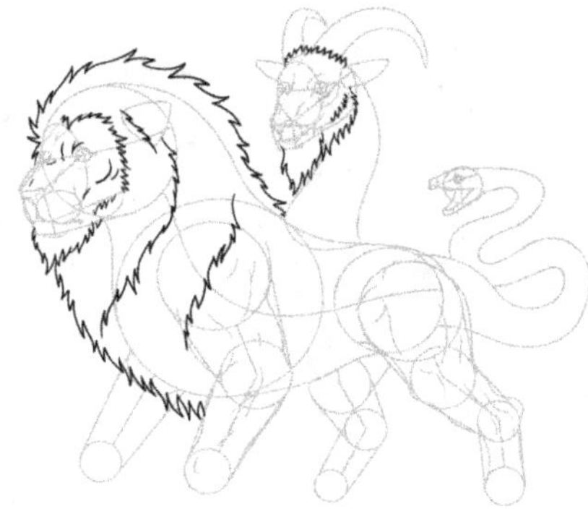

08

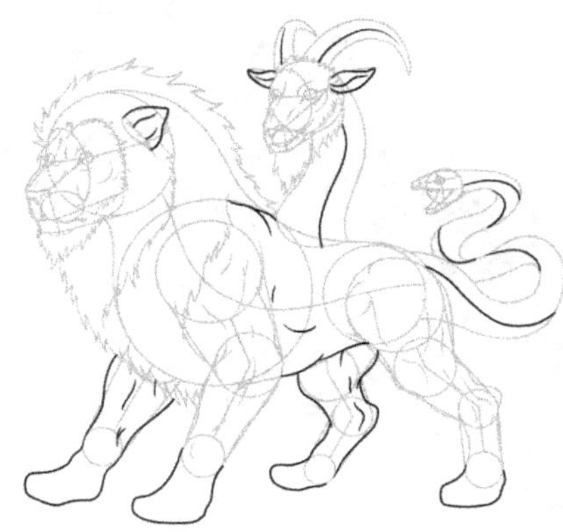

09

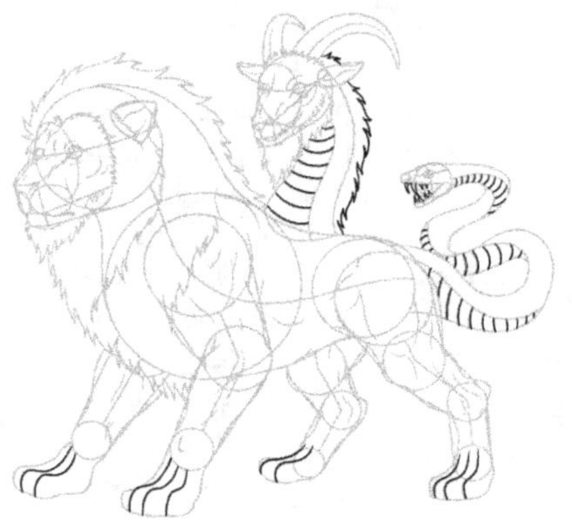

10

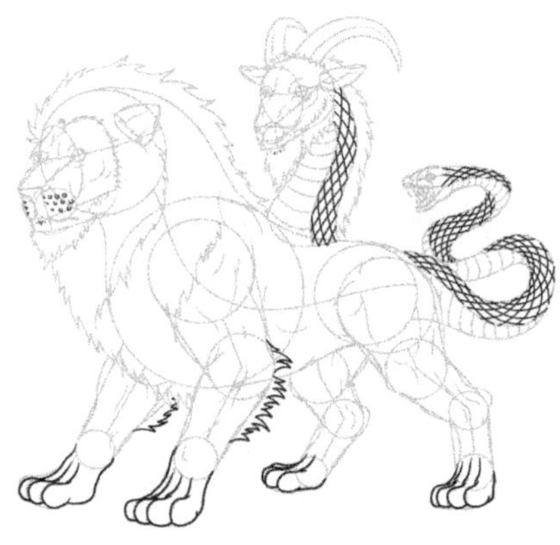

11

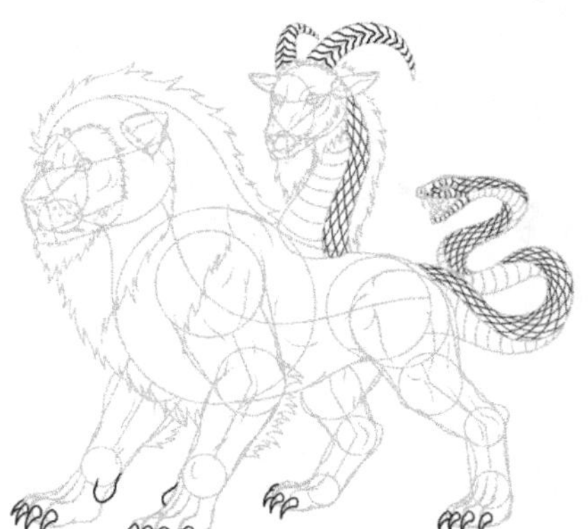

12

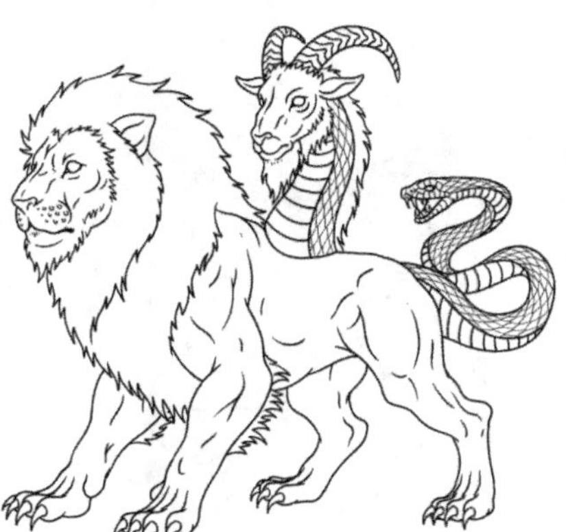

GRIFFIN

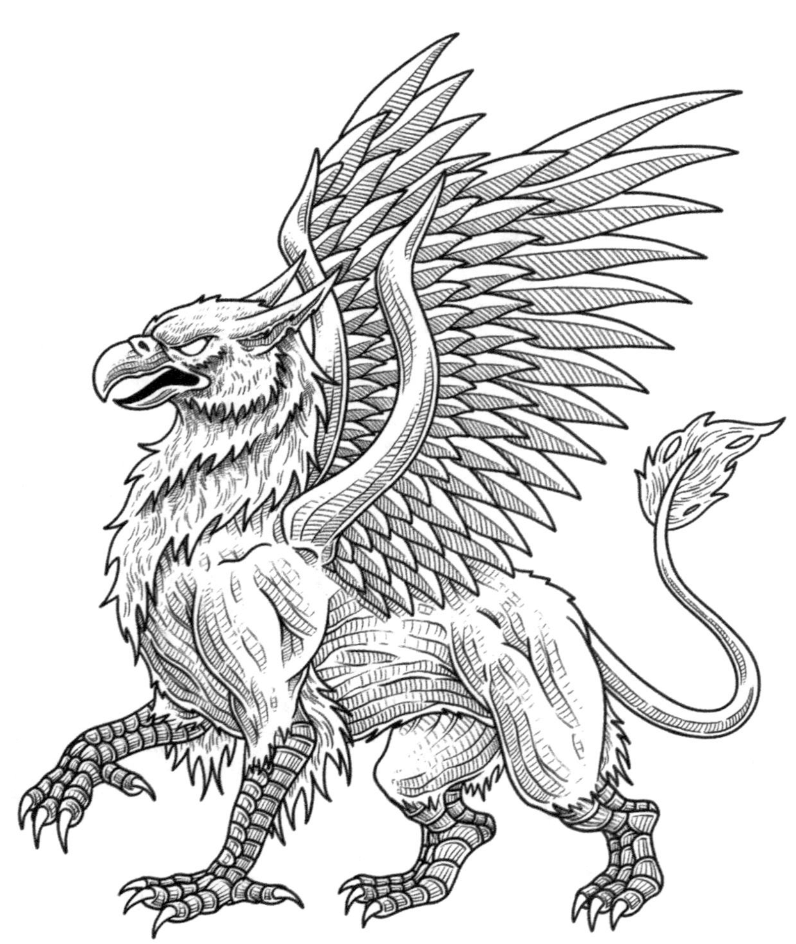

Pro tip: scale the wings to match the body's mass

The Griffin's wings should be about one and a half times the length of the body from beak to rump. When raised, they should reach roughly double the height of the torso. These proportions give the wings enough visual weight to balance the creature's powerful, lion-like body and create a convincing silhouette.

01   02   03

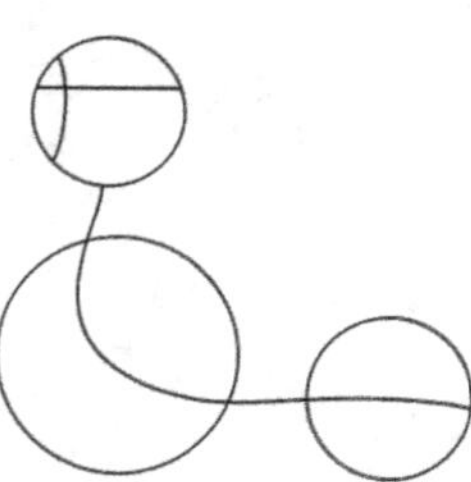

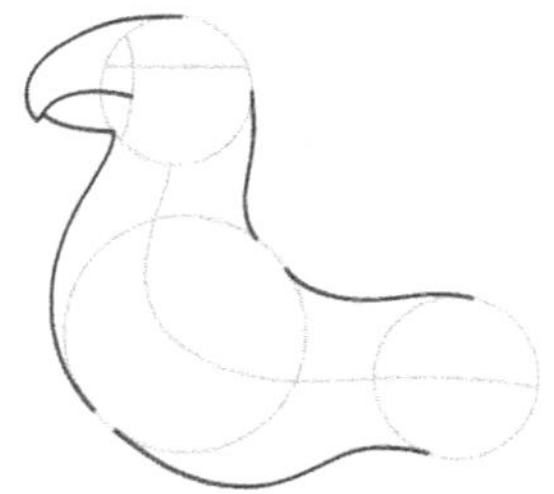

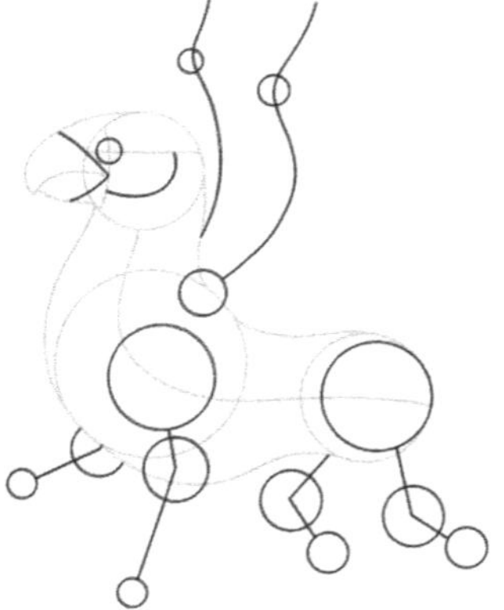

04

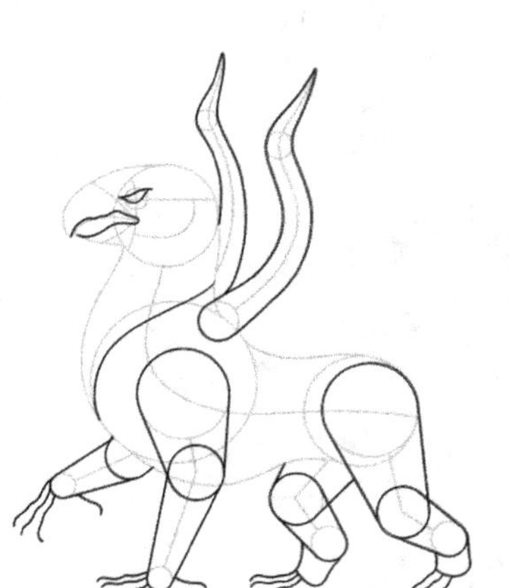

05

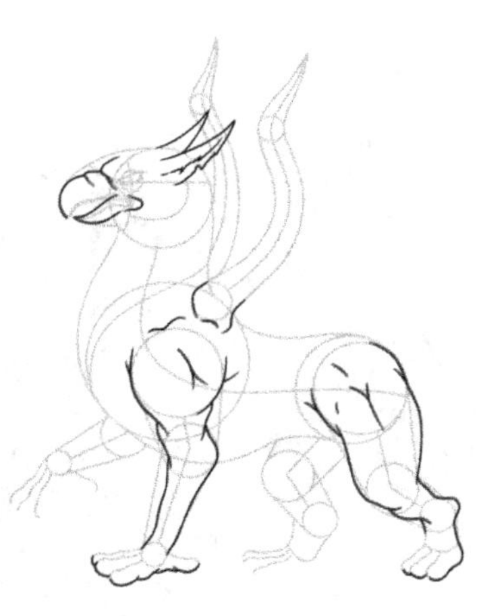

06

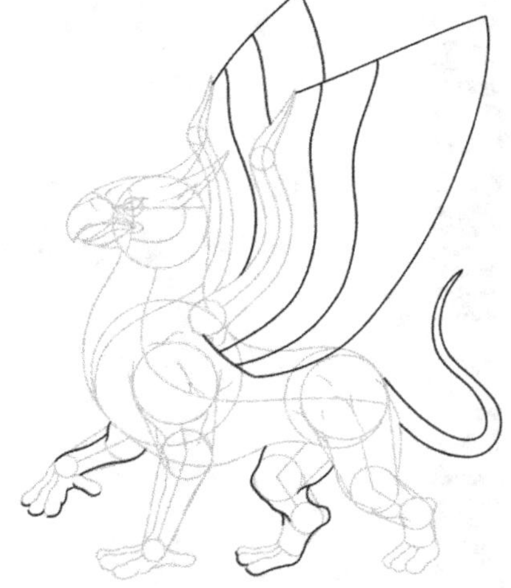

07

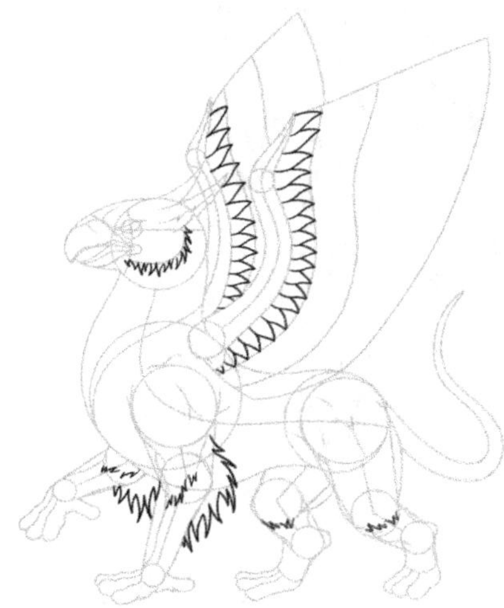

08

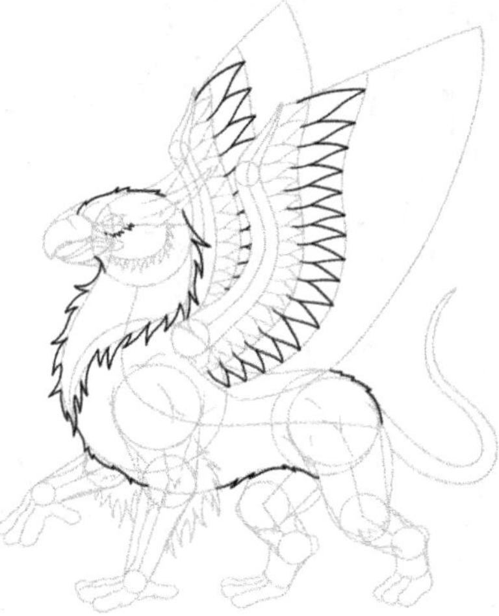

09

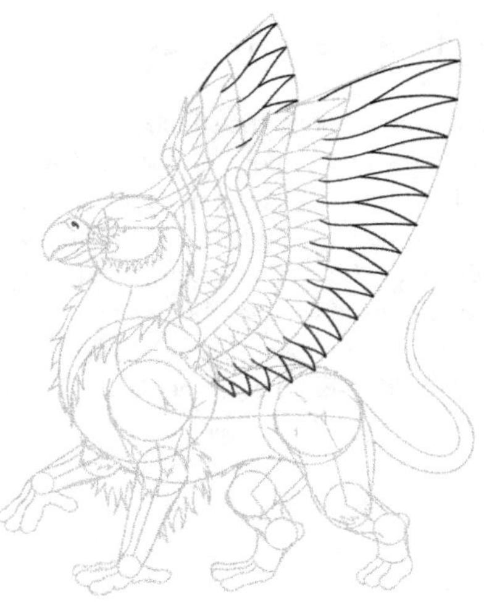

10

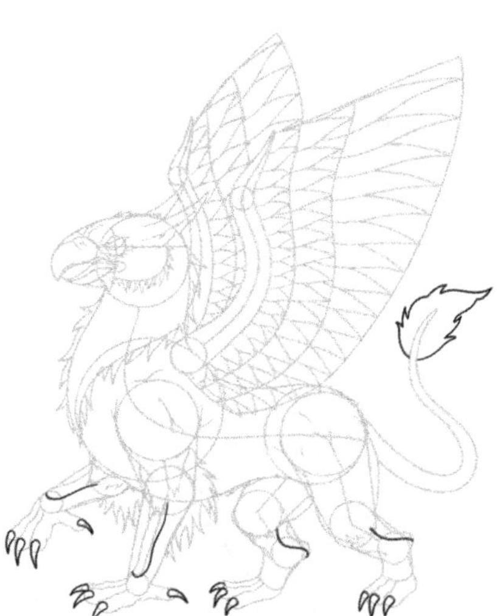

11

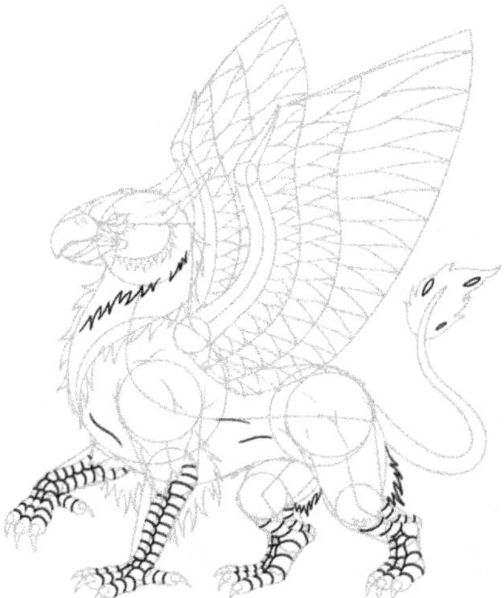

12

HOW TO DRAW MONSTERS & BEASTS

HEADLESS HORSEMAN

Pro Tip: define main masses early

Use simple geometric shapes to block in the horse's head, neck, and torso. Start with a large oval for the ribcage, a smaller one for the hindquarters, and a tapered box for the head. Connecting these with clean, flowing lines for the neck and back establishes the overall posture early, making it easier to layer the rider and limbs accurately later on.

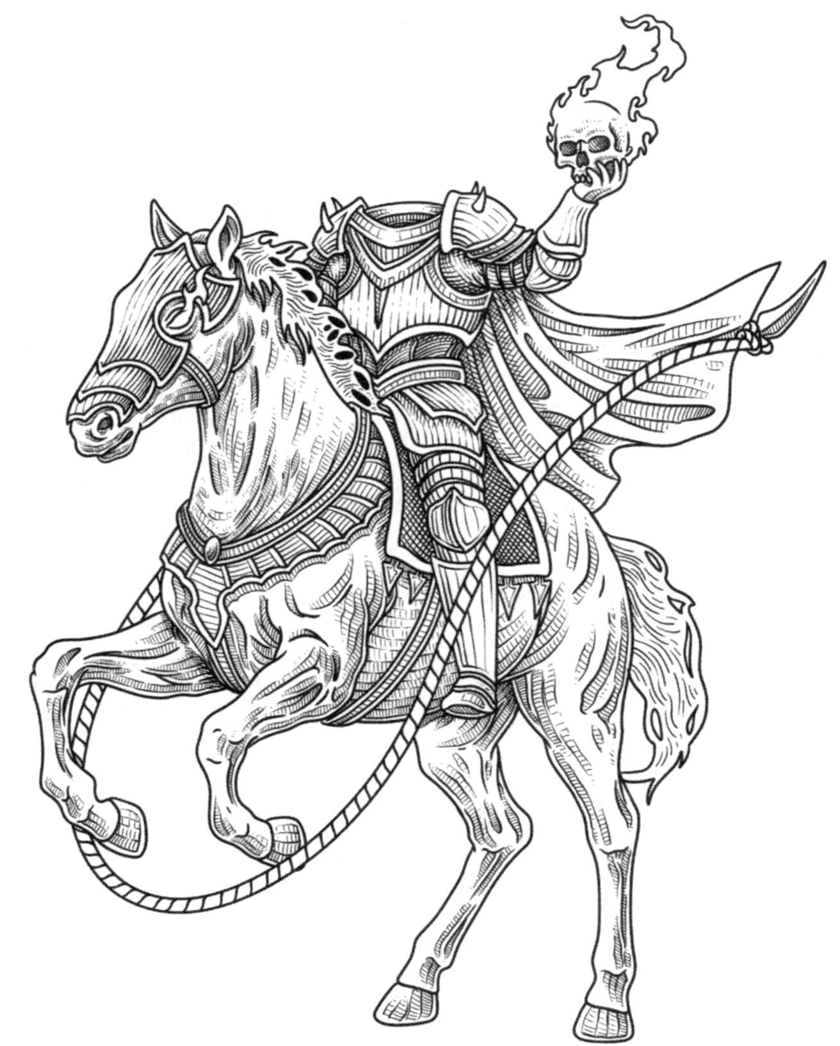

01

02

03

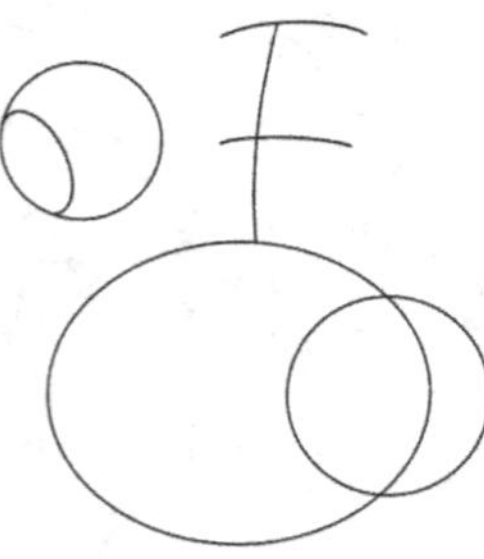

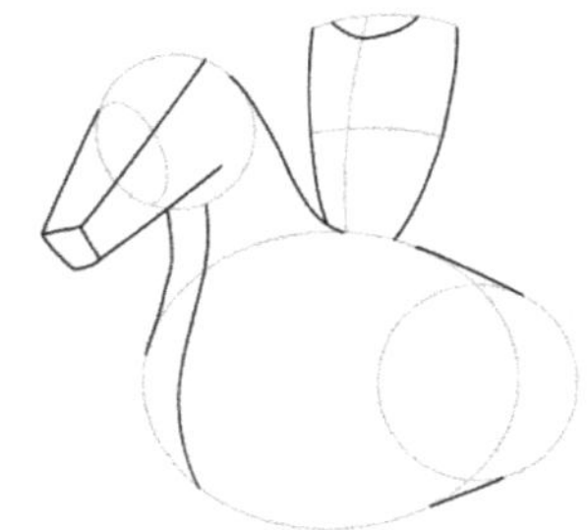

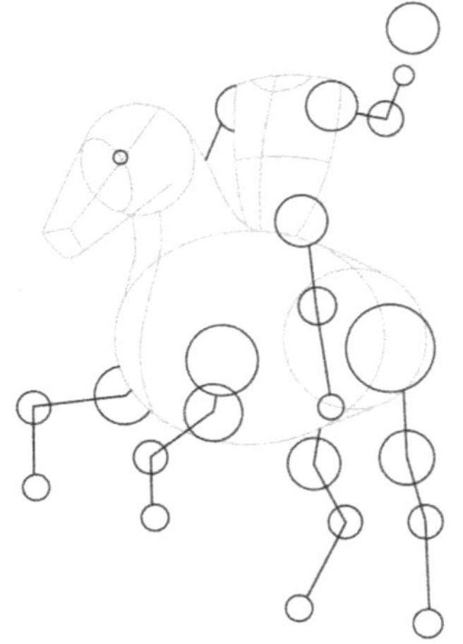

04

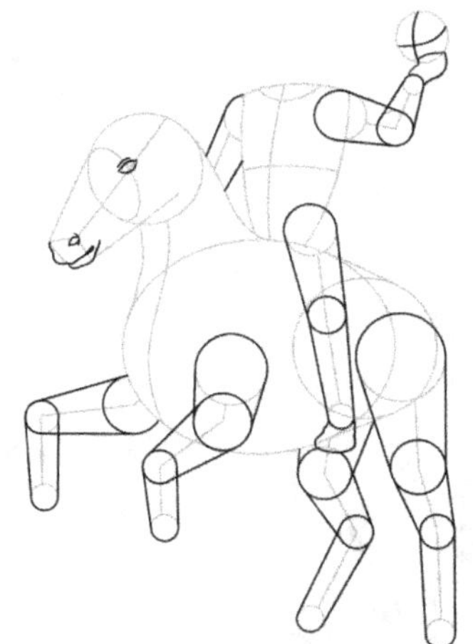

05

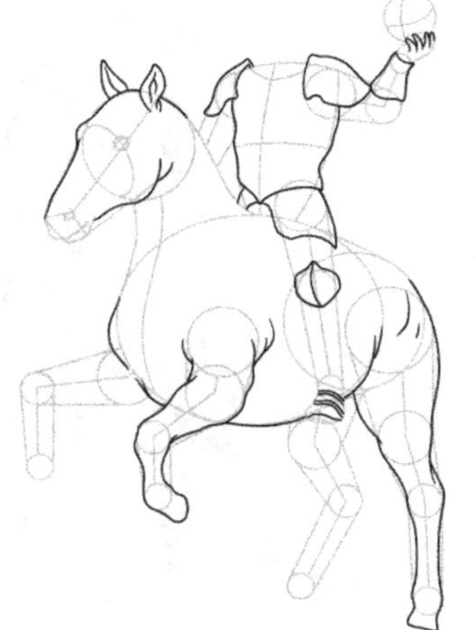

06

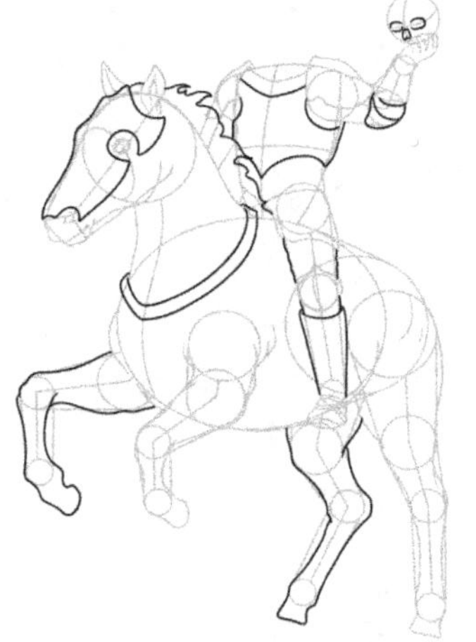

07

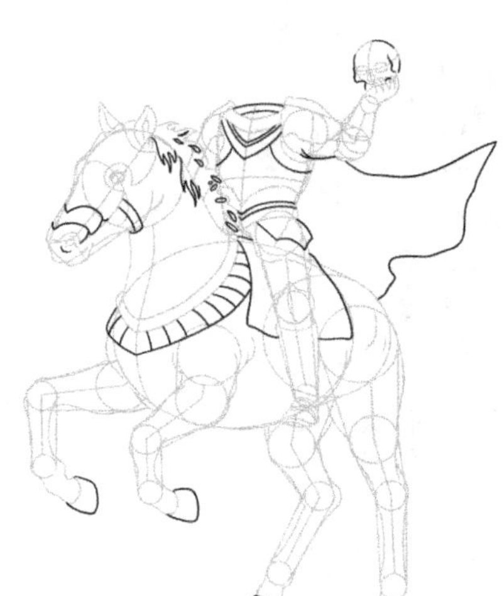

08

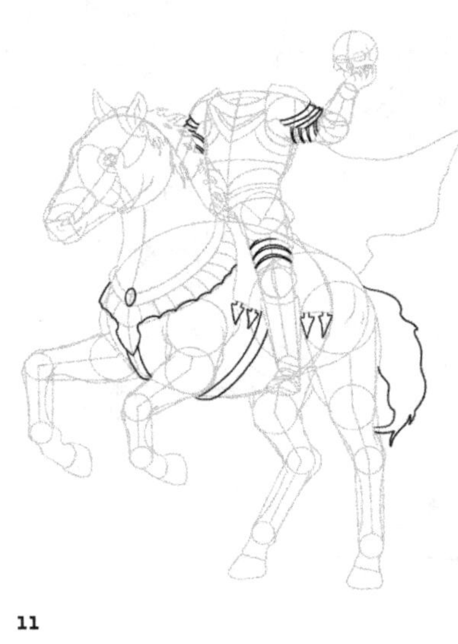

09

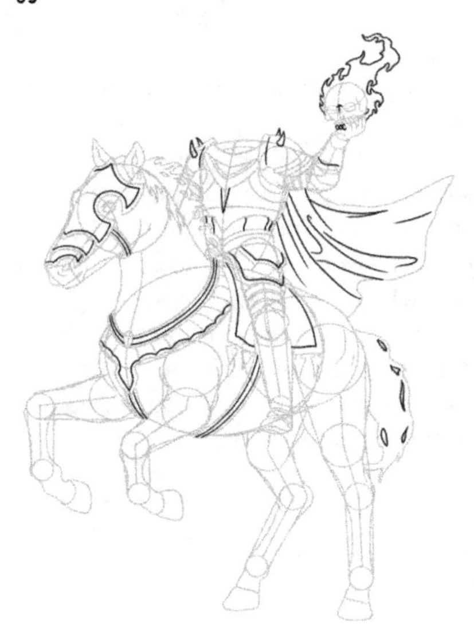

10

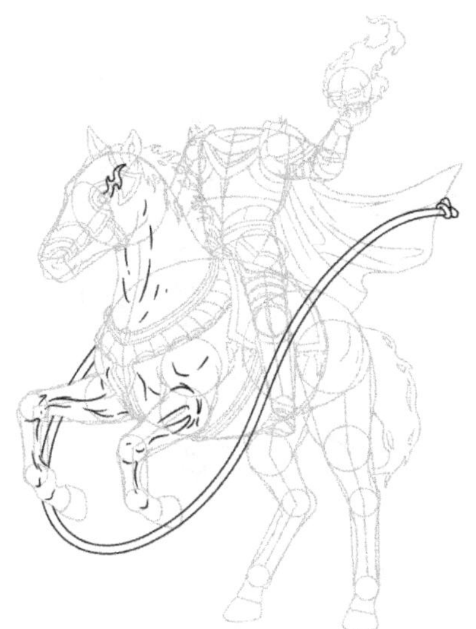

11

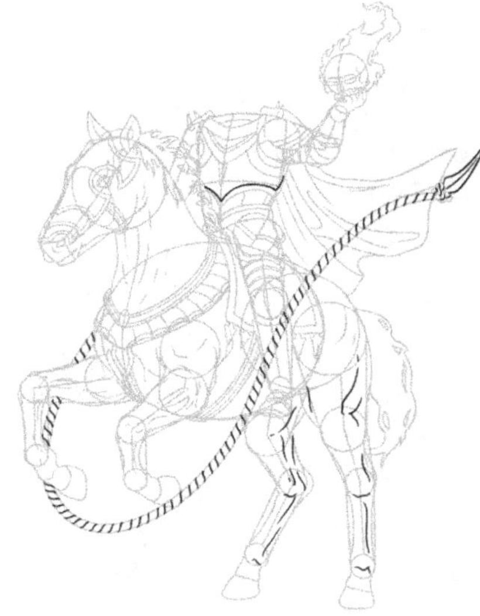

12

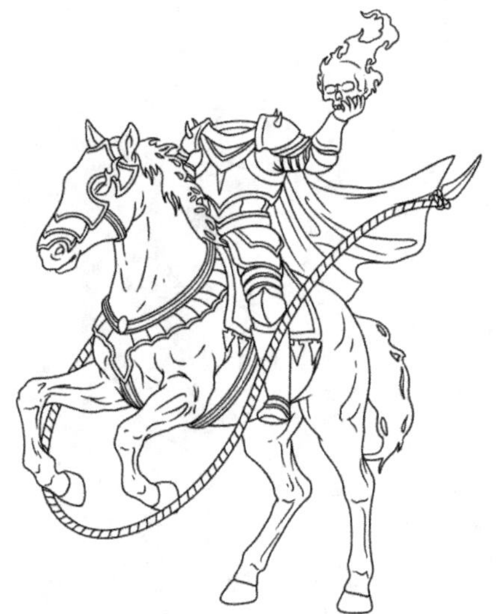

FOREST GUARDIAN

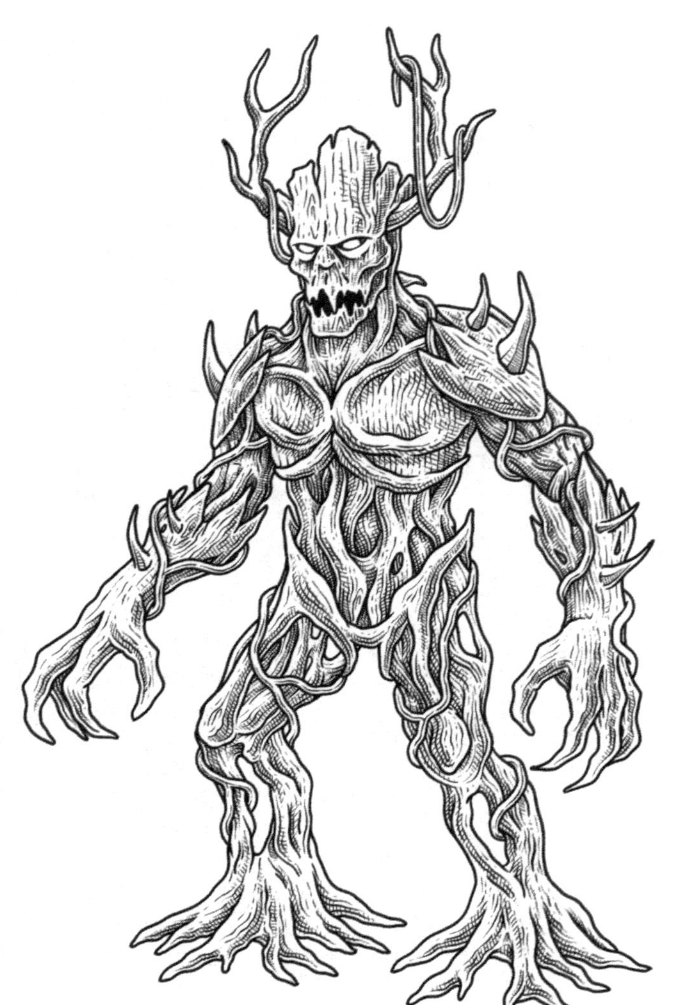

Pro tip: use head units to establish torso height

Measure the torso using the head as your basic unit. For this figure, the torso from the base of the neck to the bottom of the pelvis is roughly 2¼ head-heights tall. Marking this early ensures the proportions stay consistent and helps you position the limbs and ribcage accurately as you refine the figure.

01

02

03

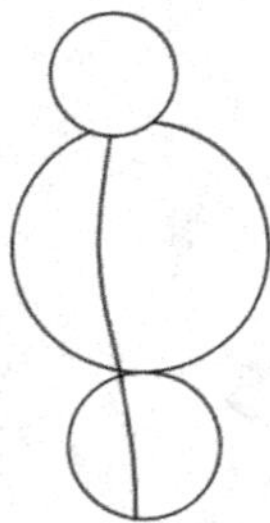

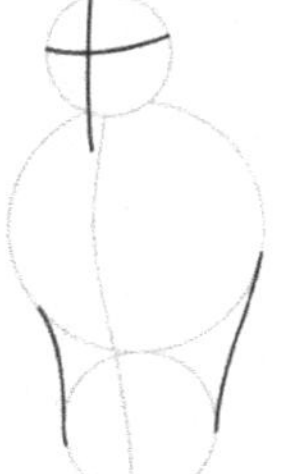

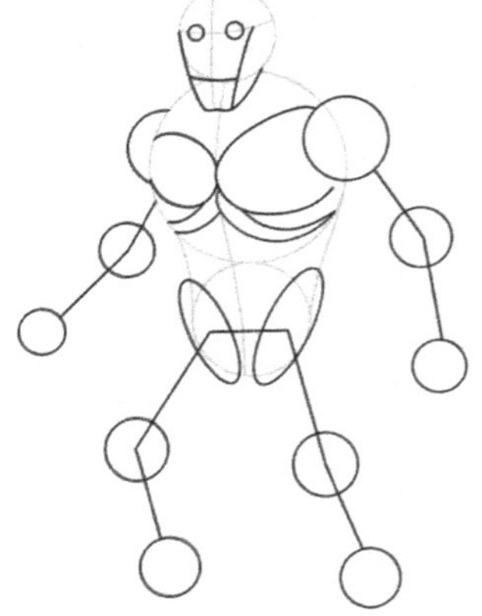

04

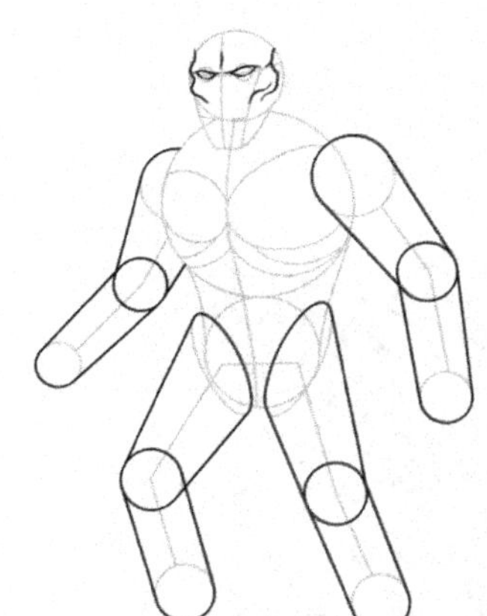

05

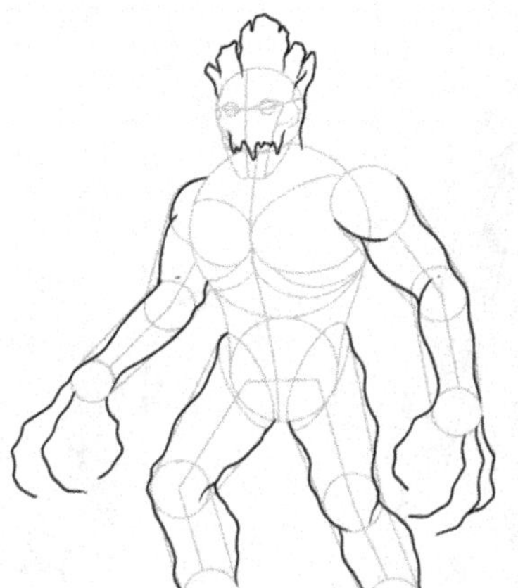

06

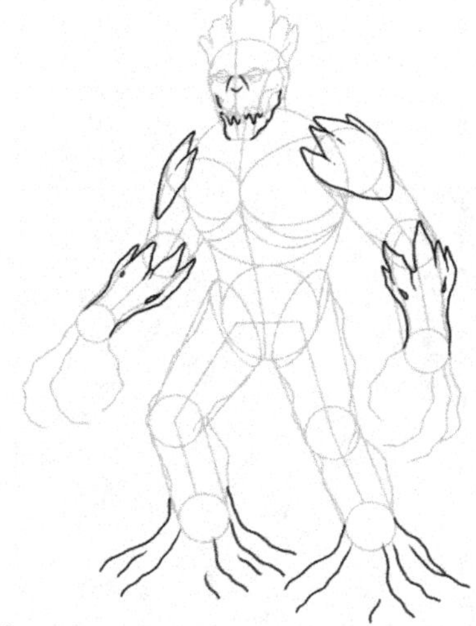

07

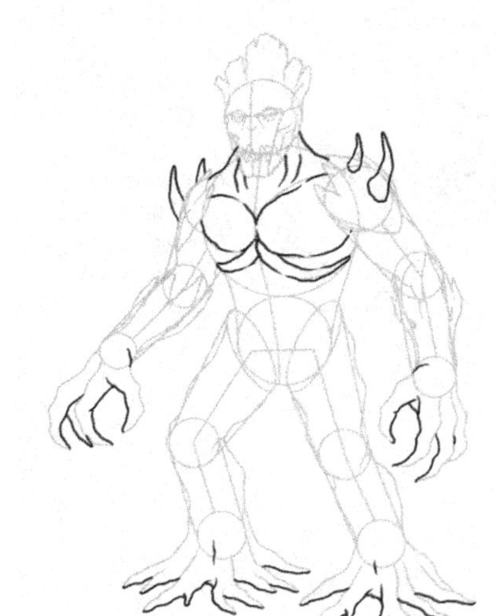

08

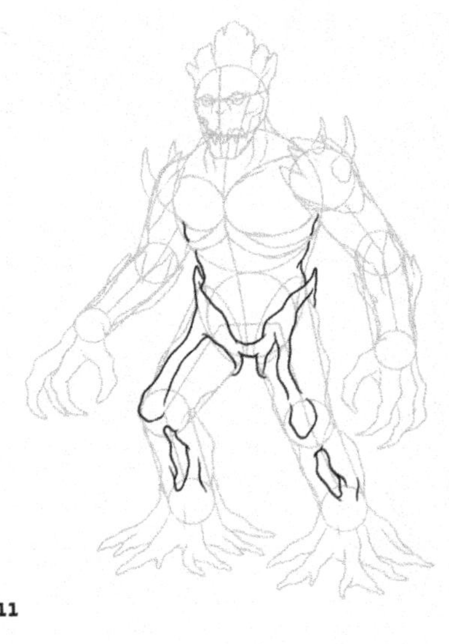

09

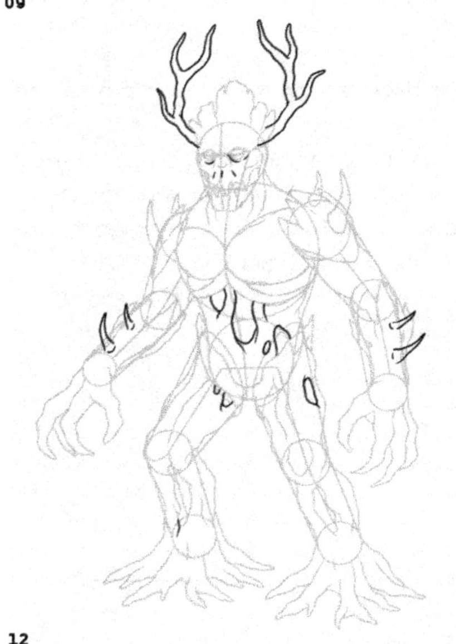

10

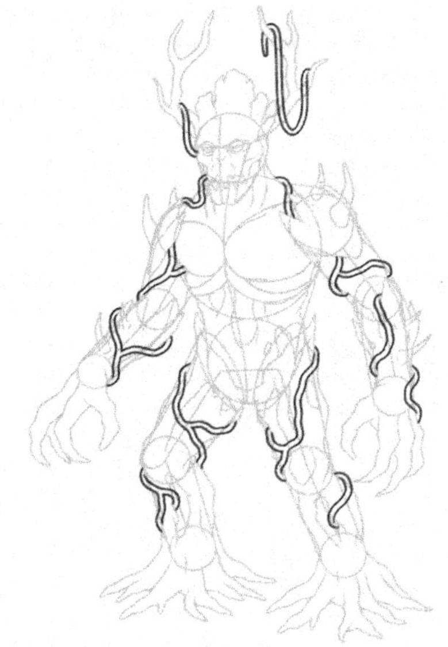

11

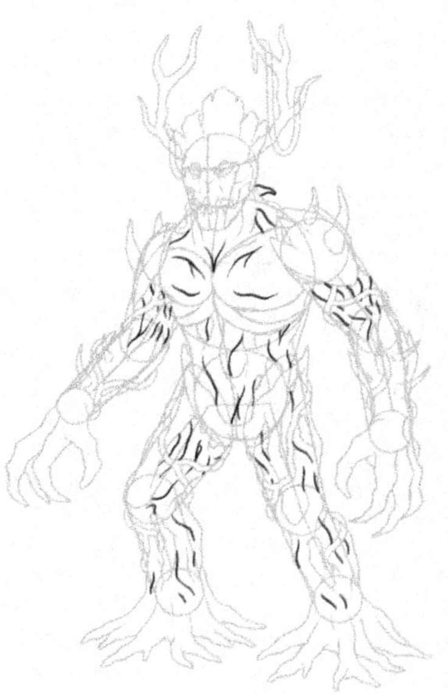

12

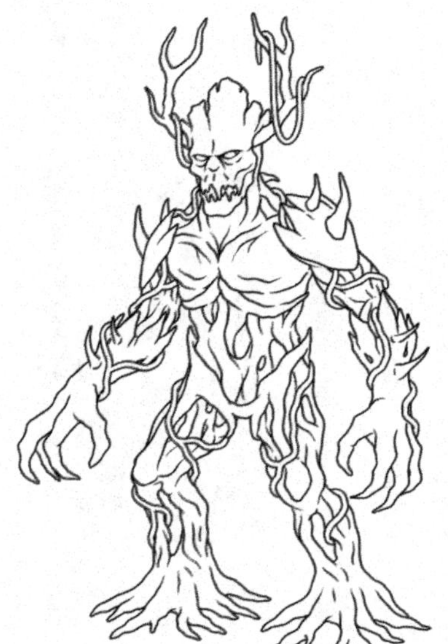

GOBLIN

Pro tip: exaggerate the head proportion

For a classic goblin silhouette, draw the head circle just slightly smaller than the torso circle. This creates an exaggerated, top-heavy proportion that instantly gives the character a mischievous and fantastical energy.

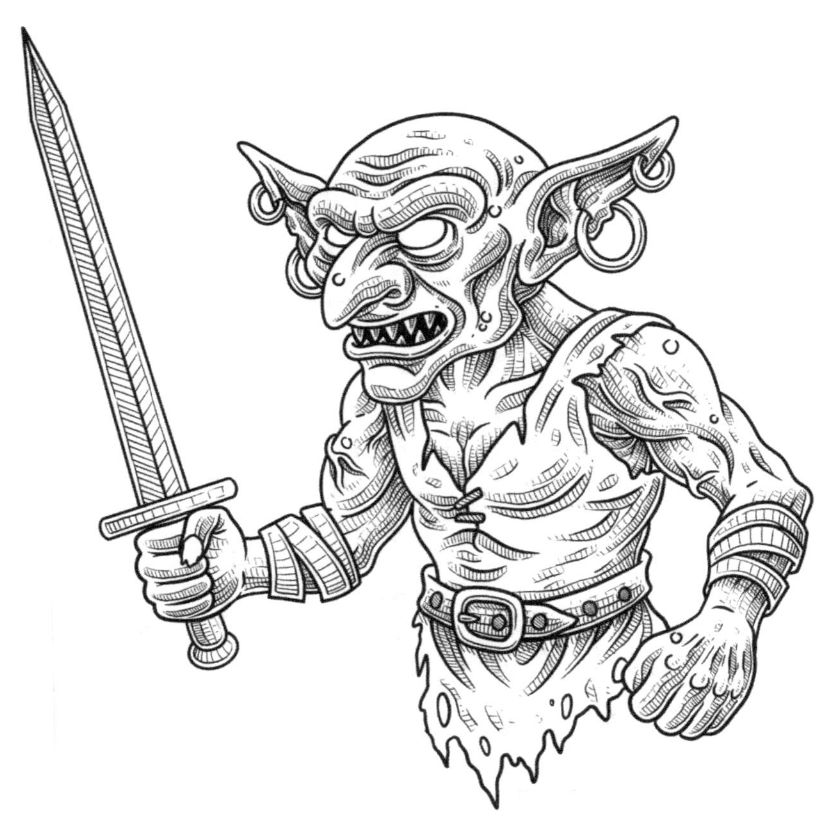

01

02

03

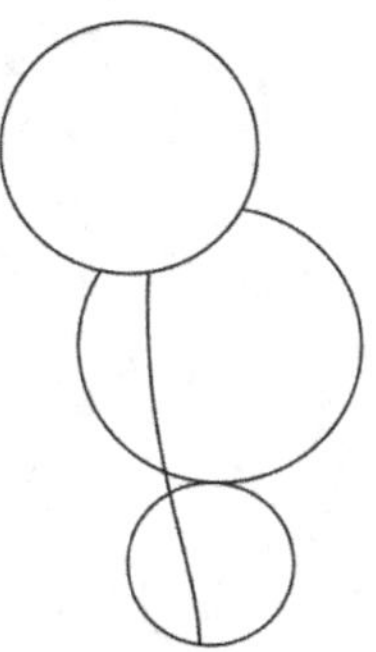

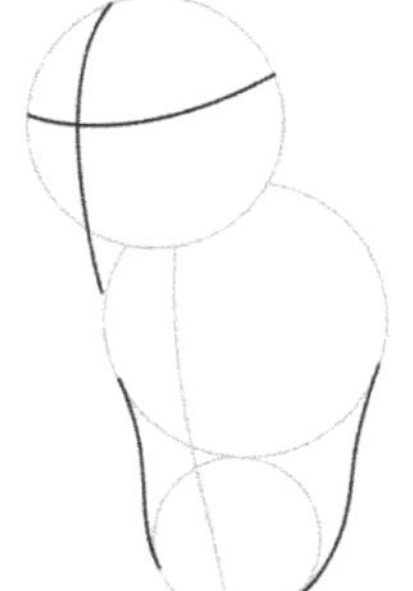

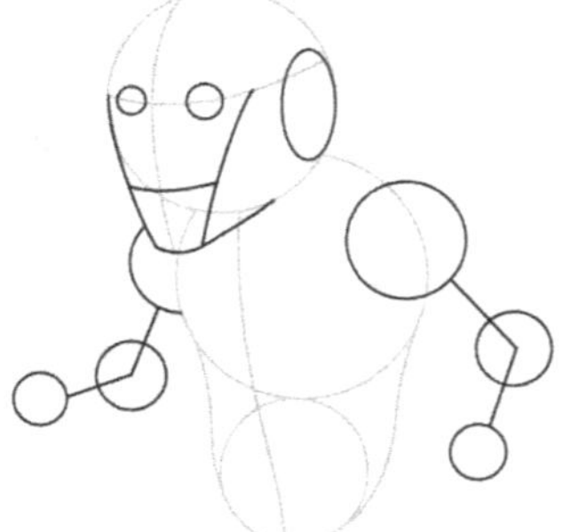

04

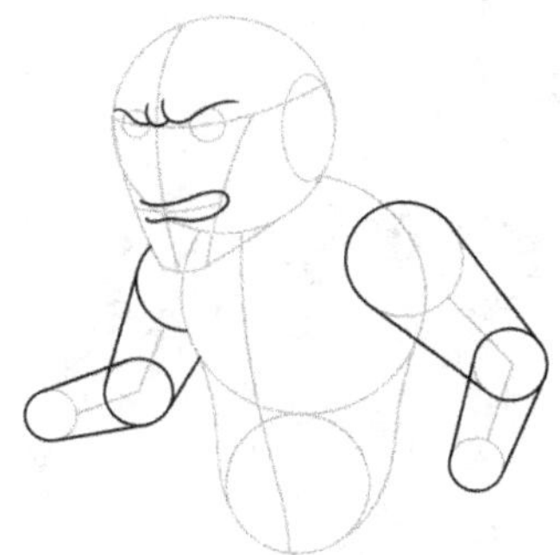

05

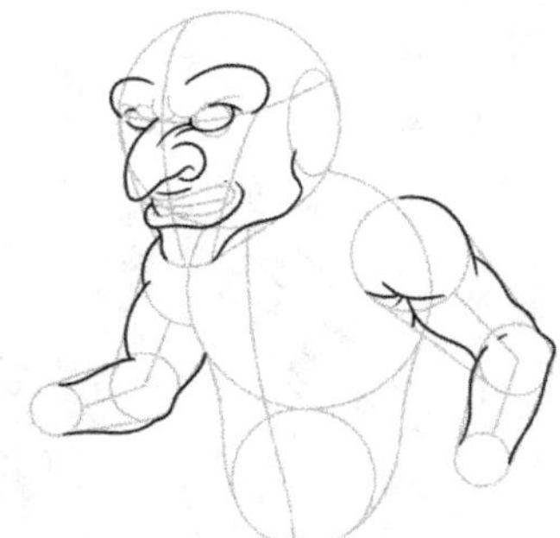

06

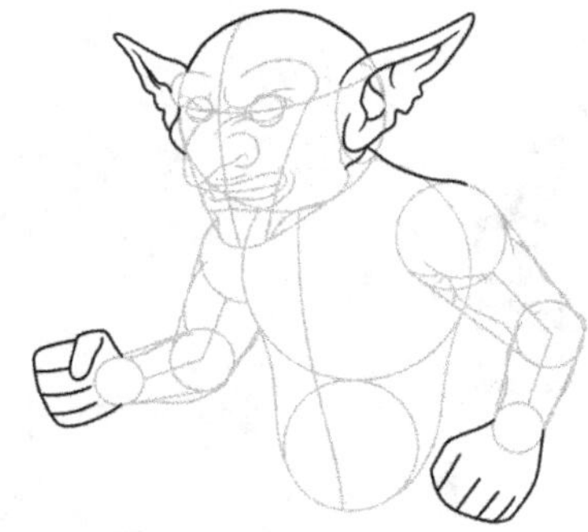

07

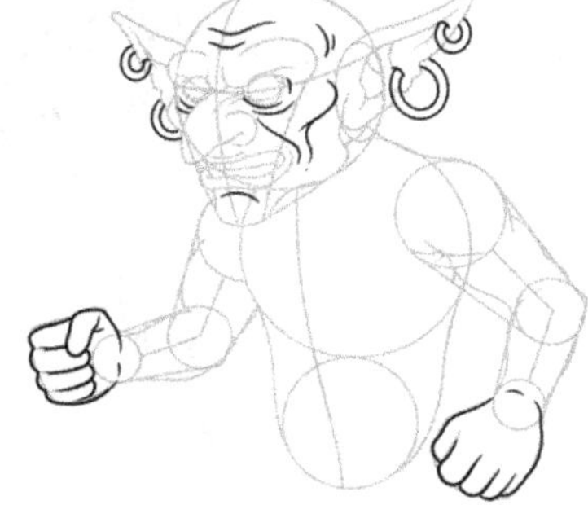

08

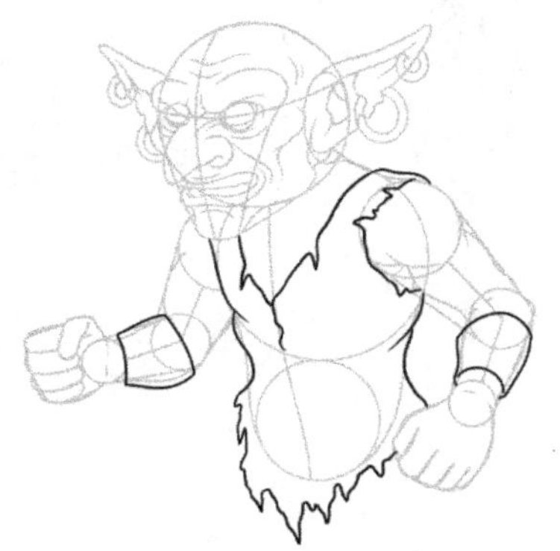

09

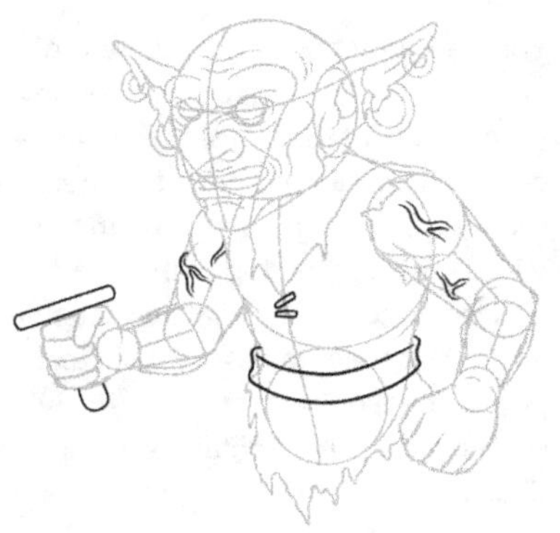

10

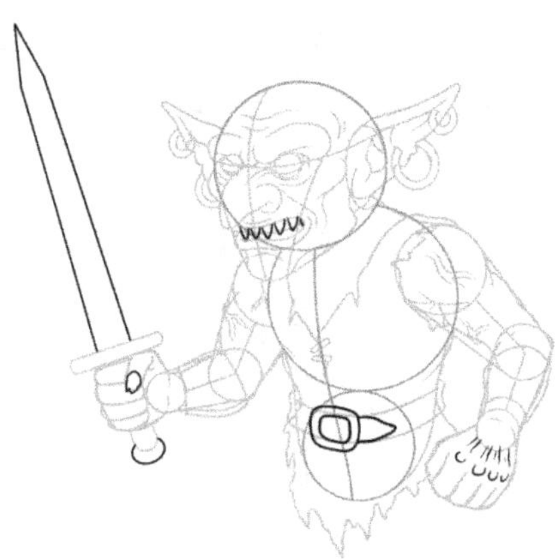

11

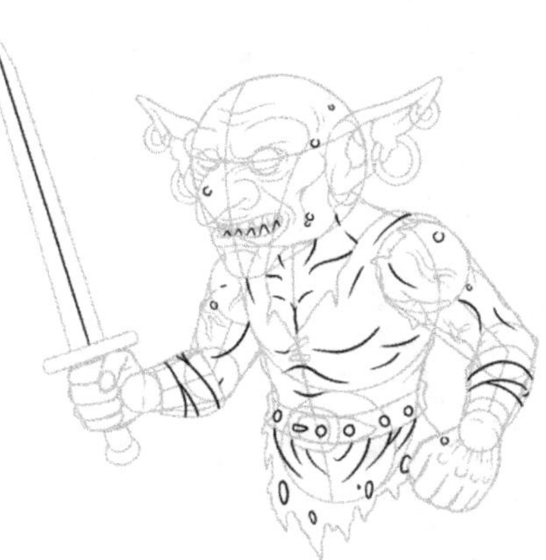

12

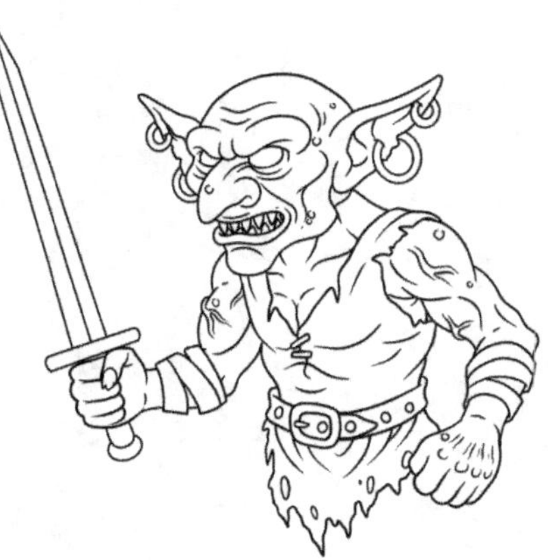

HARPY

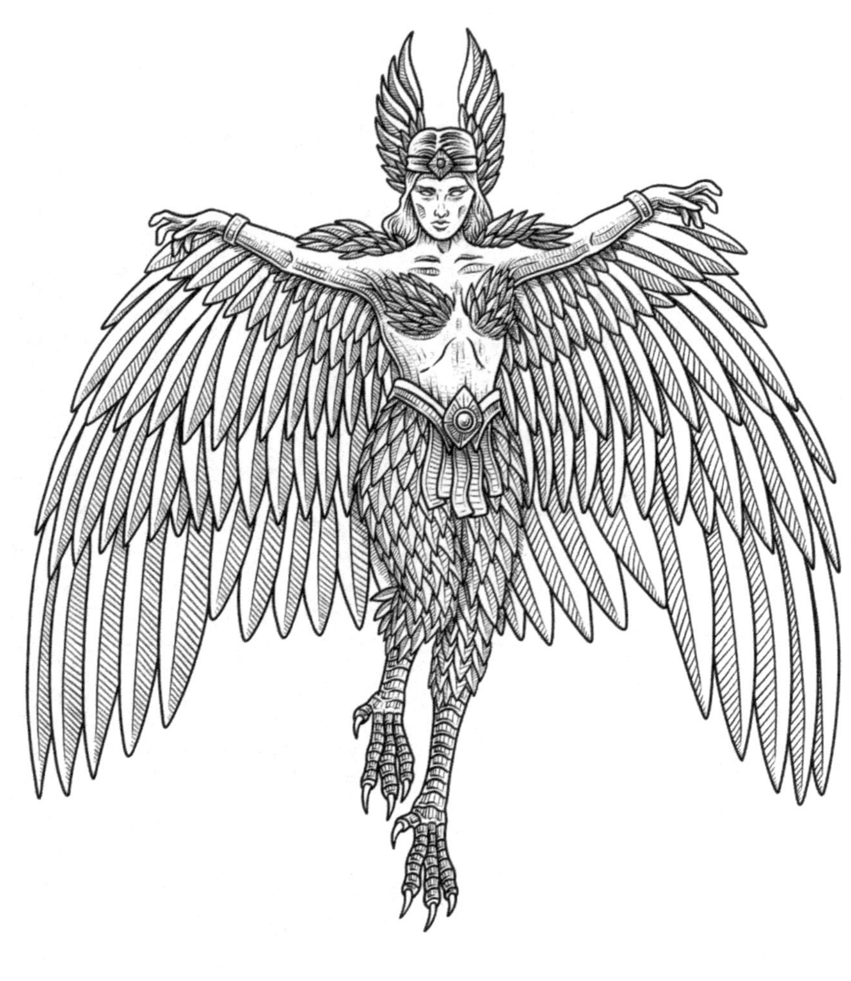

Pro tip: use a triangle method to size the wings (Step 10)

For the Harpy's wings, measure the vertical height from the shoulder down to the ankle of the viewer's right leg—this sets the overall wing height. To determine the width, draw an equilateral triangle with its apex at the top of the head and the base line intersecting the right ankle. This triangle gives you a clean, proportional guide for how far the wings should extend horizontally, ensuring the design feels balanced.

01

02

03

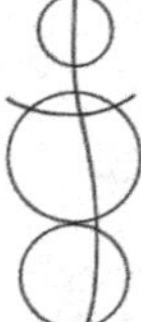

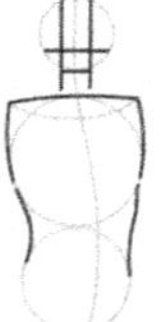

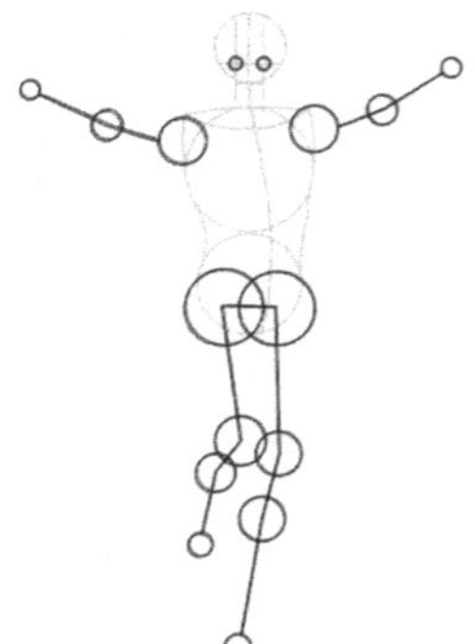

04

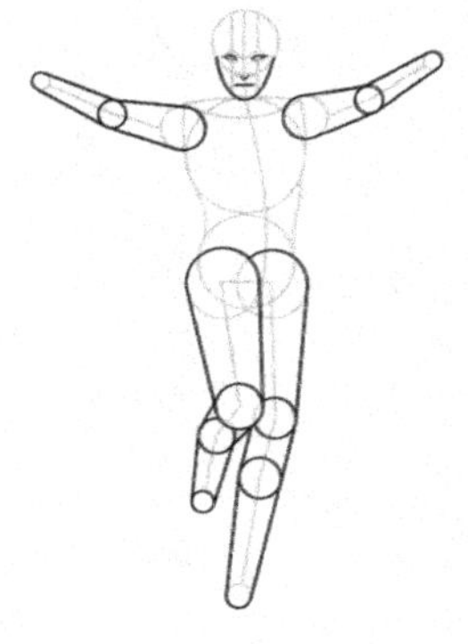

05

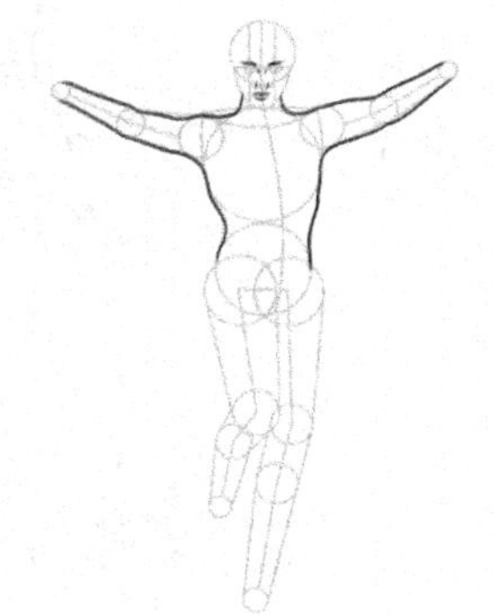

06

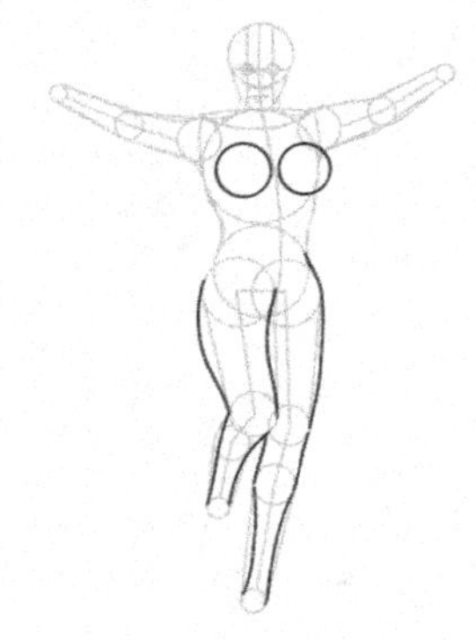

07

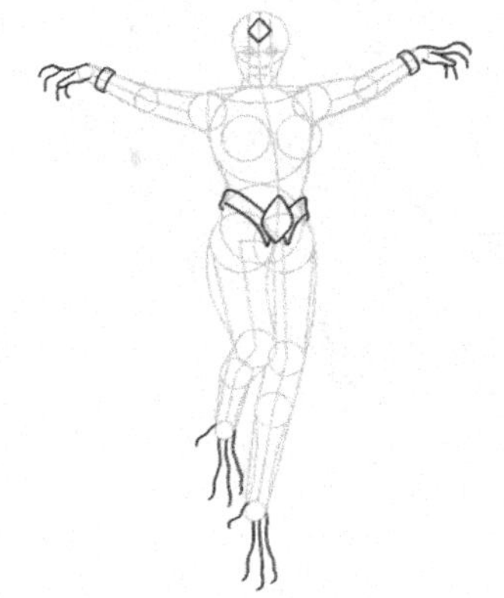

08

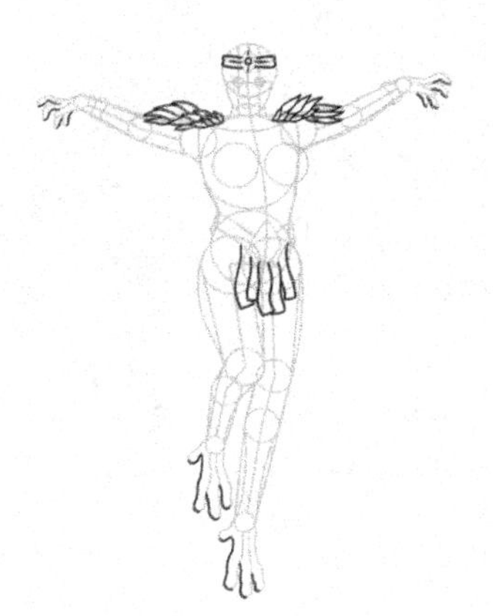

09

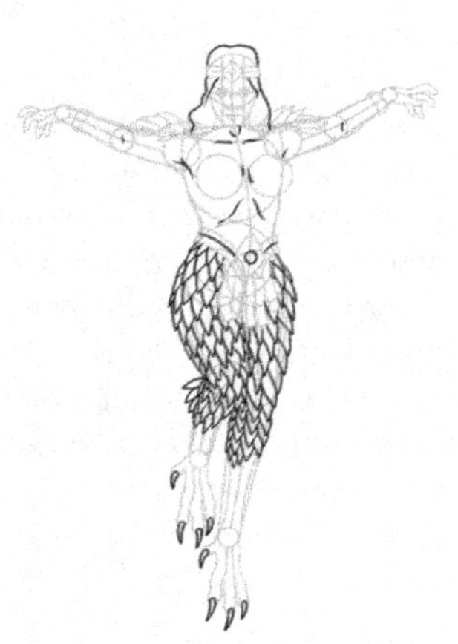

10

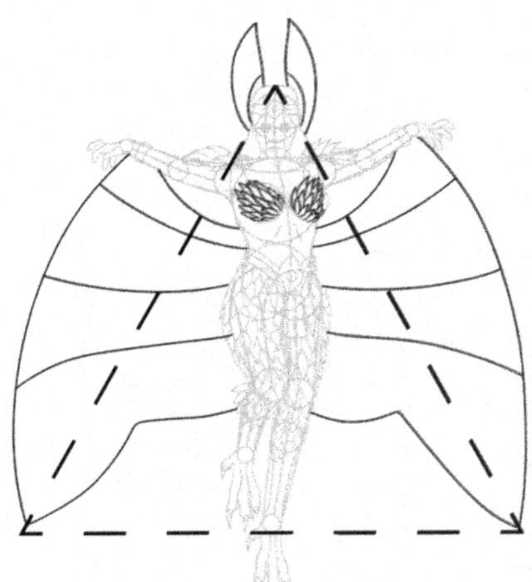

11

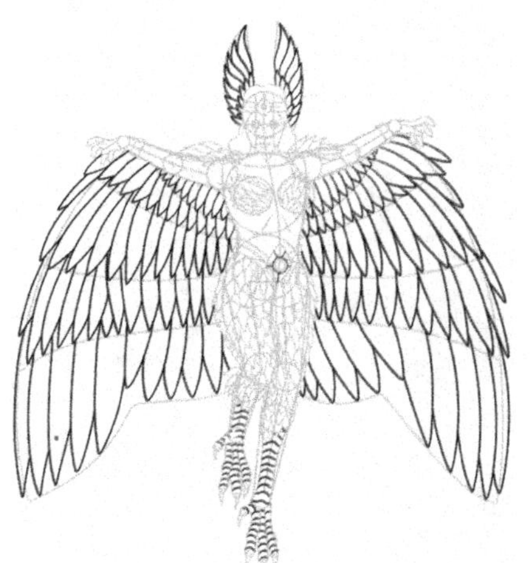

12

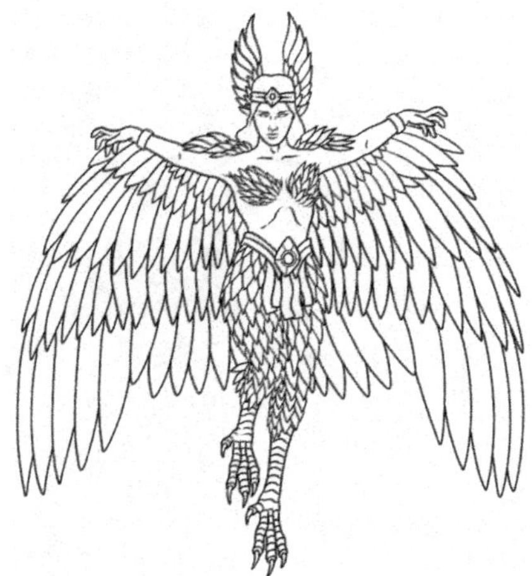

KELPIE

Pro tip: flow the body around a single spine line

Use a long, sweeping spine line to guide the Kelpie's entire body, from the tip of the head down through the tail. This continuous curve gives the creature its elegant, serpentine movement and helps you position the torso, limbs, and tail so they all follow the same fluid rhythm. Keeping everything anchored to this line ensures the pose feels dynamic.

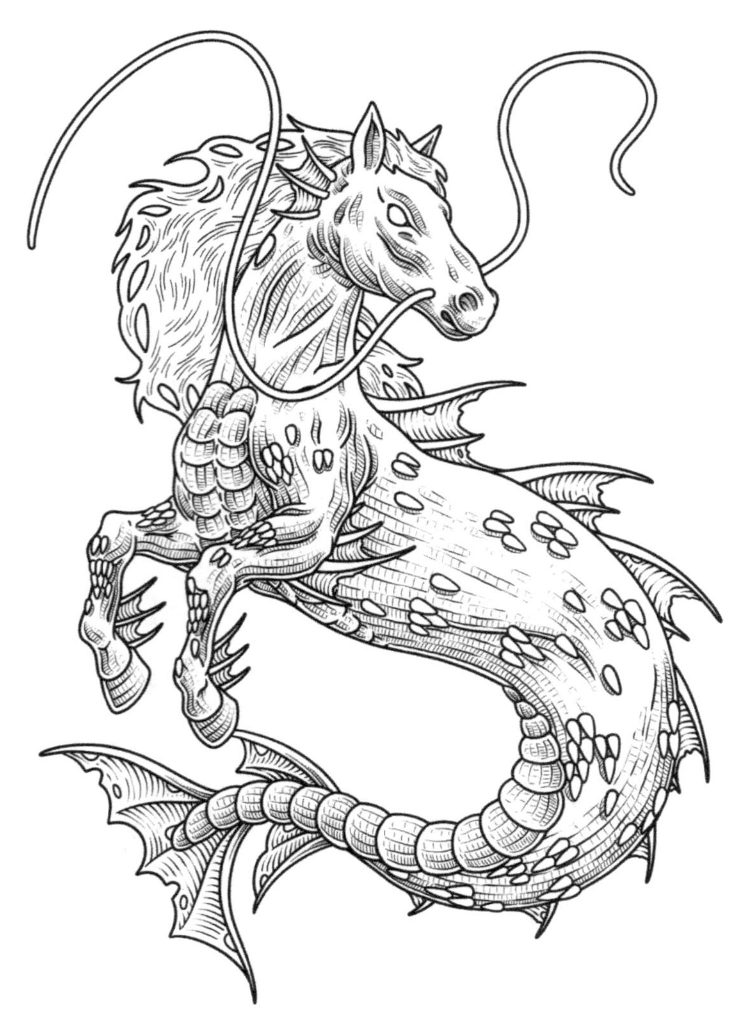

01

02

03

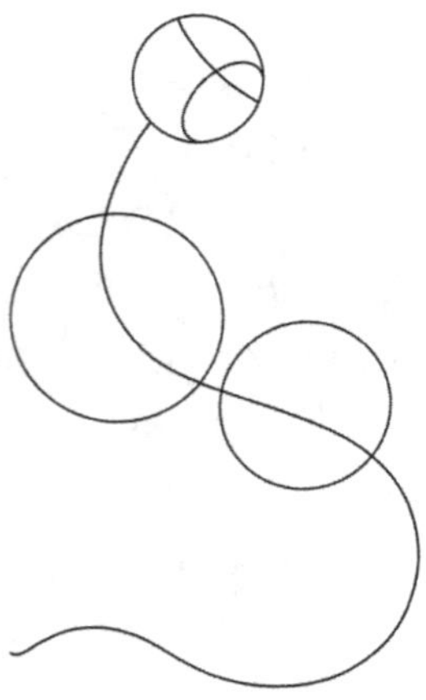

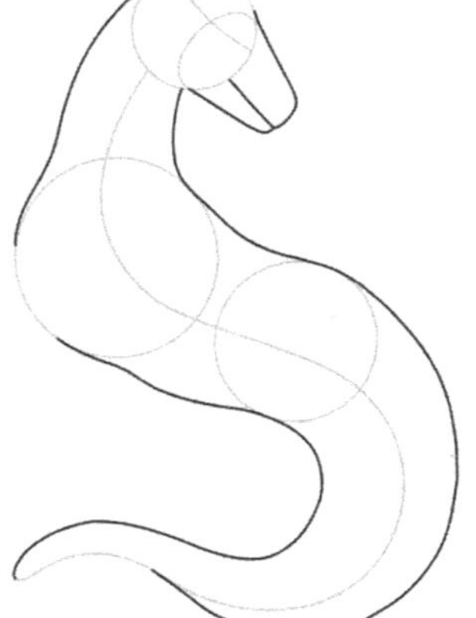

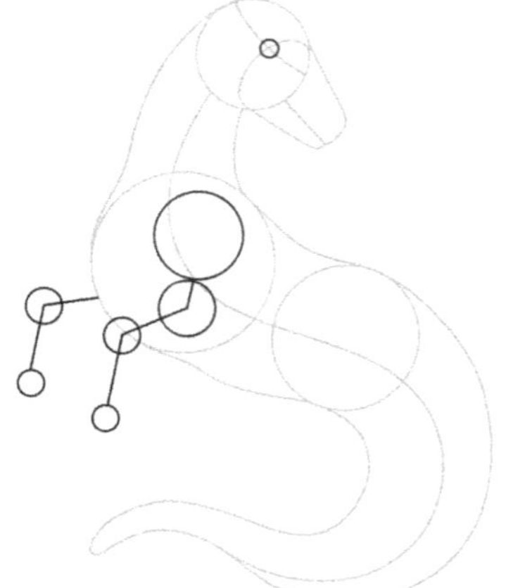

04

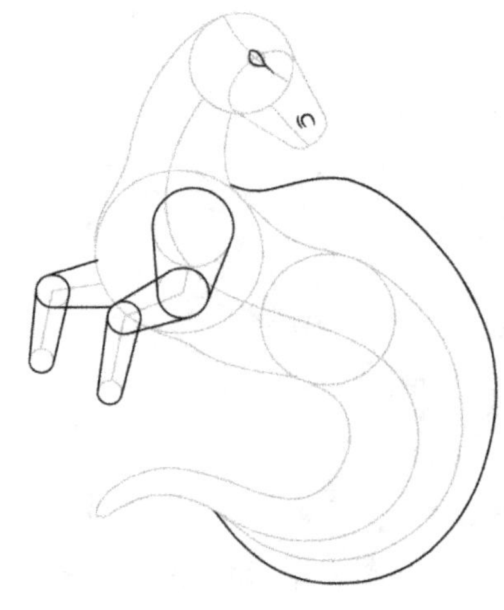

05

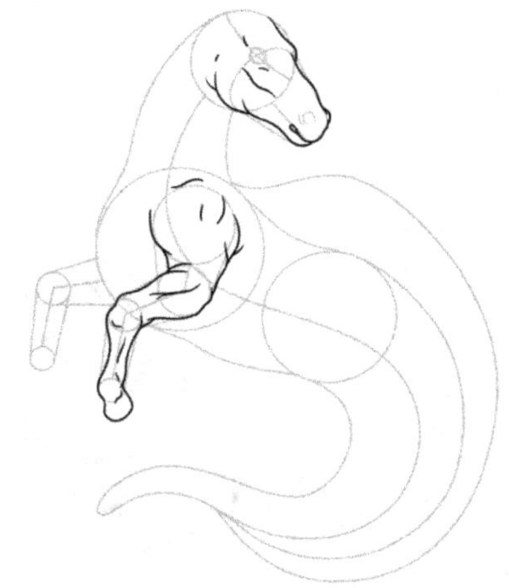

06

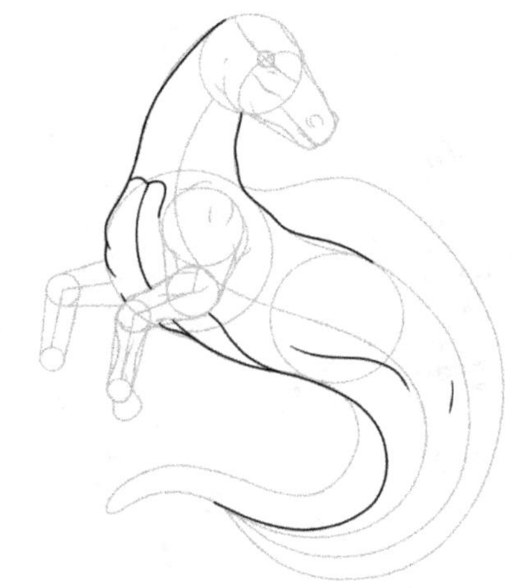

07

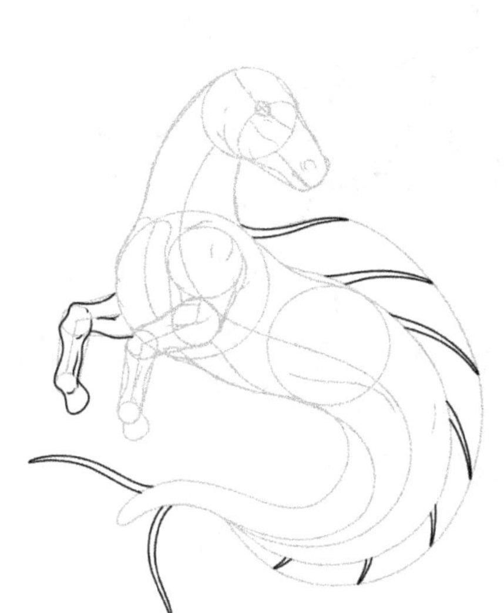

08

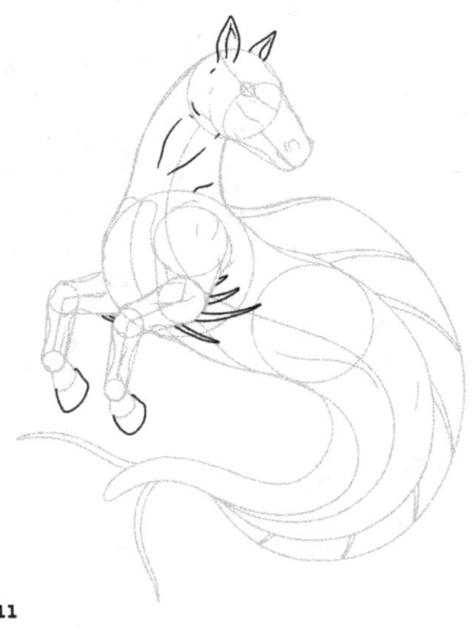

09

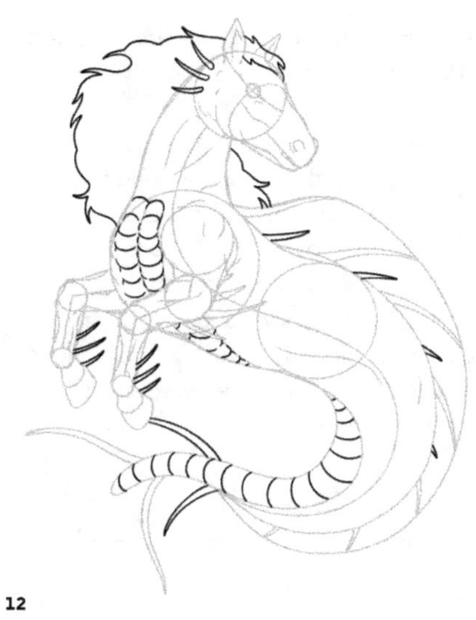

10

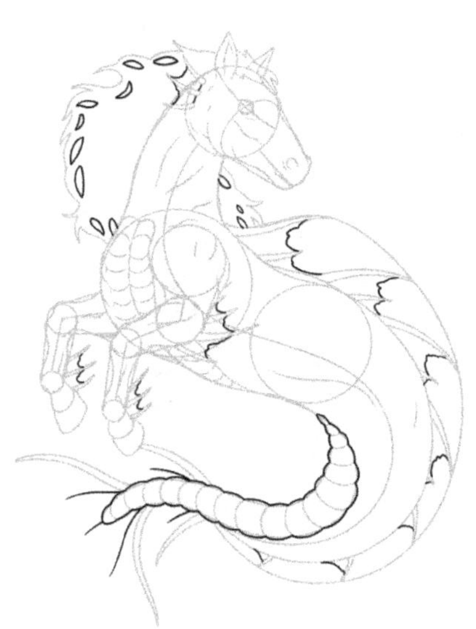

11

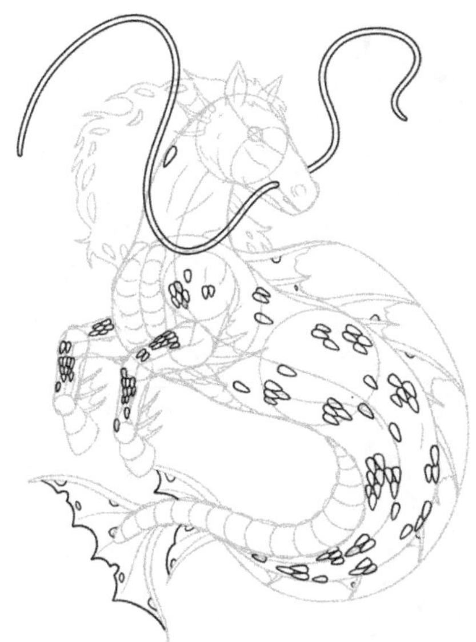

12

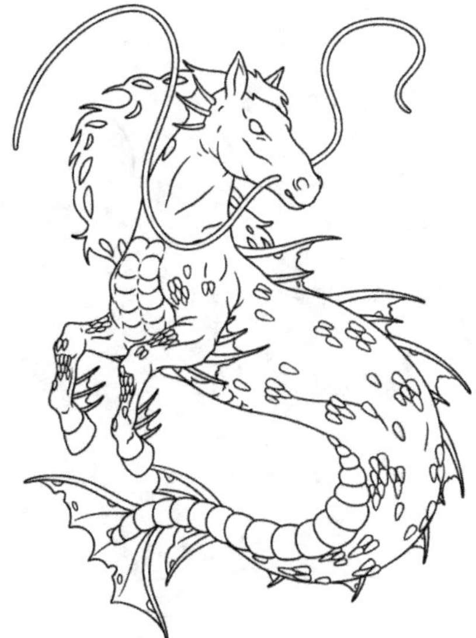

HOW TO DRAW MONSTERS & BEASTS

LEVIATHAN

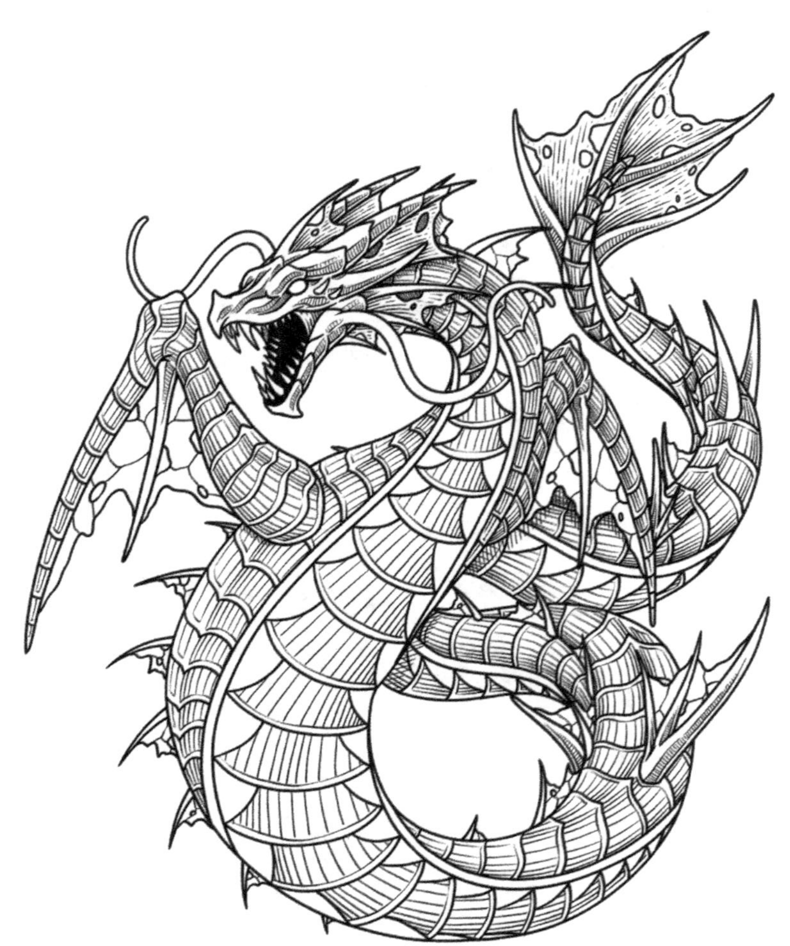

Pro tip: build the body around a central flow line

Start with a long, continuous curve running from the tip of the head through to the tail. This single line sets the Leviathan's movement and posture. Wrap the body forms around this spine to keep the massive, serpentine structure cohesive, then layer the fins and limbs on top, following the same directional flow to unify the design.

01

02

03

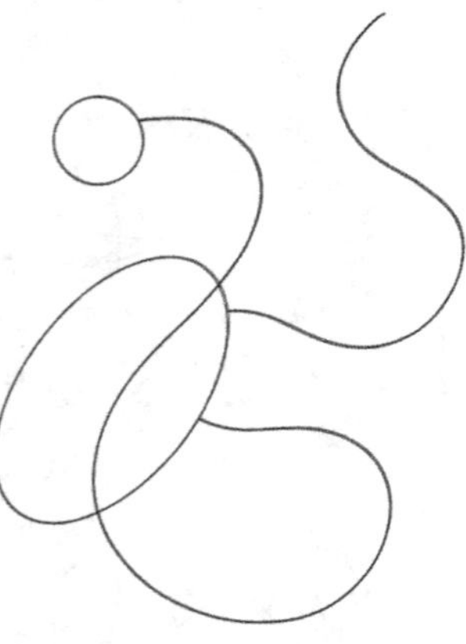

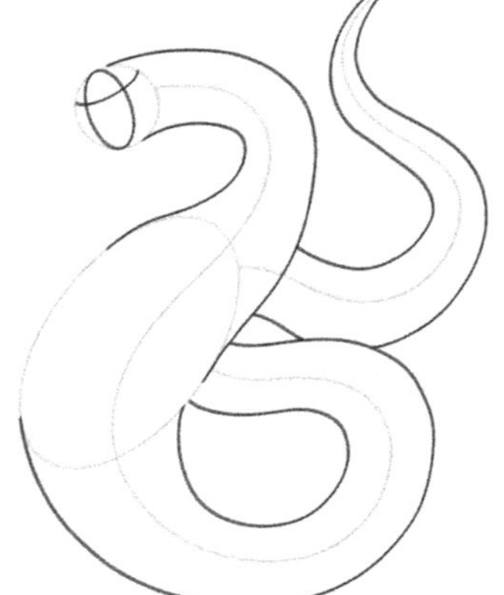

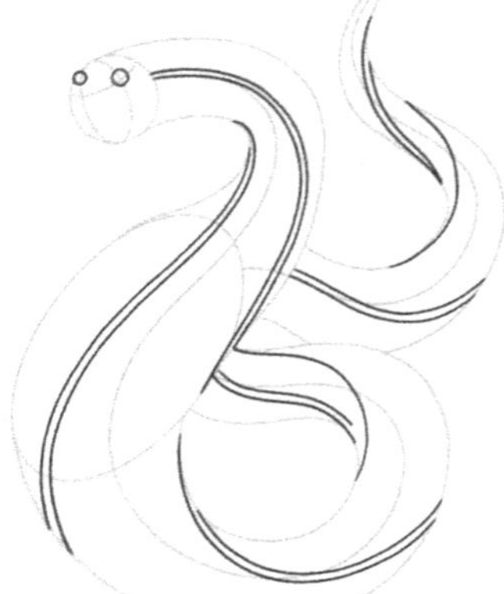

04

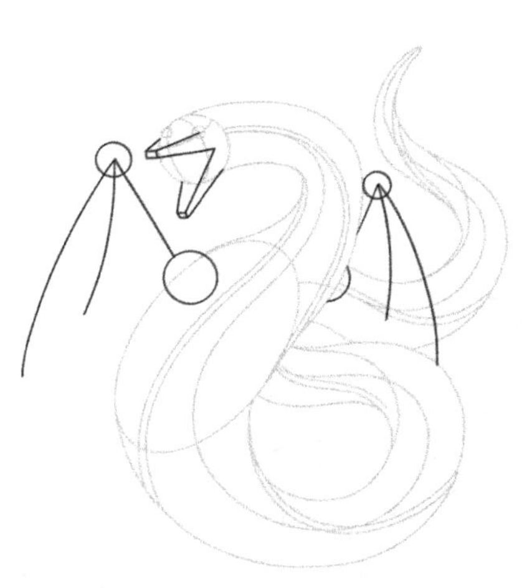

05

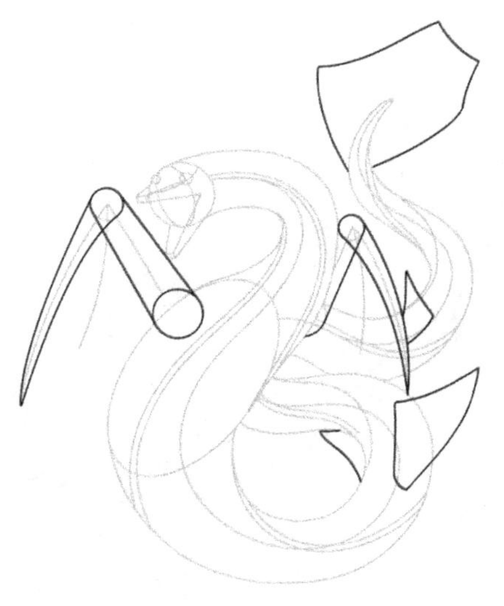

06

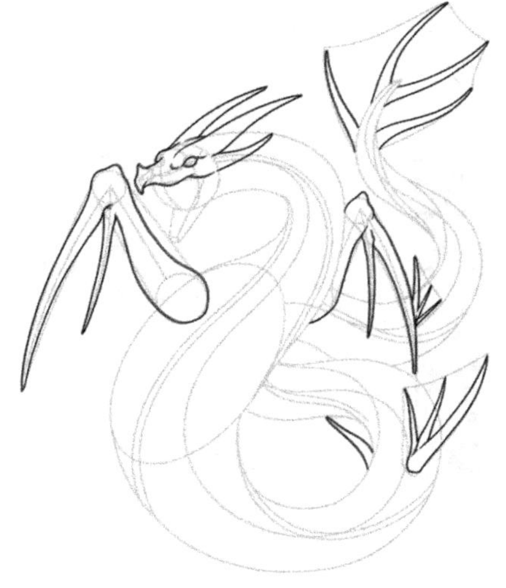

07

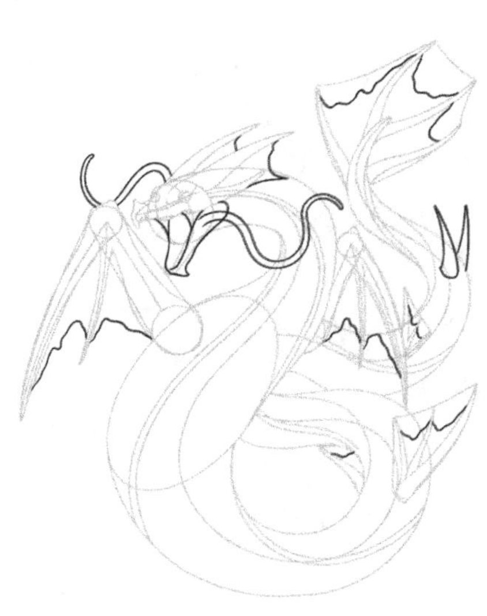

08

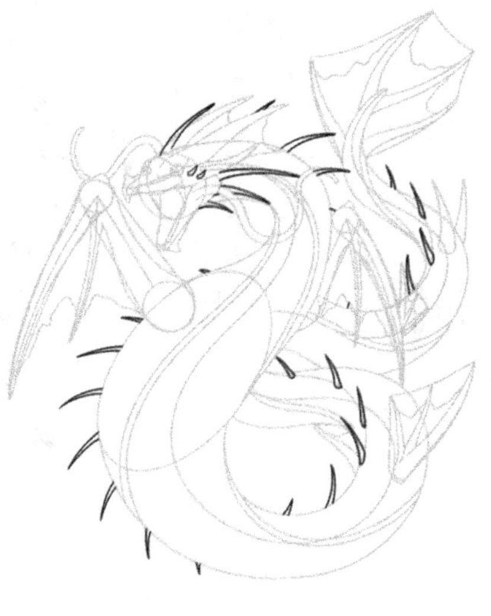

09

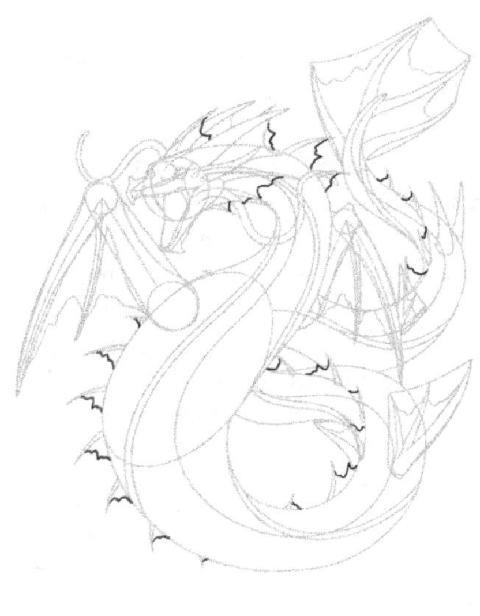

10

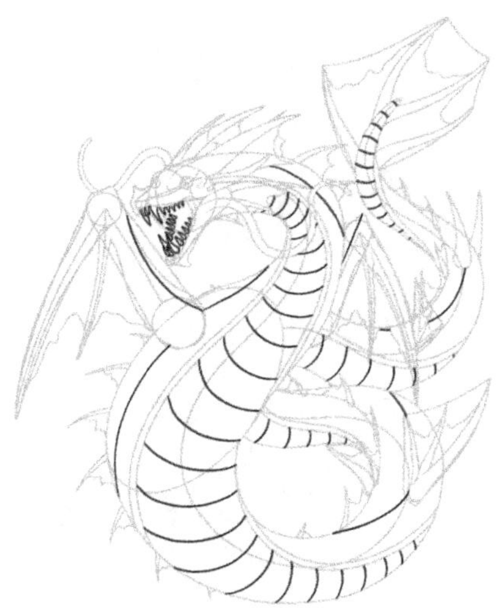

11

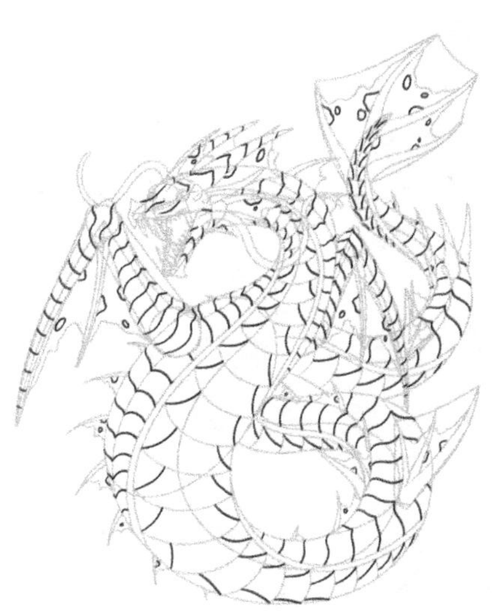

12

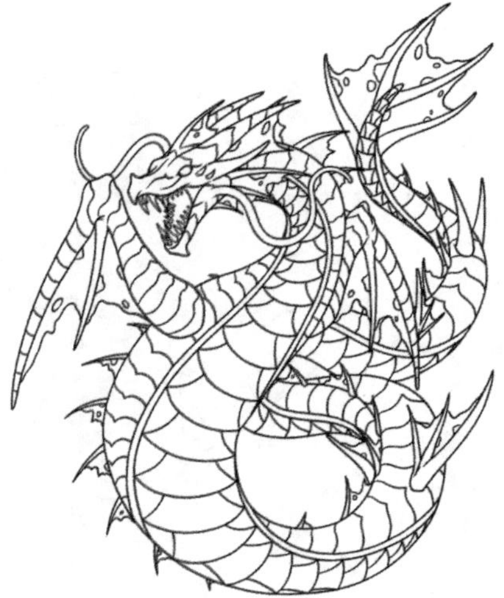

MANTICORE

Pro tip: establishing the anchor point and direction of the wings

Place the wing base at the midpoint of the ribcage circle. This ensures the wings attach to a structurally strong area, giving the impression they're rooted into the creature's back, not floating off the shoulders. Angle the wings slightly back and outward, following the spine's direction. This integrates the wings naturally into the creature's posture and avoids them looking pasted on.

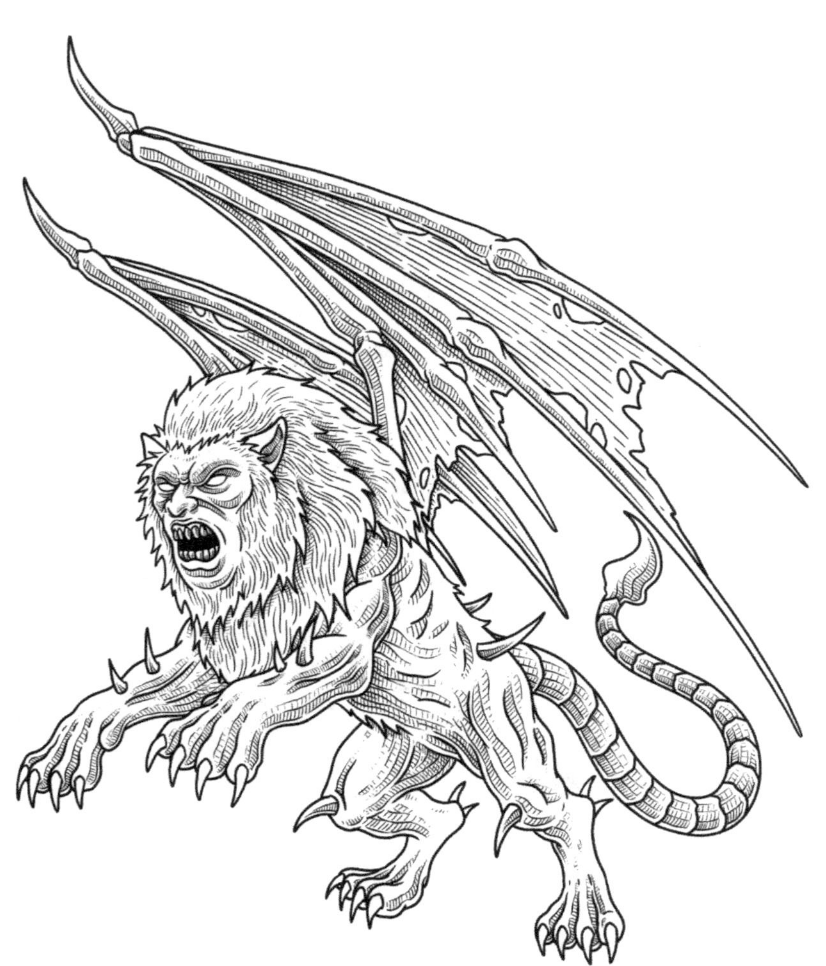

01

02

03

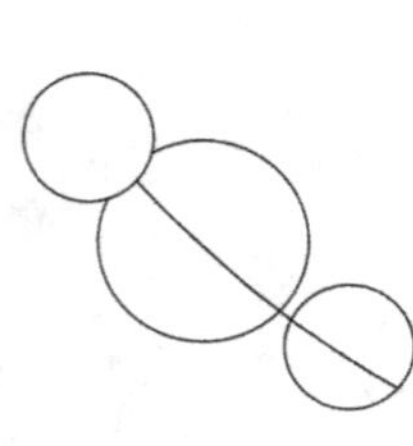

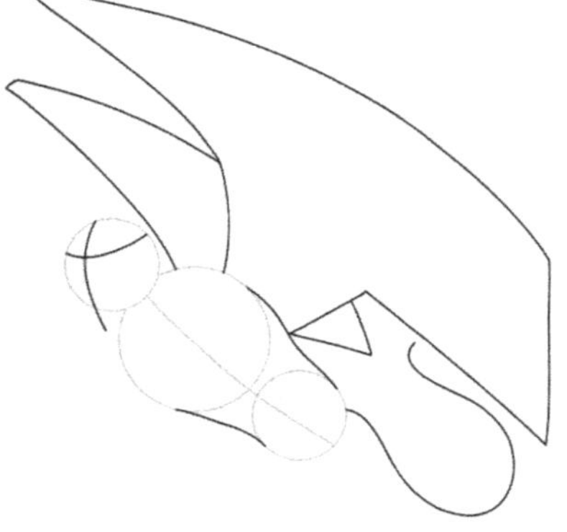

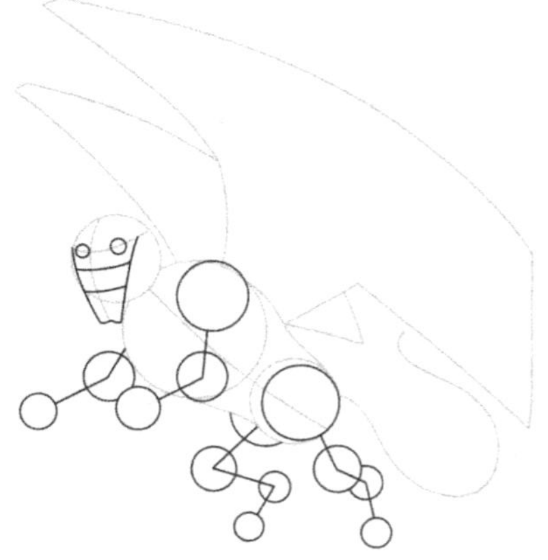

04

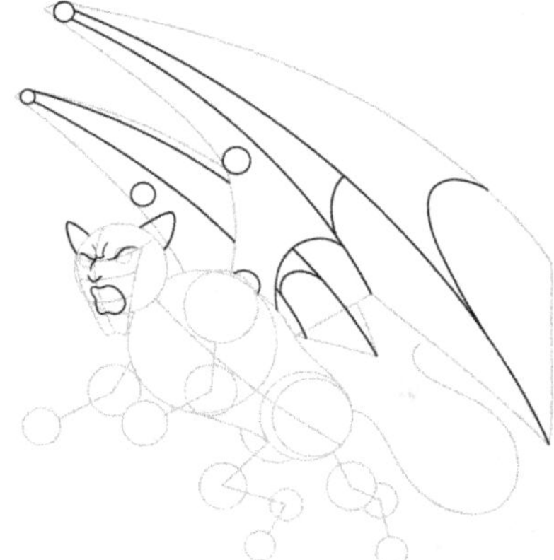

05

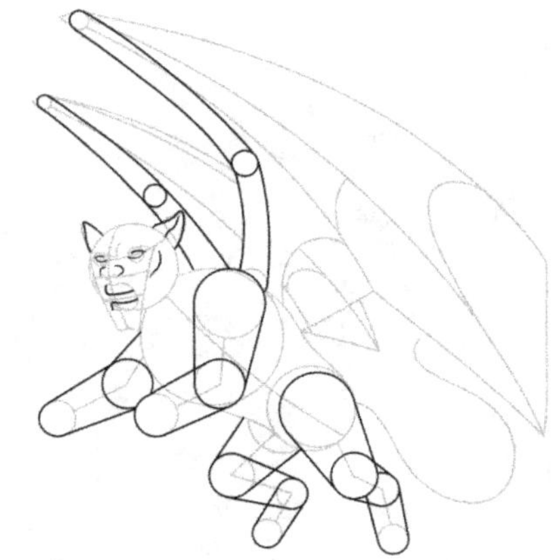

06

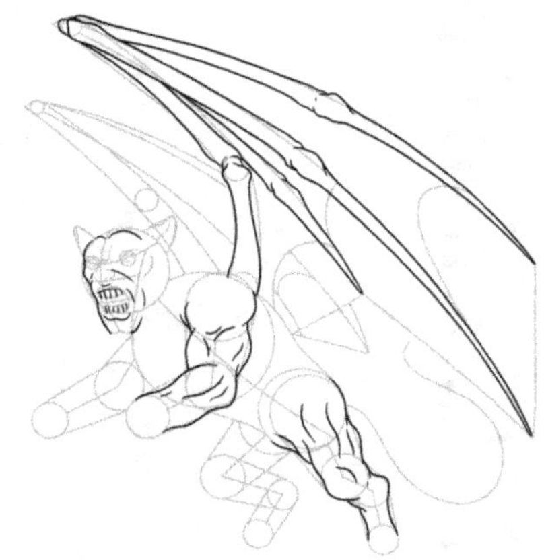

07

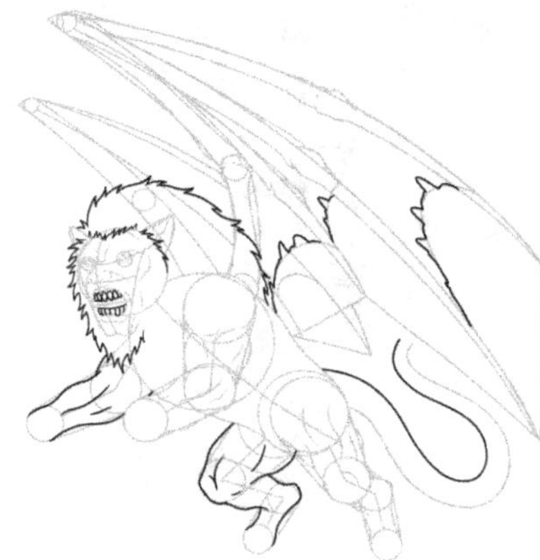

08

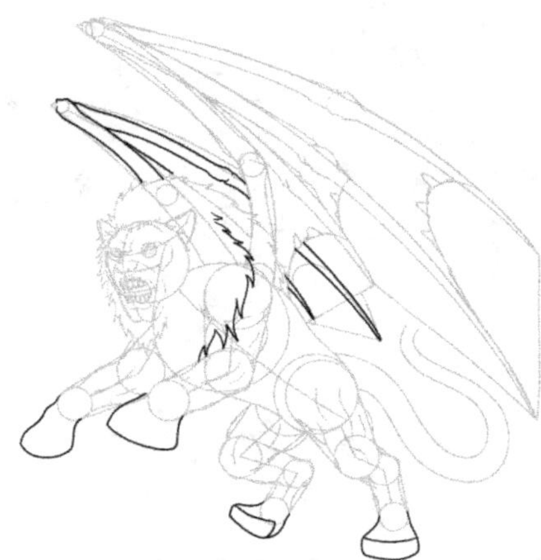

09

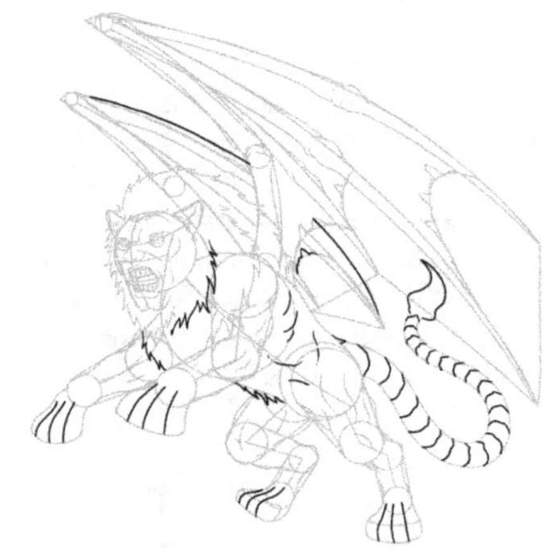

10

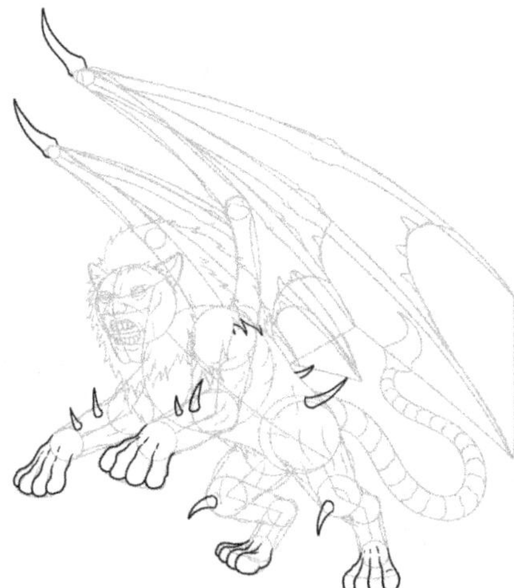

11

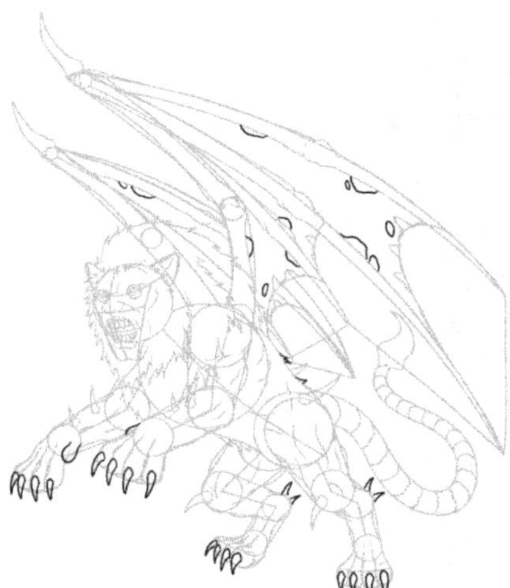

12

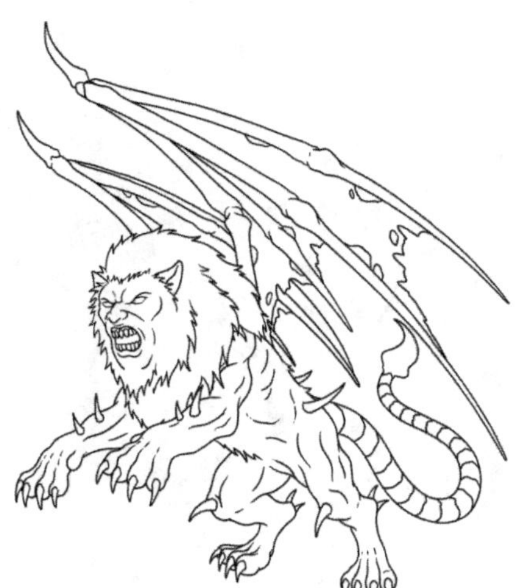

REPTILIAN MONSTER

Pro tip: emphasise the forward lean

Angle the torso forward so the head, shoulders, and hips align along a diagonal spine line. This creates a powerful, grounded stance typical of large reptilian creatures. Make sure the legs are positioned beneath the body to support this forward weight, and angle the arms slightly outward to enhance the creature's imposing posture.

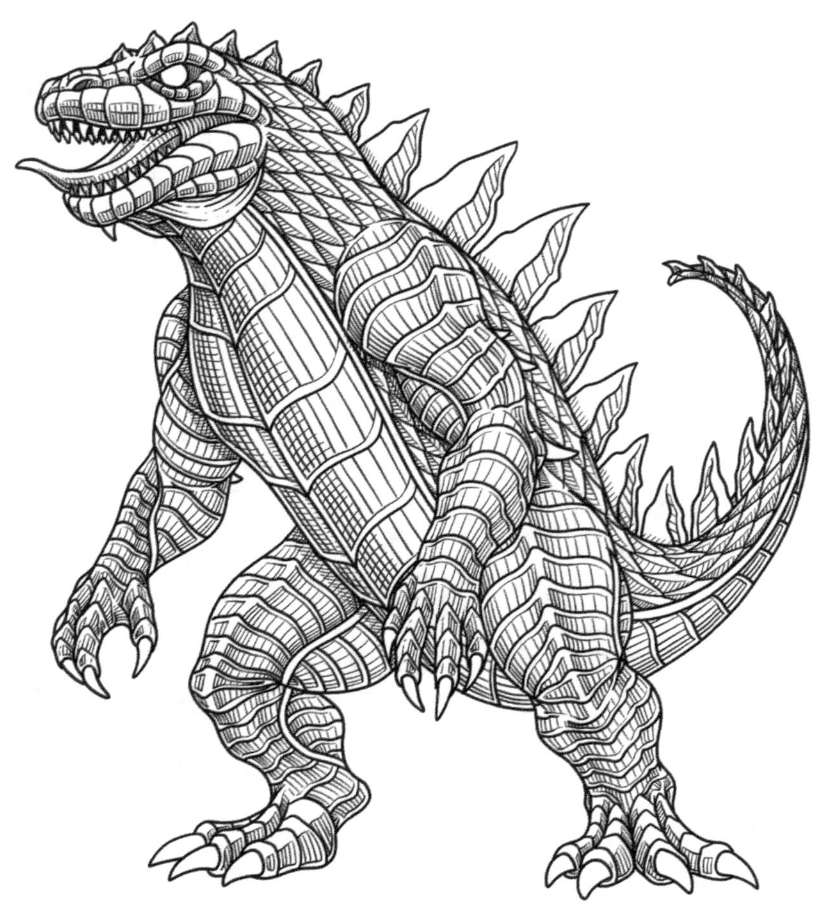

01

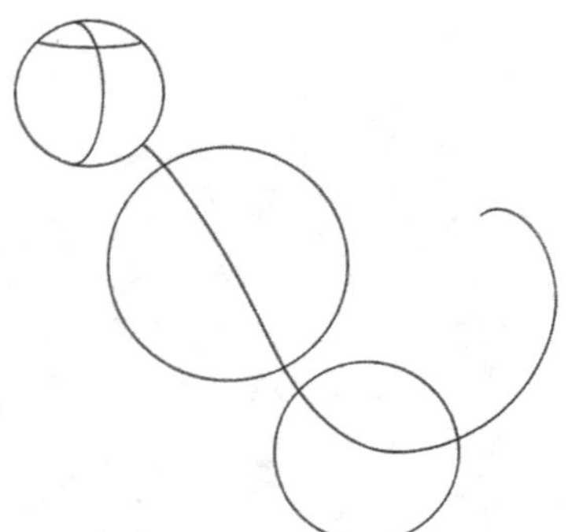

02

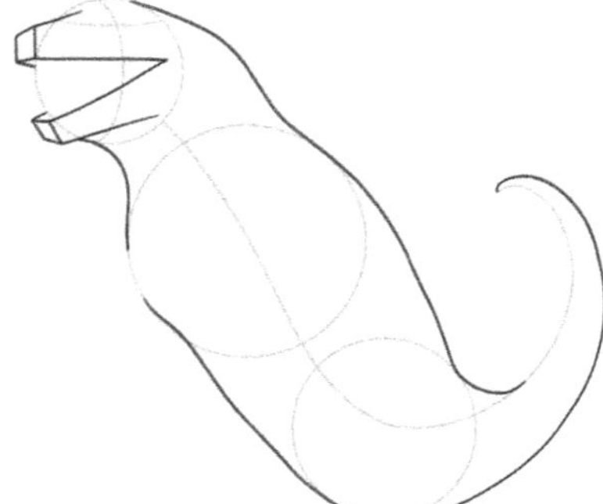

03

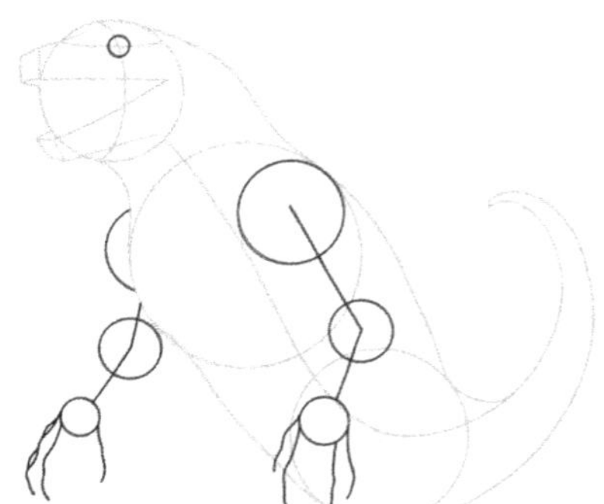

04

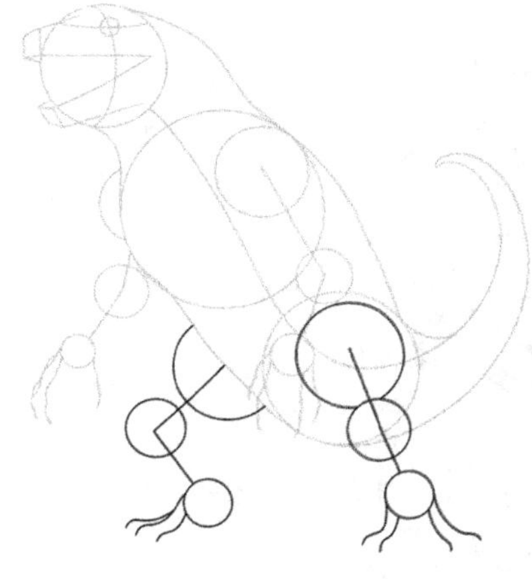

05

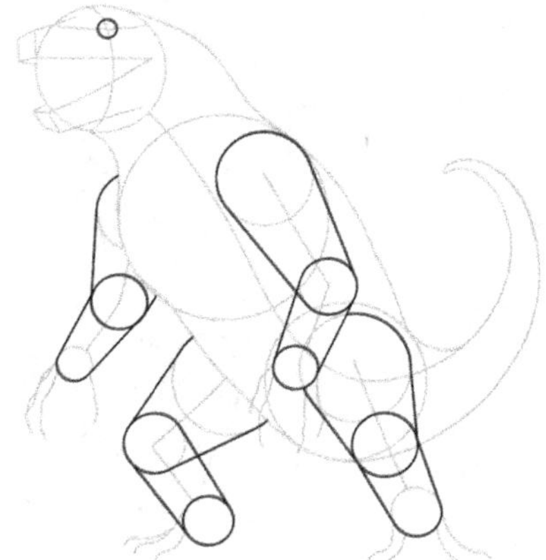

06

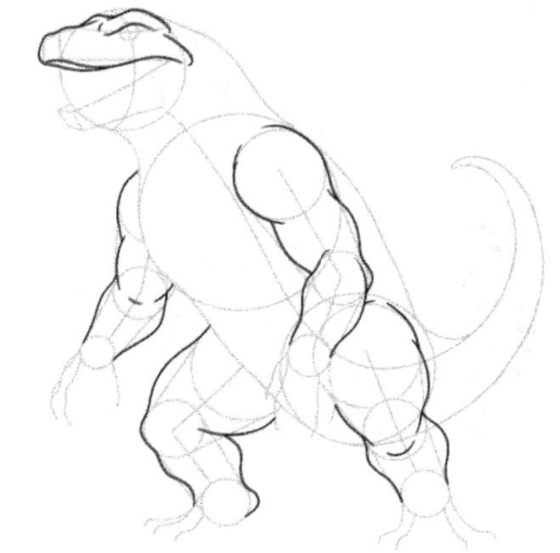

07

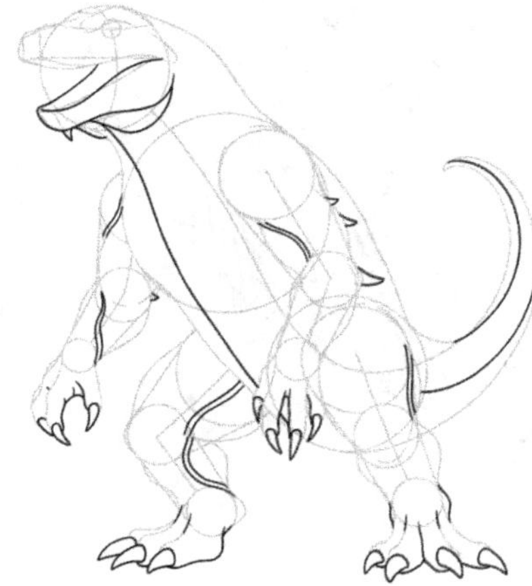

08

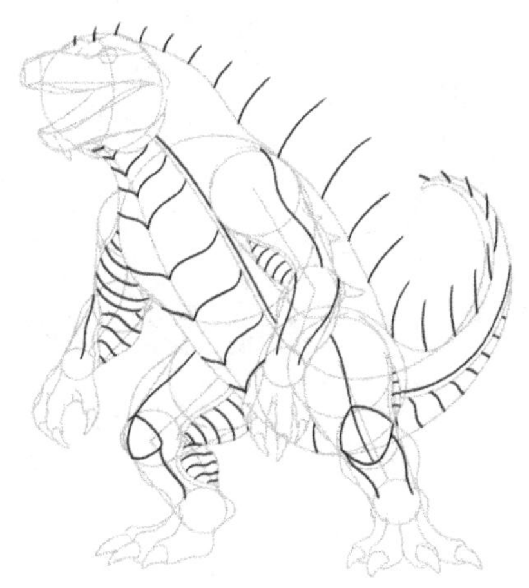

09

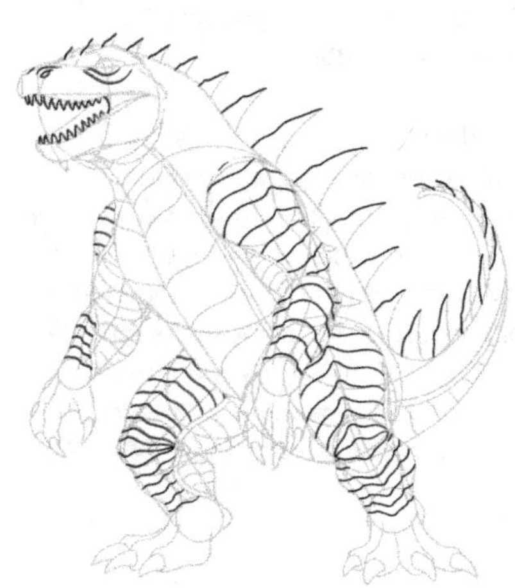

10

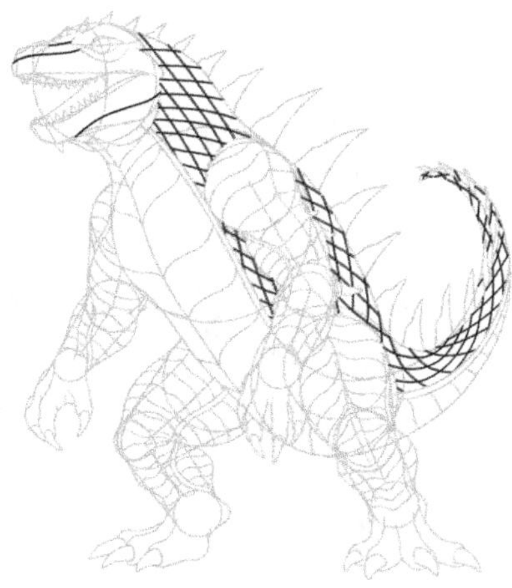

11

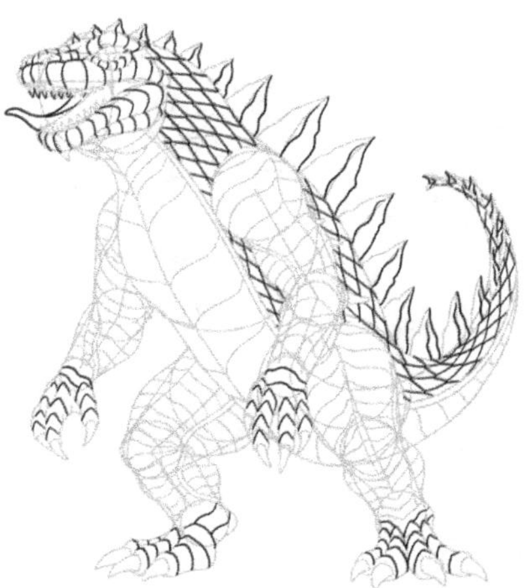

12

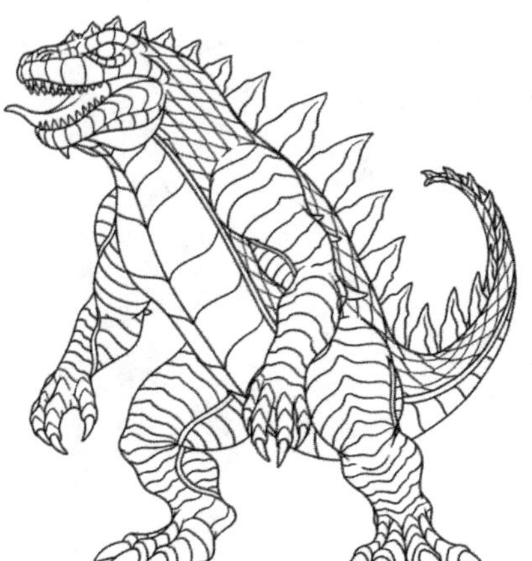

CYCLOPS

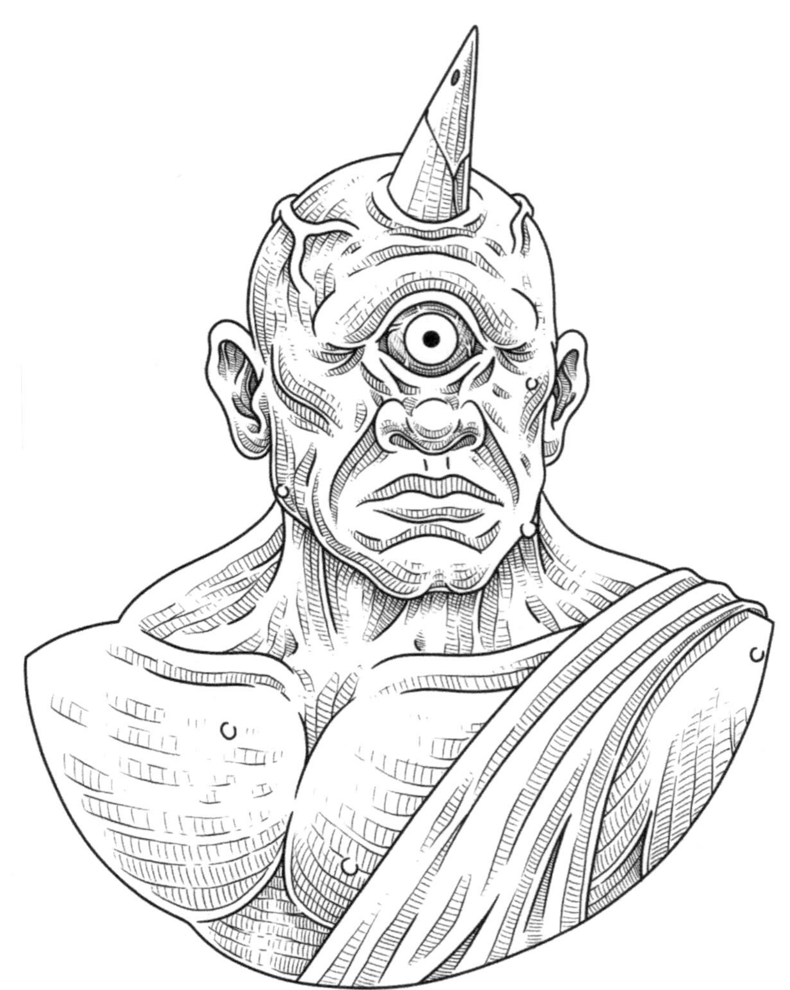

Pro tip: centre the eye using the horizontal midline

For the Cyclops, place the single eye directly on the horizontal midline of the head, aligned with the vertical centre line. This ensures the eye sits naturally within the structure rather than drifting too high or low. Use a circle that spans roughly one-third of the head's width to give the eye a dominant, powerful presence without overwhelming the face.

01

02

03

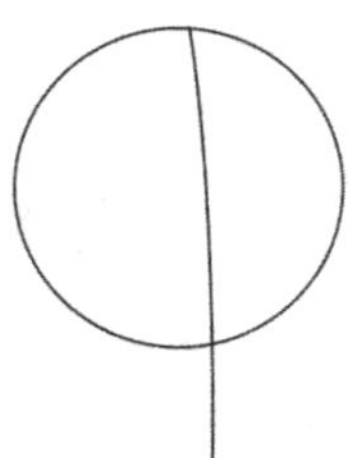

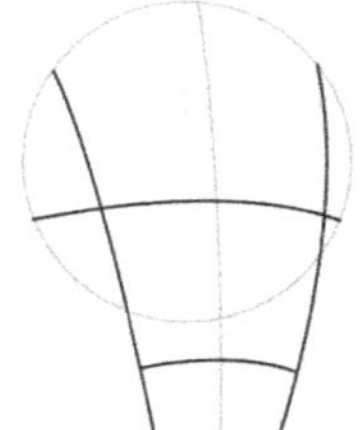

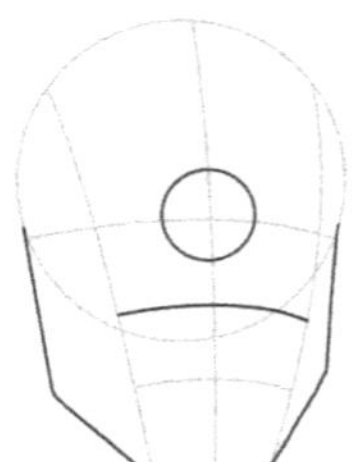

04

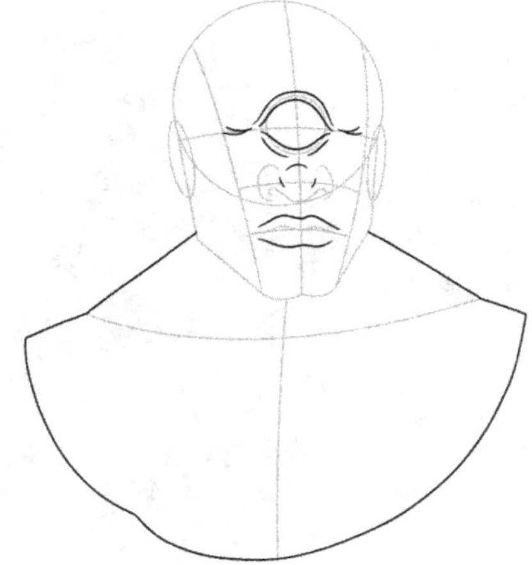

05

06

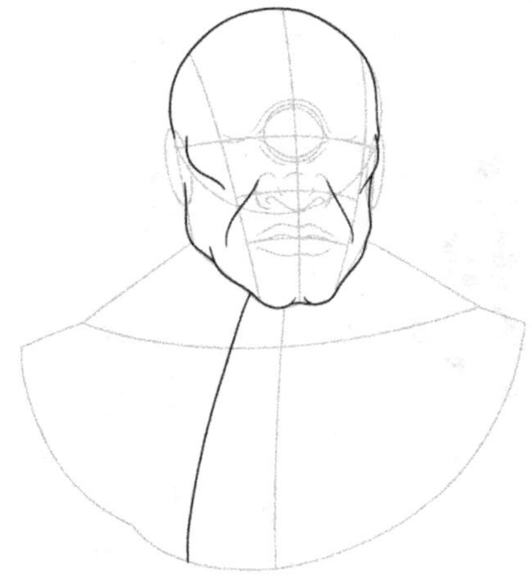

07

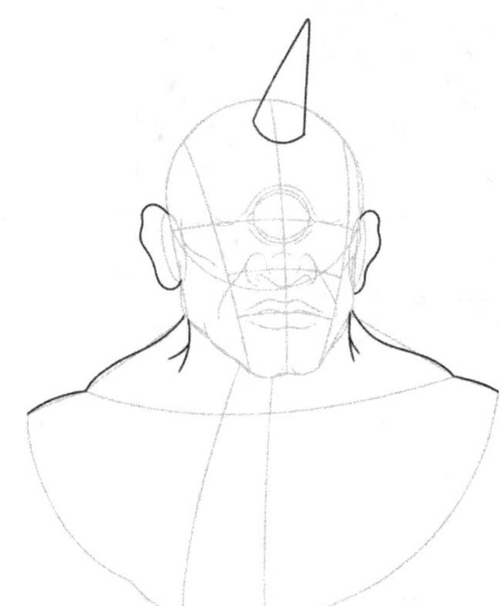

08

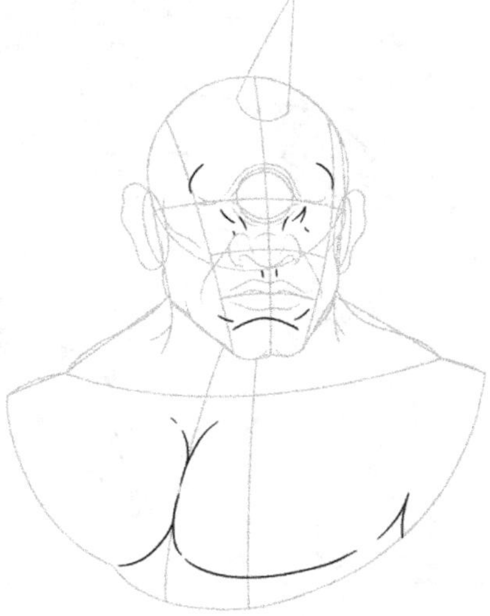

09

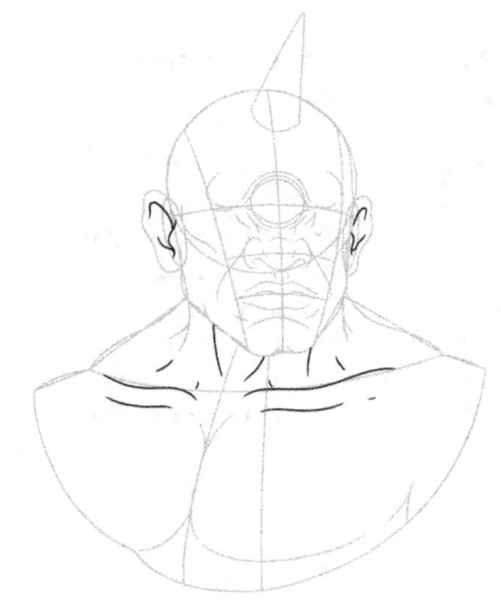

10

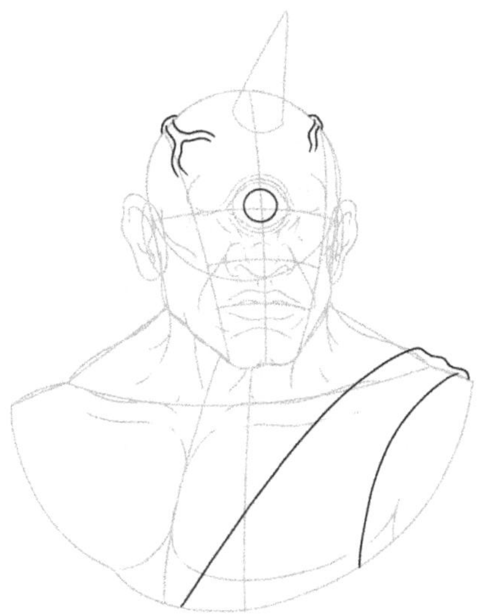

11

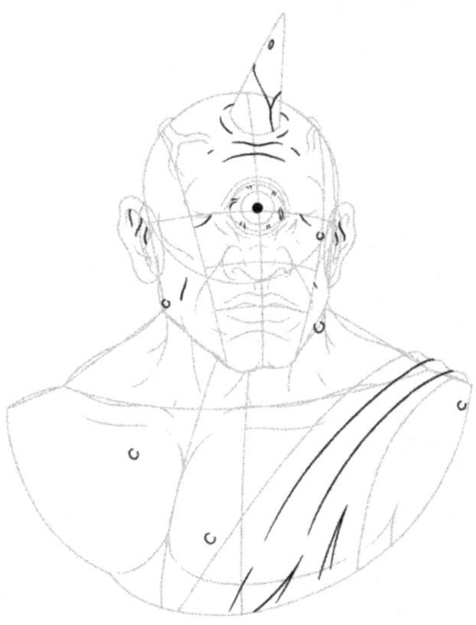

12

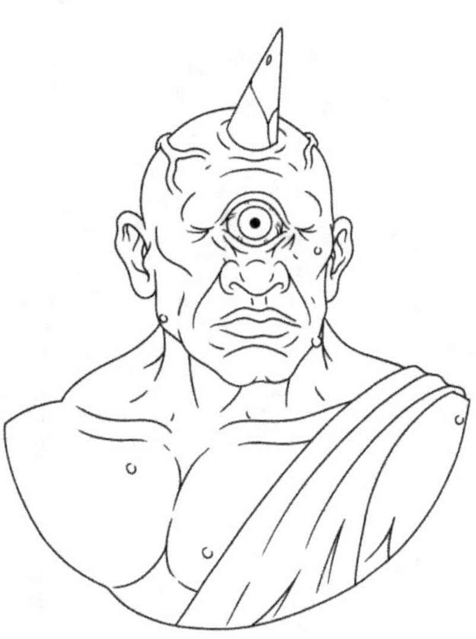

MEDUSA

Pro tip: use a circle to arrange the snakes evenly

Draw a large circle around the head to act as a placement guide for the snakes. This helps you space them evenly and control their flow, ensuring they radiate out in a balanced, harmonious pattern rather than clumping awkwardly. You can use the circle as a reference line to vary the angles while maintaining an overall pleasing silhouette.

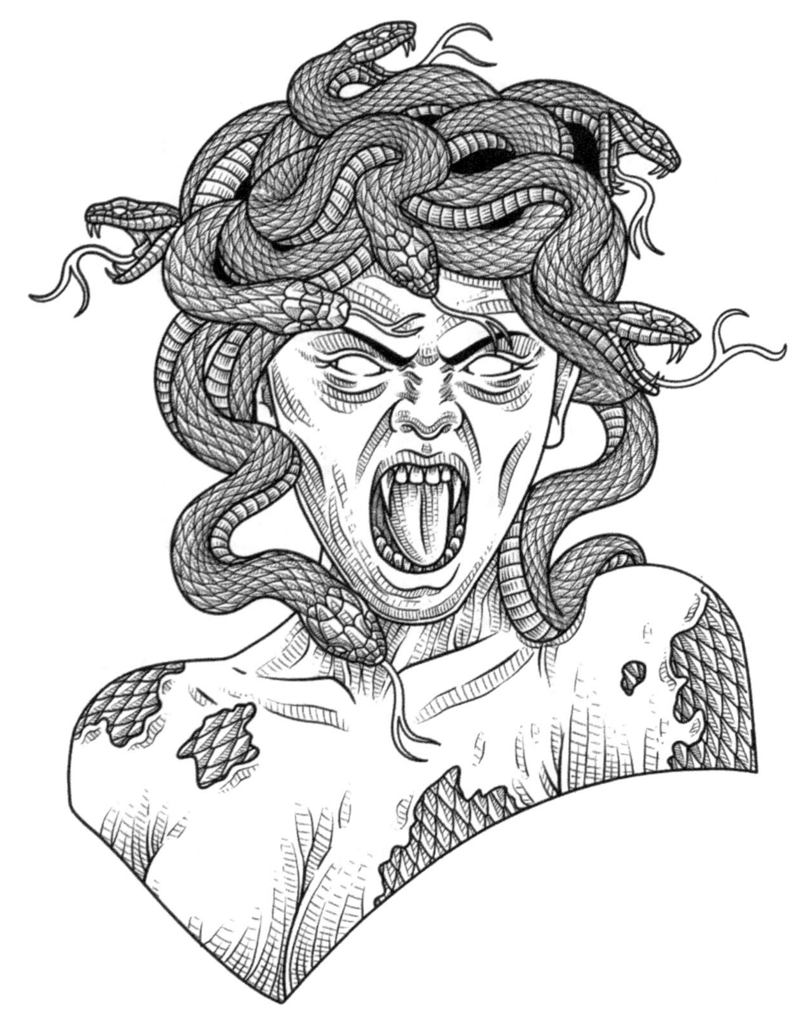

---

01 **02** **03**

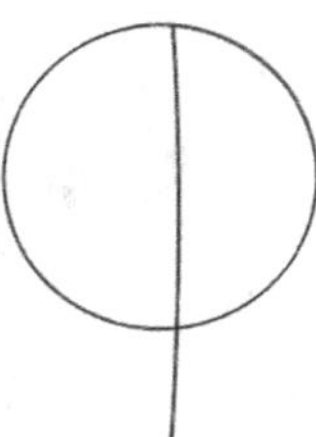
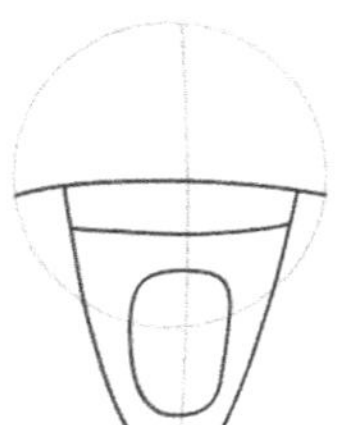
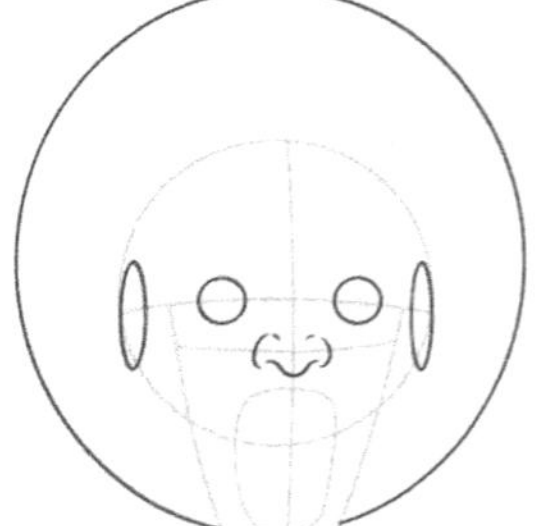

04

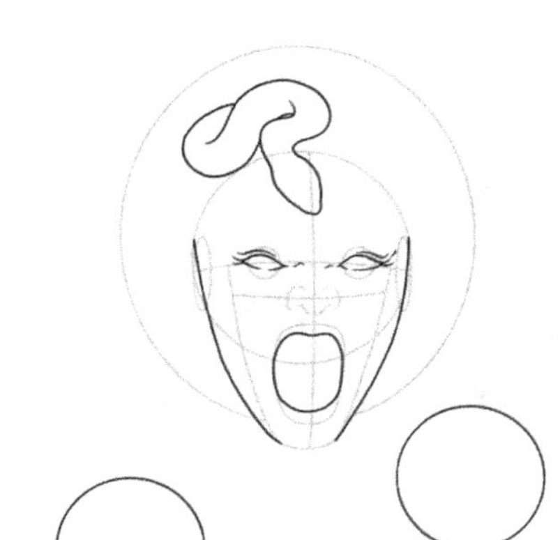

05

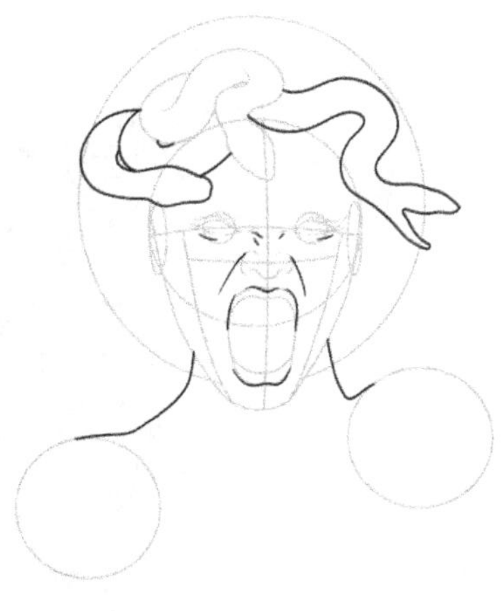

06

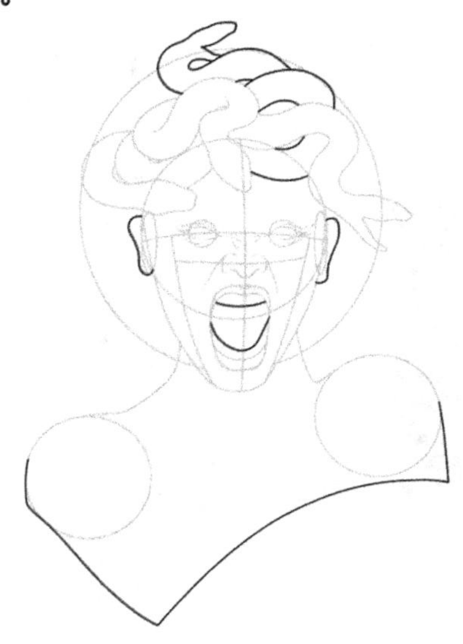

07

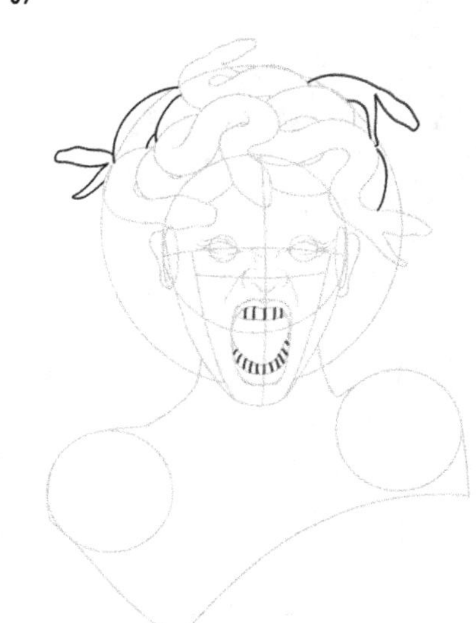

08

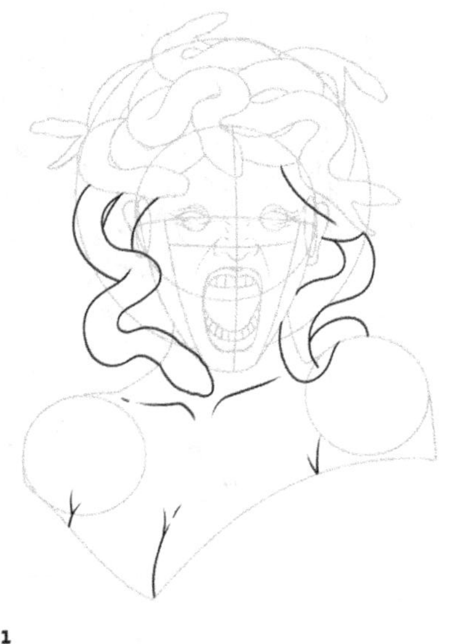

09

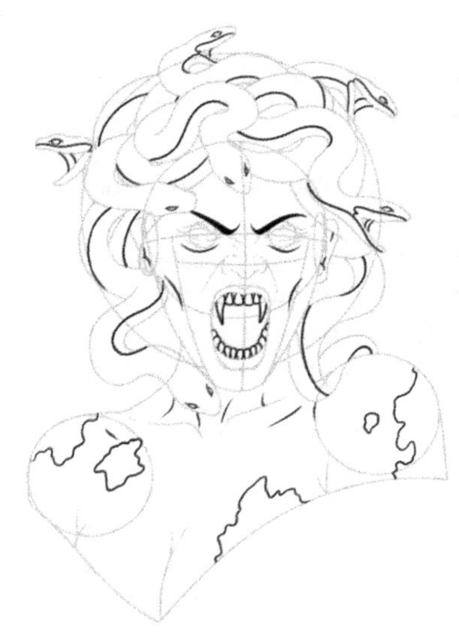

10

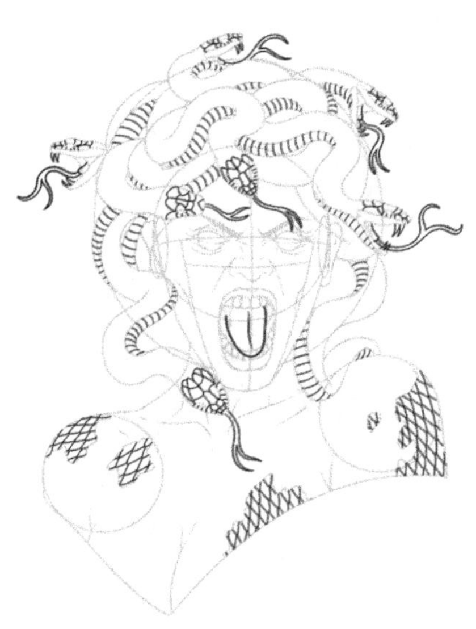

11

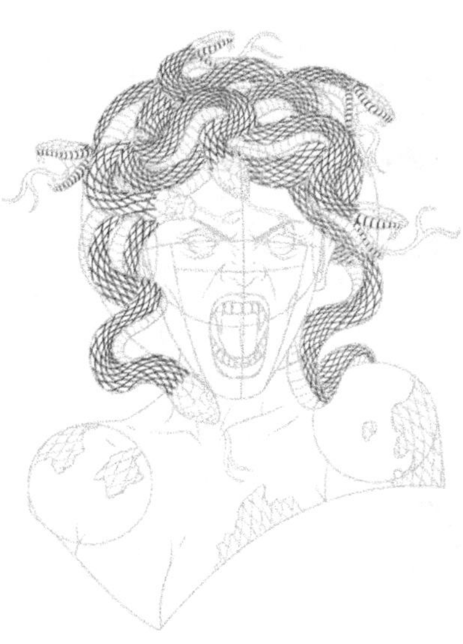

12

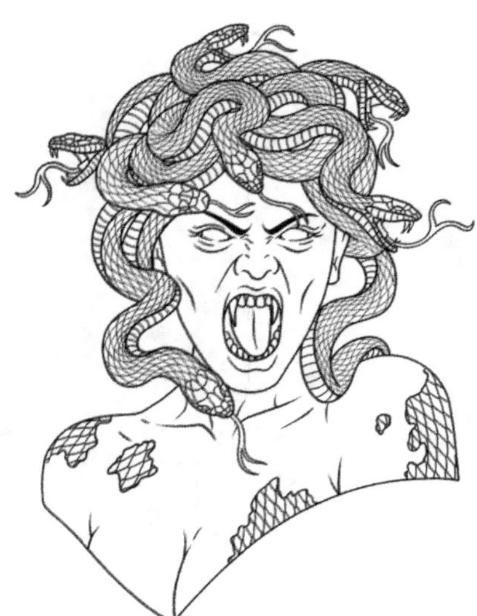

MINOTAUR

Pro tip: use head-width multiples to set the torso width

To give the Minotaur its powerful build, measure the width of the torso at the shoulders as roughly 2½ head-widths. This simple proportional rule keeps the figure broad and imposing while maintaining anatomical balance.

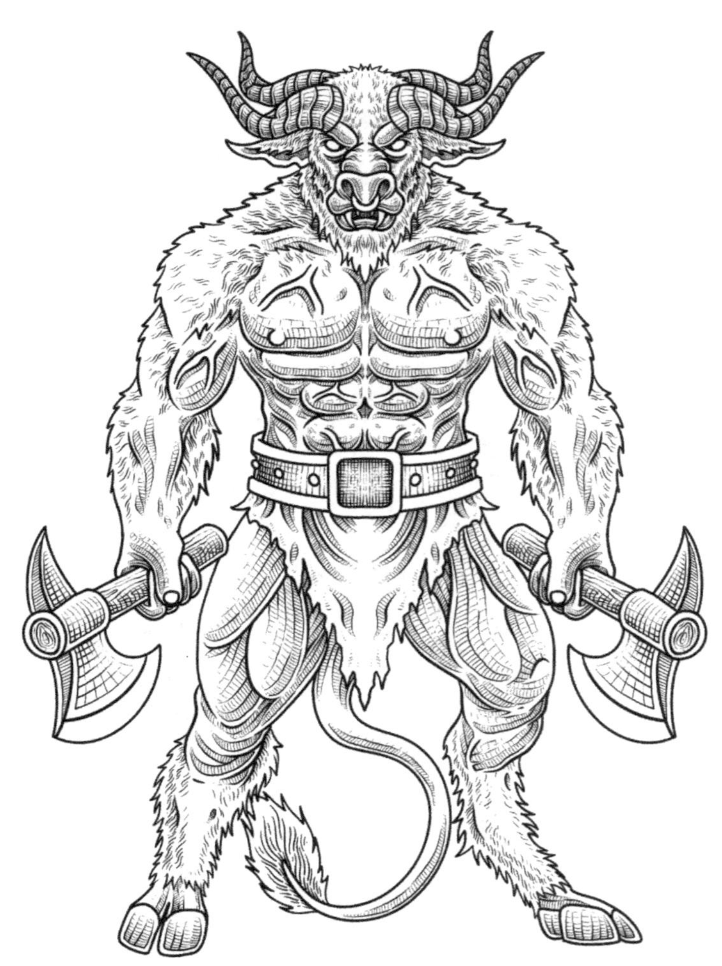

01

02

03

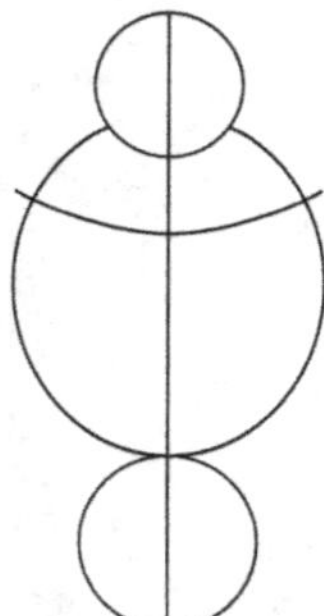
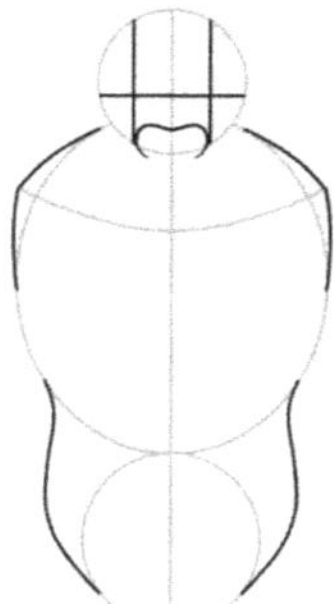
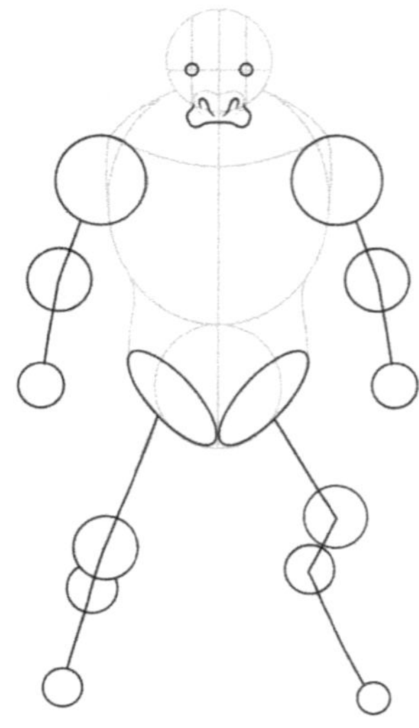

04

05

06

07

08

09

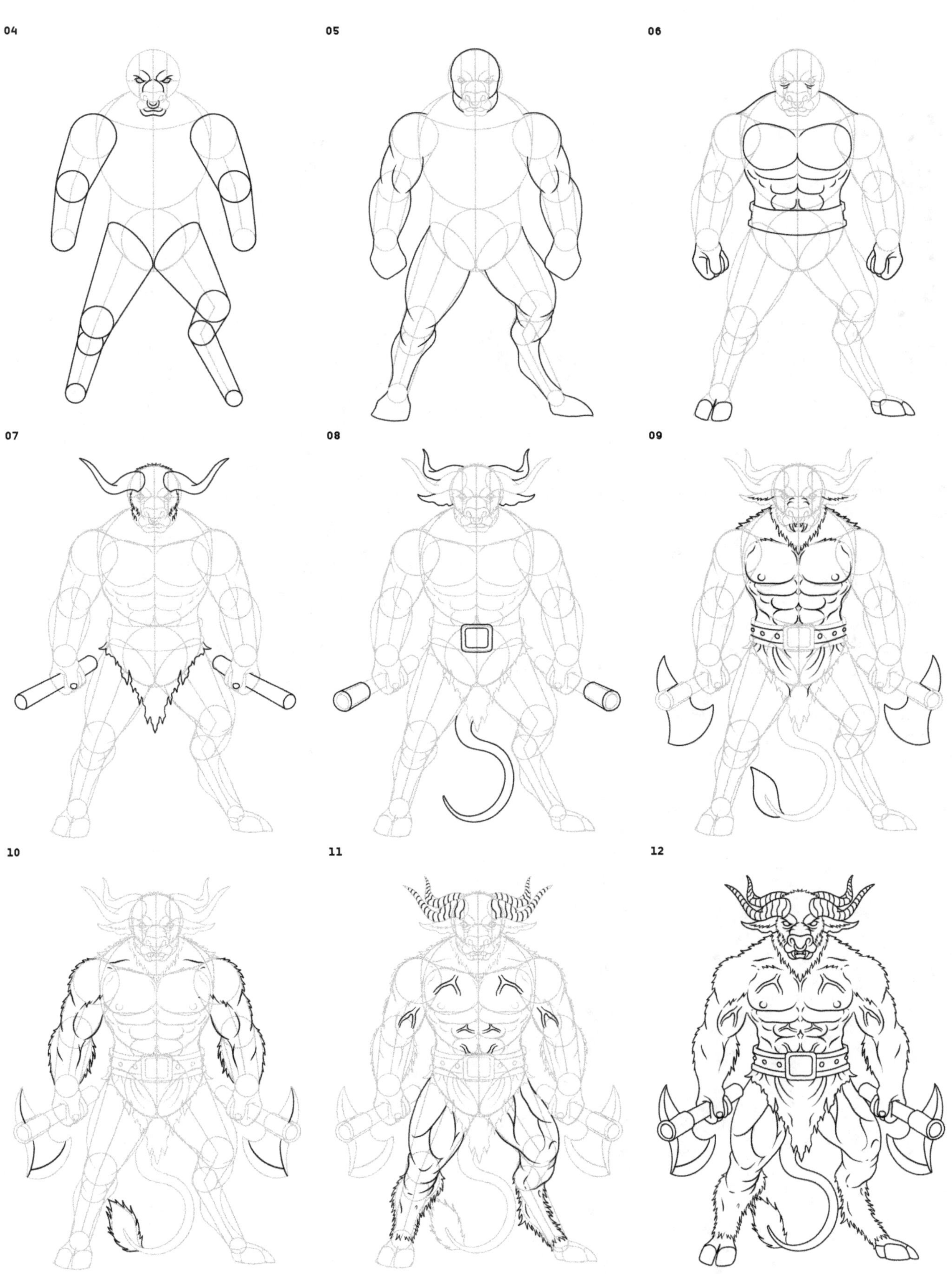

10

11

12

DARK PEGASUS

Pro tip: use the body length to set wing size

Measure from the head to the base of the tail, and use this distance to determine the length of each wing from base to tip. This creates wings that are proportionally large enough to feel powerful while staying visually balanced with the body. Establishing this measurement early makes it easier to keep the wings symmetrical and correctly scaled as you refine the drawing.

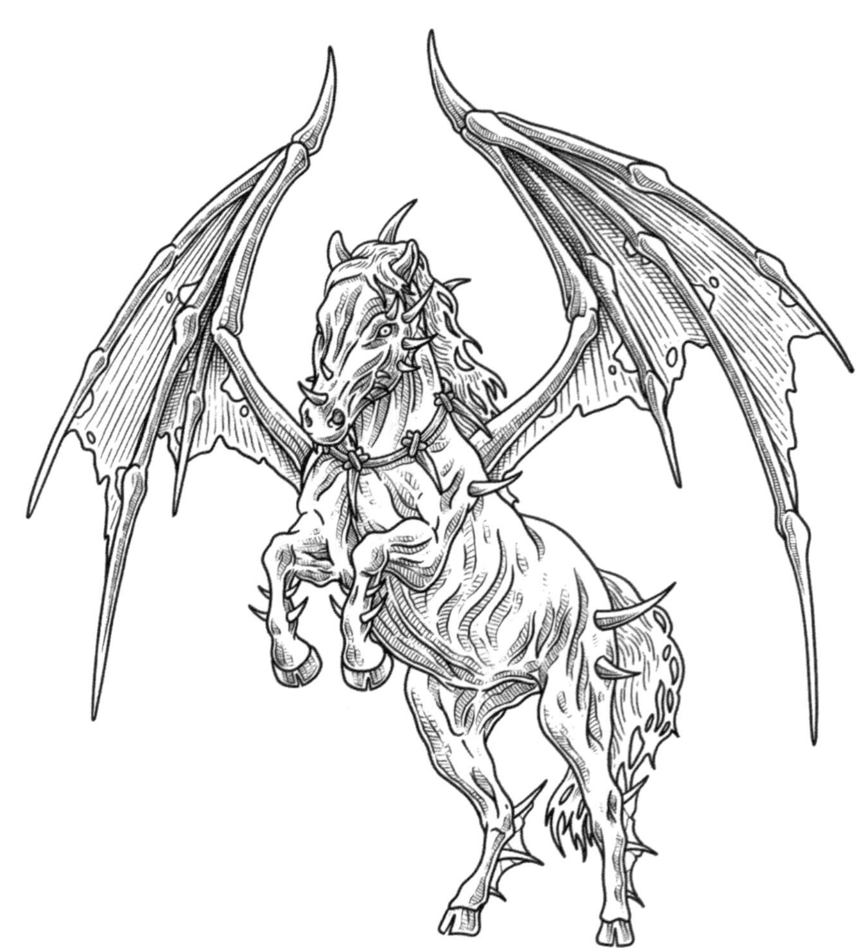

01

02

03

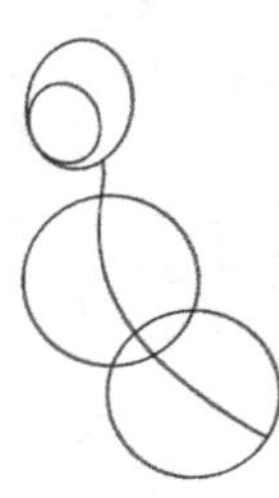

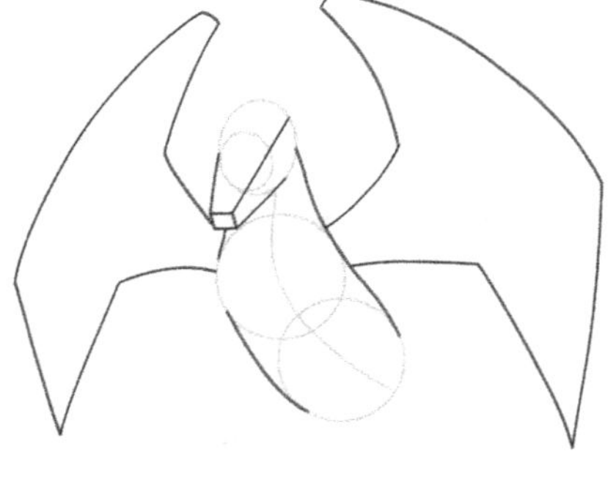

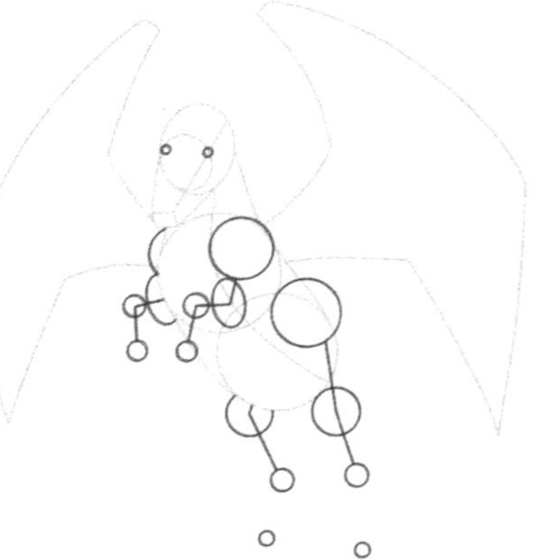

04

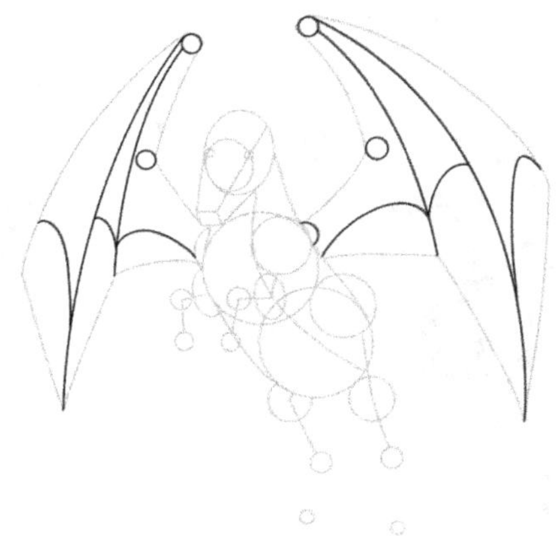

05

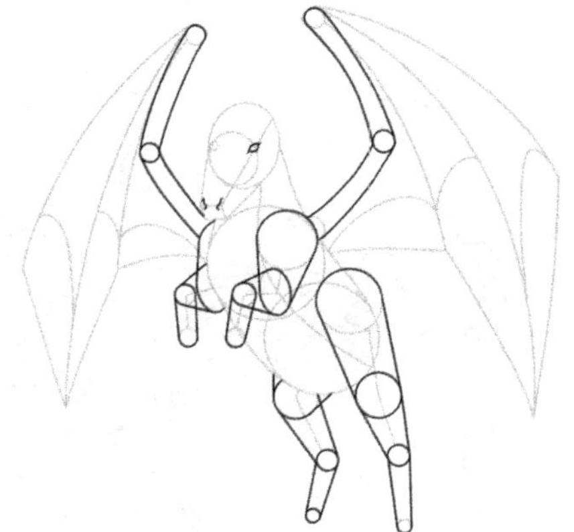

06

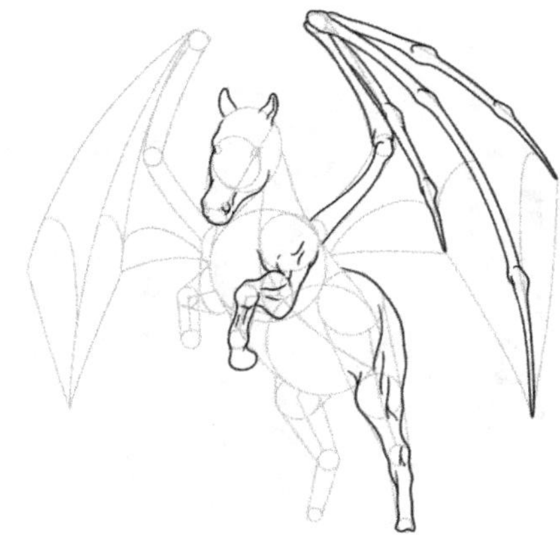

07

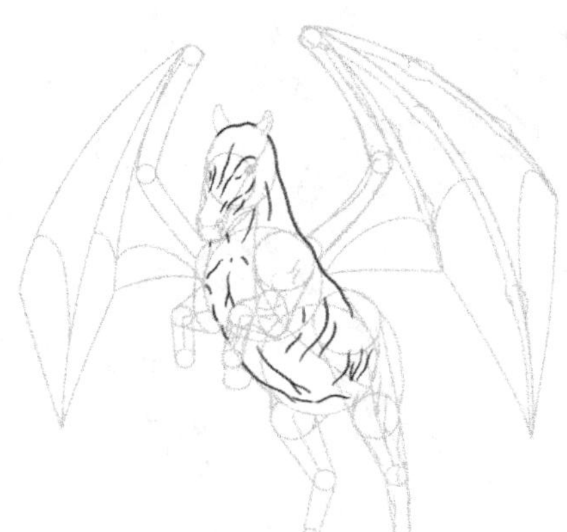

08

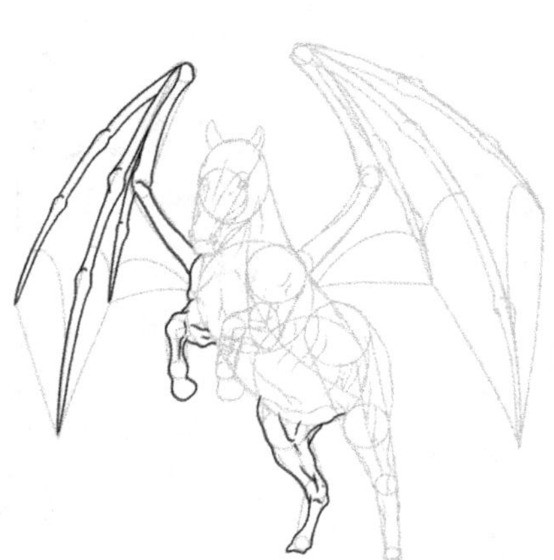

09

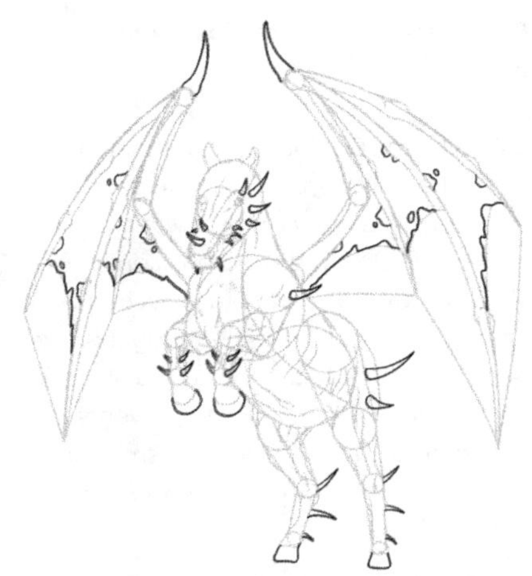

10

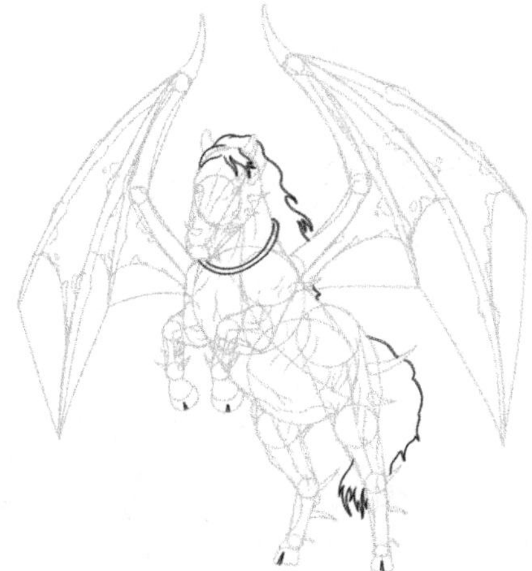

11

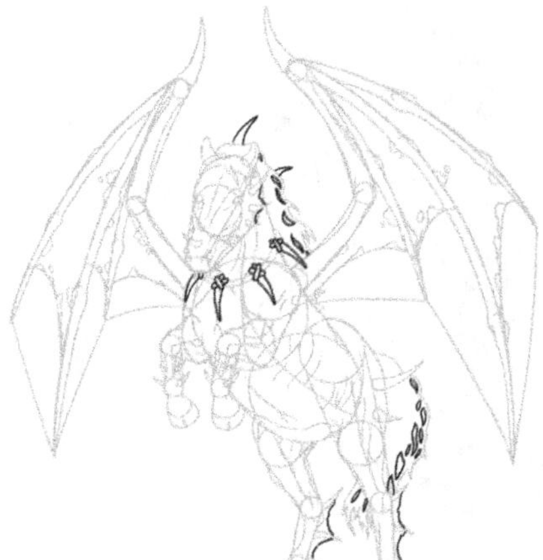

12

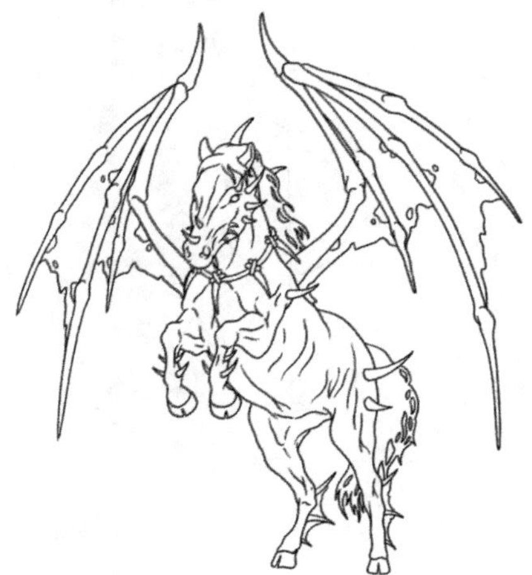

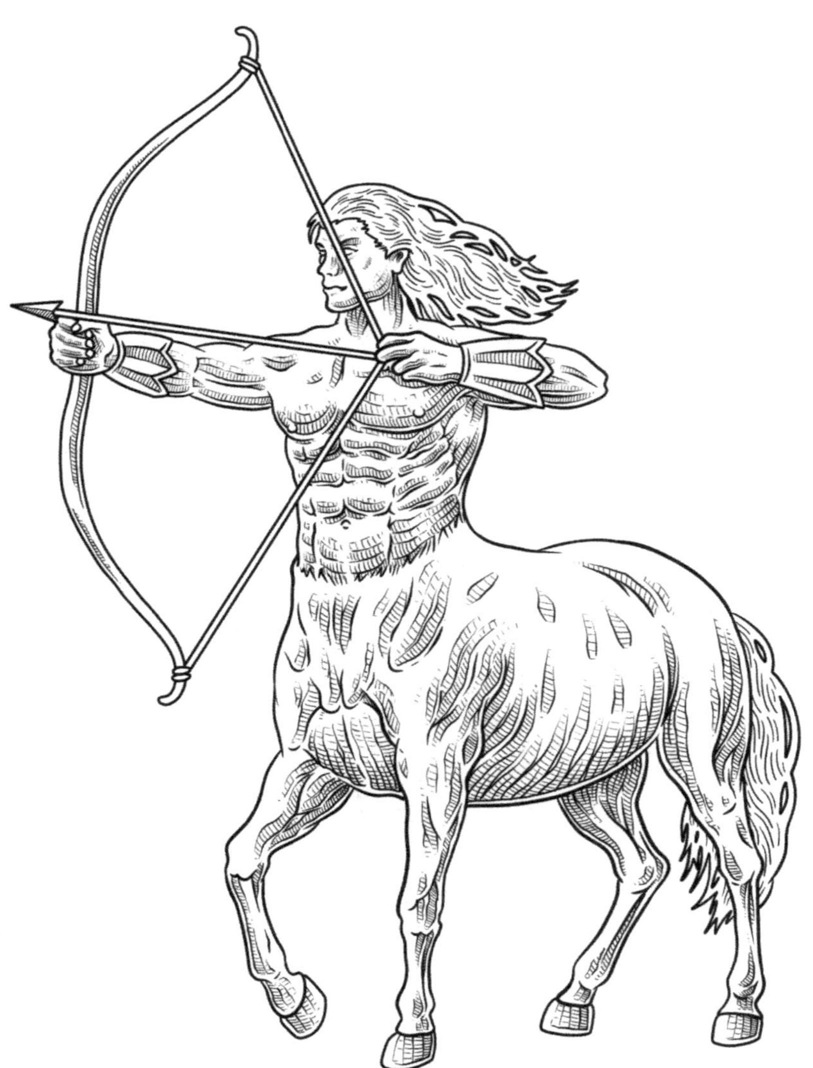

CENTAUR

Pro tip: use circle sizes to lock in proportions

Establish the Centaur's proportions by using the human ribcage circle as your base unit. The horse body circle should be roughly 1½ larger, and positioned slightly lower to create a natural transition between the two forms. Keeping this size relationship consistent helps maintain anatomical believability and prevents the human torso from looking too small or the horse body from overpowering the human figure.

01   **02**   **03**

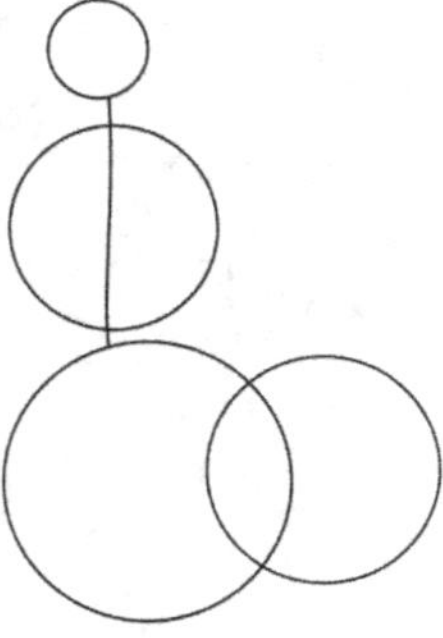

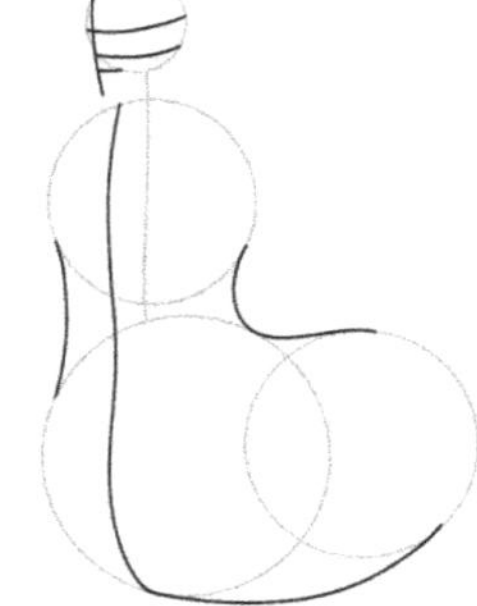

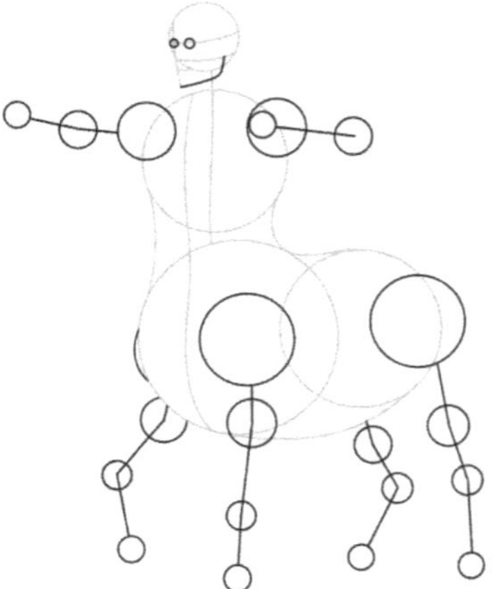

04

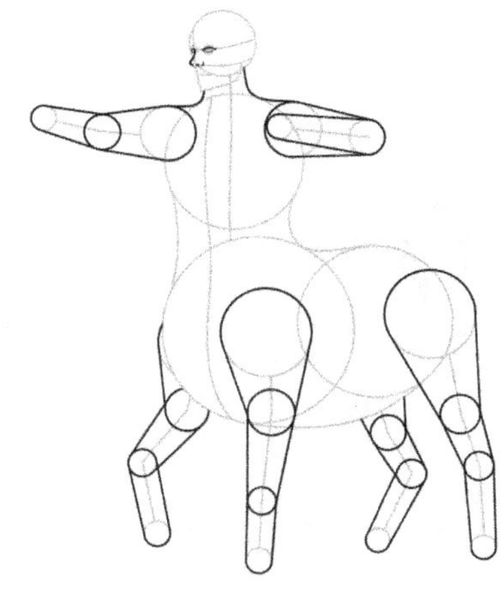

05

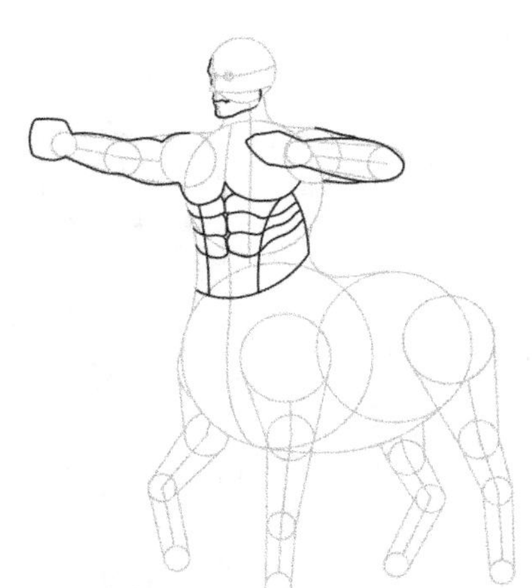

06

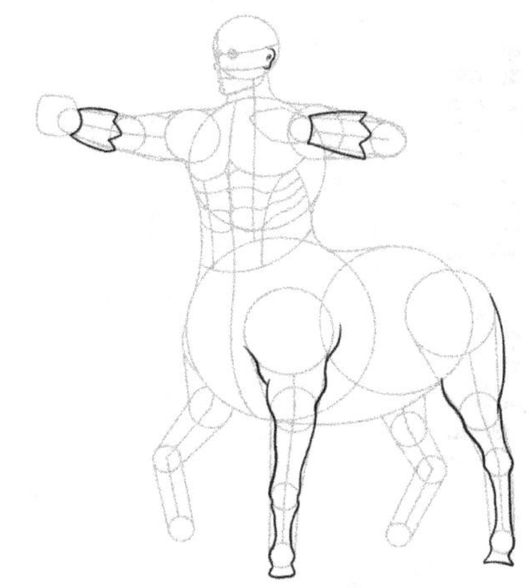

07

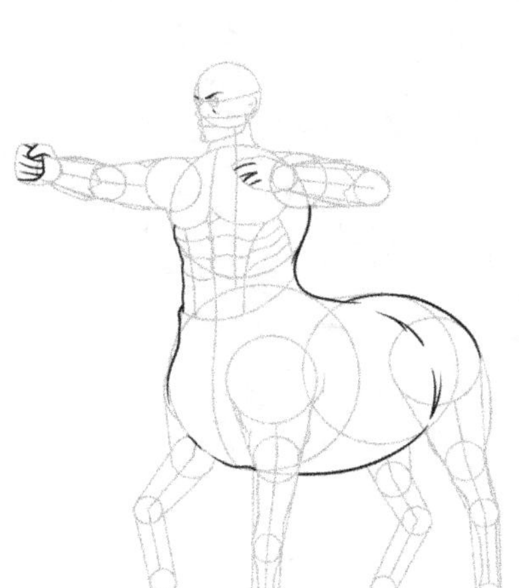

08

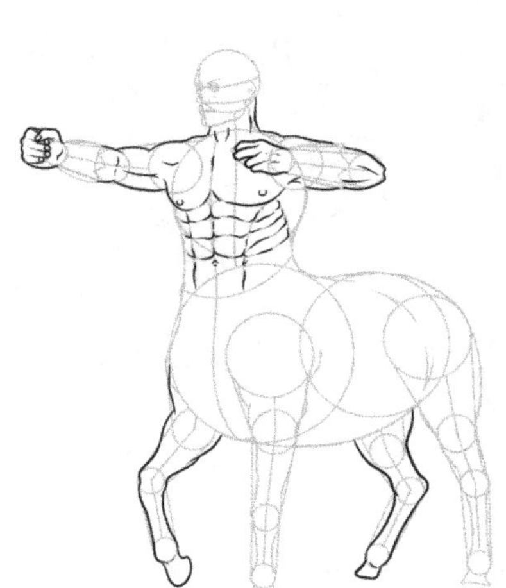

09

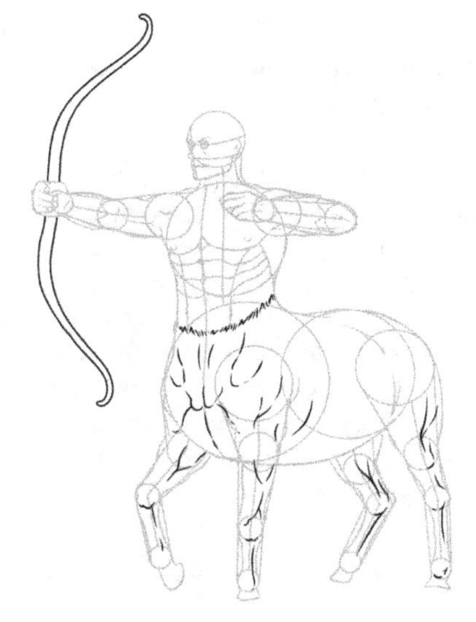

10

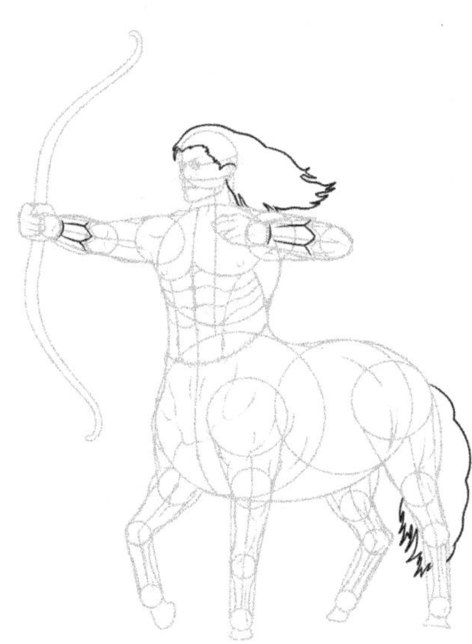

11

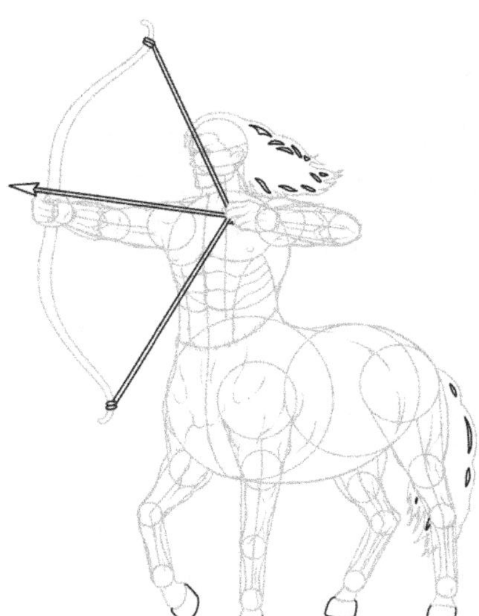

12

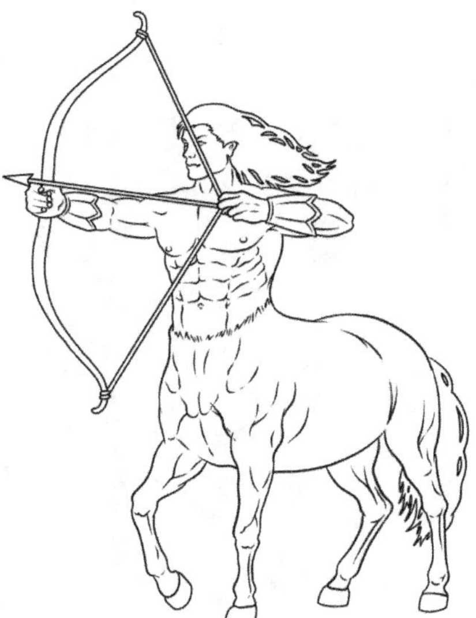

ZOMBIE MUMMY

Pro tip: use the guidelines to place the eyes and jaw

Position the eyes along the central horizontal guideline wrapping around the head, ensuring they sit evenly on either side of the vertical centre line. Place the bottom of the jaw about half a head-height below the base of the head circle, tapering inward to form a narrow, sunken chin. This placement creates the gaunt, skeletal structure characteristic of the Zombie Mummy.

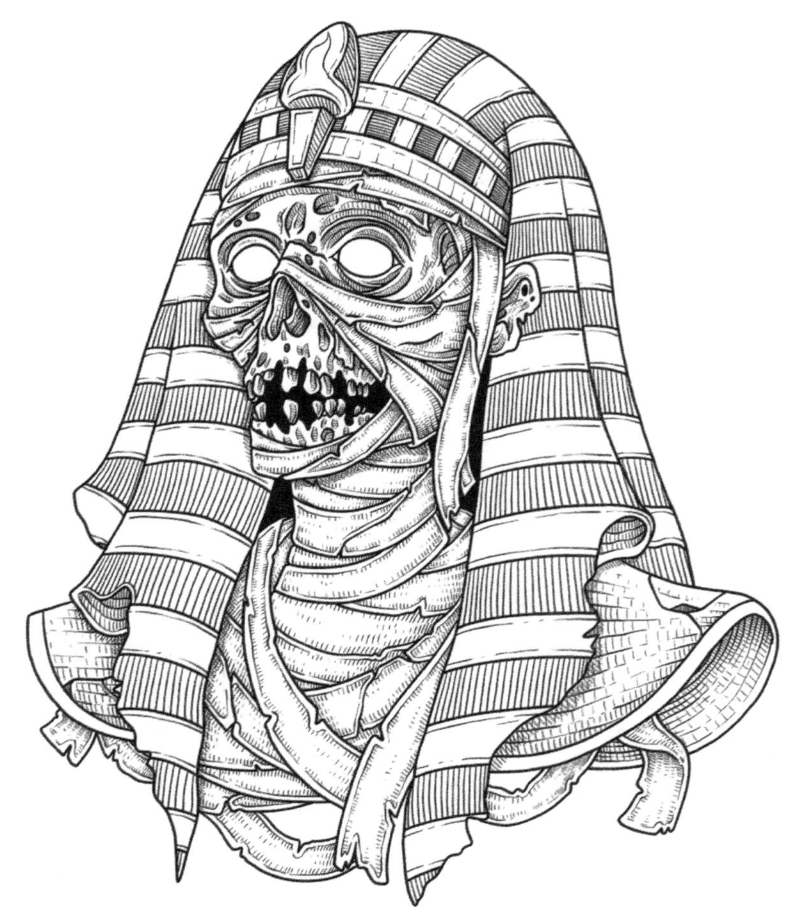

01

02

03

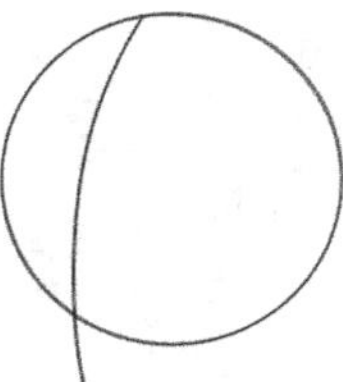

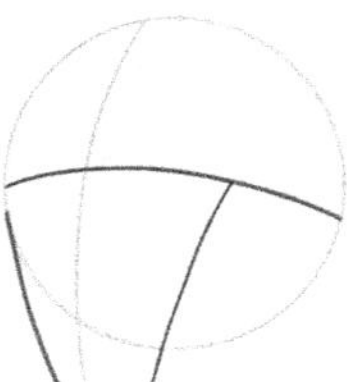

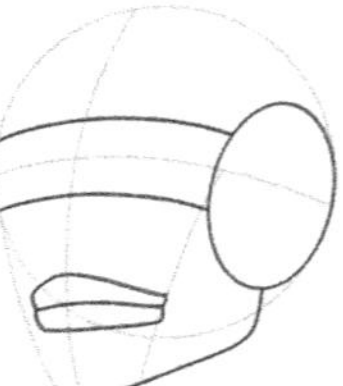

04

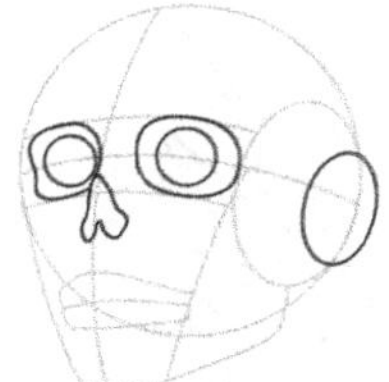

05

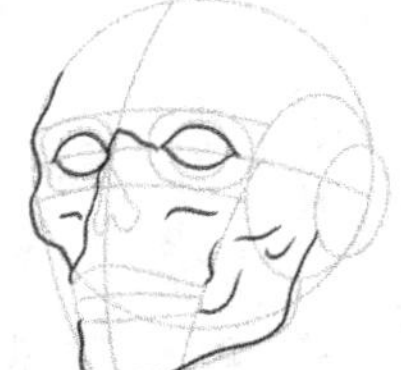

06

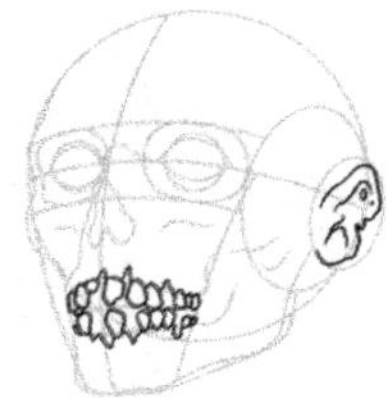

07

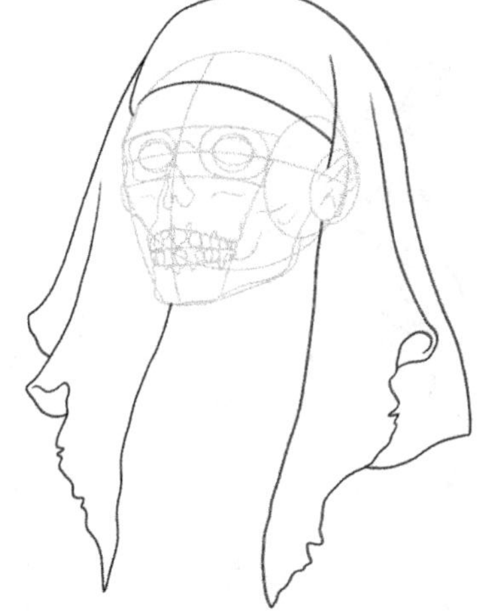

08

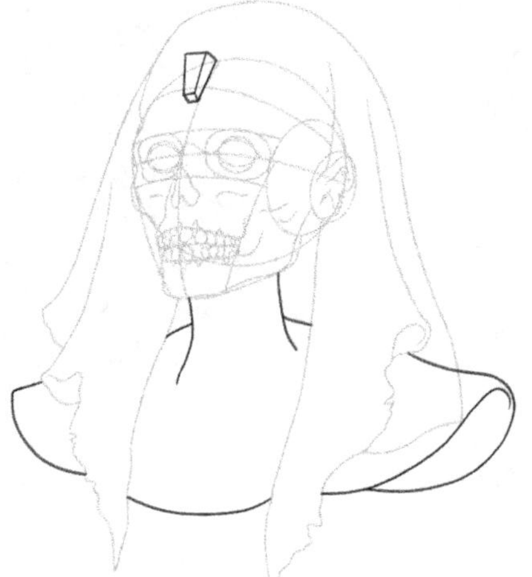

09

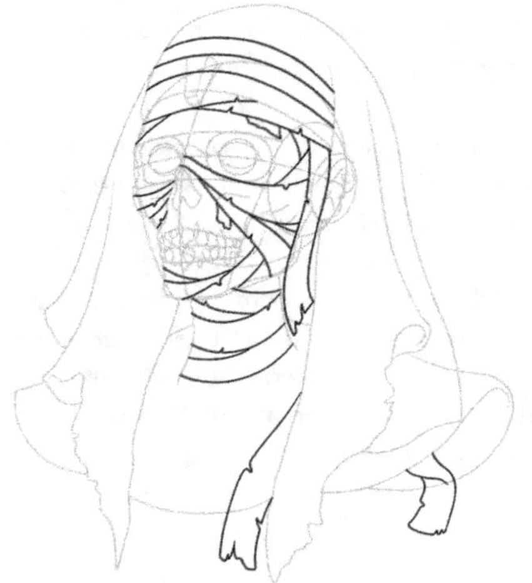

10

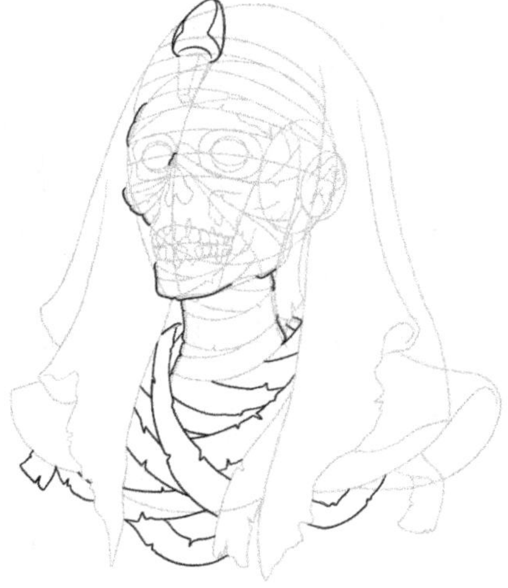

11

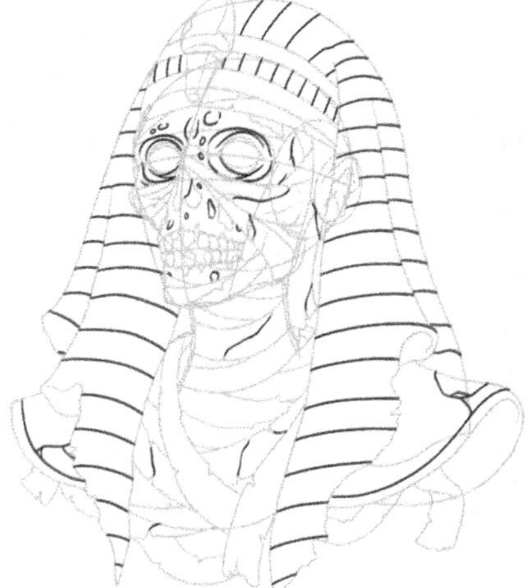

12

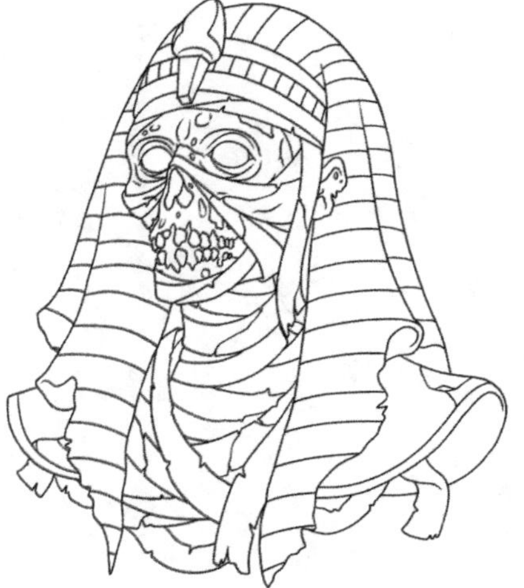

PHOENIX

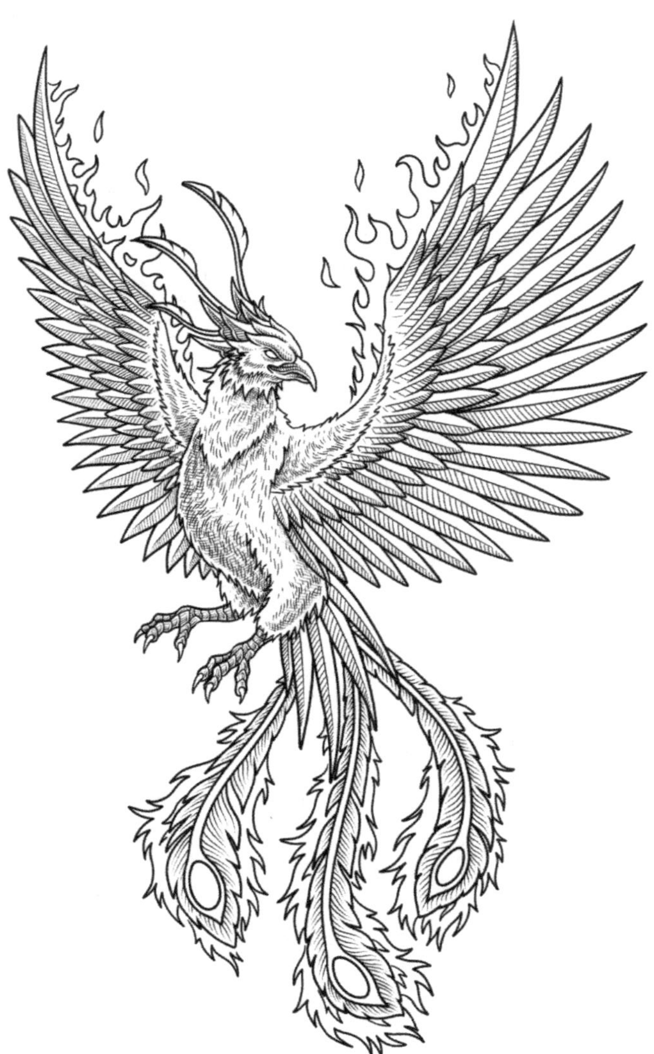

Pro tip: at step 04, block in the feather layers

Mark in the feather groupings across the wings, starting from the outer edge and working inward. The outer feathers should be broad and sweeping, while each inner layer becomes progressively narrower and shorter as it approaches the body. This layered construction will give the wings structure and rhythm, making the final detailing phase much easier and more harmonious.

01

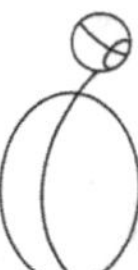

02

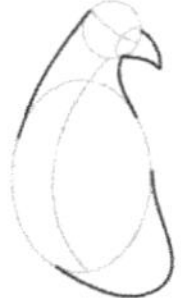

03

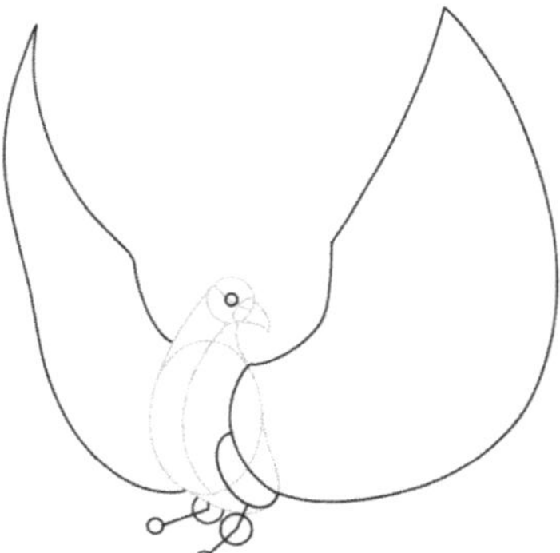

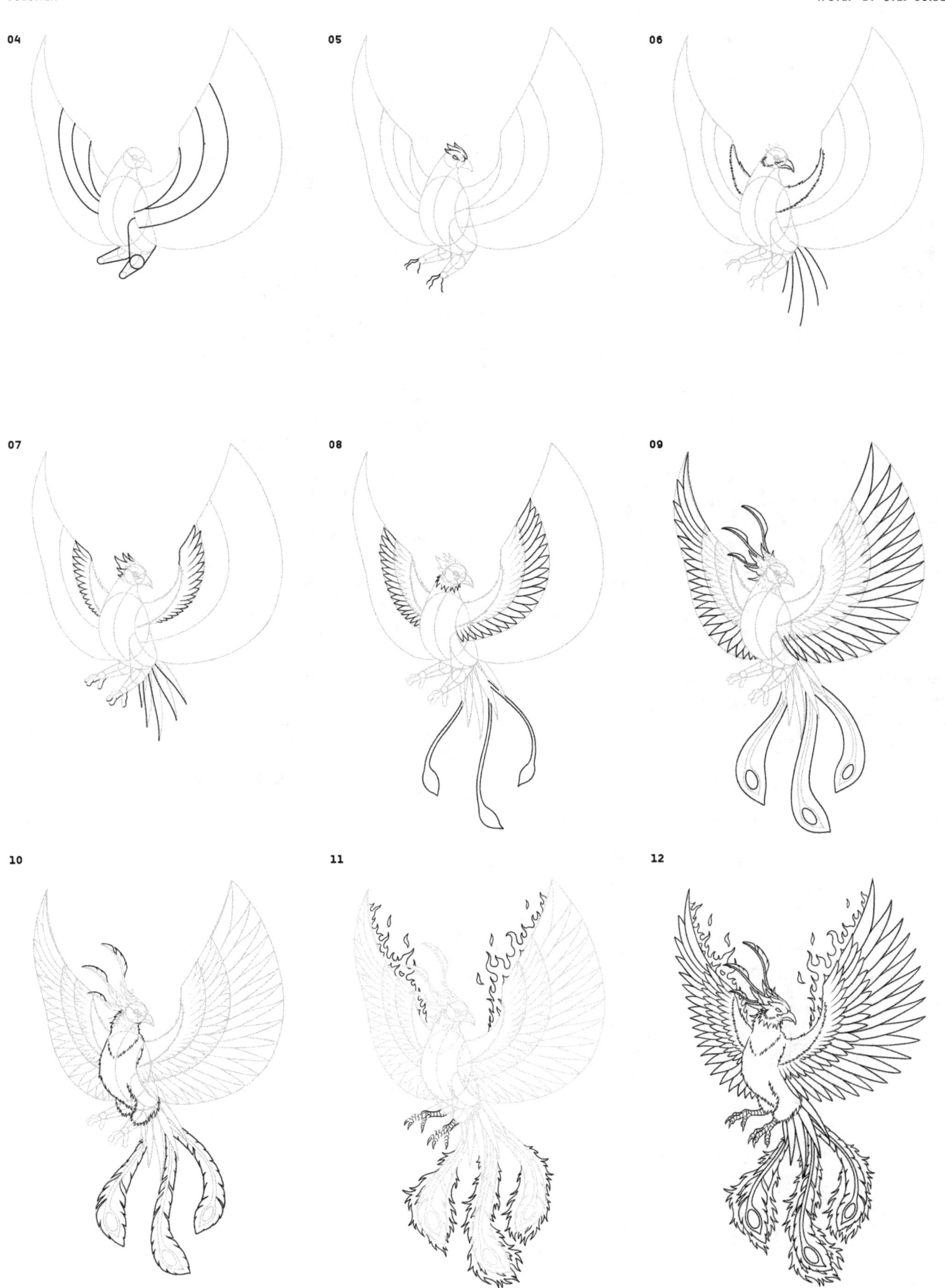

04
05
06
07
08
09
10
11
12

SATYR

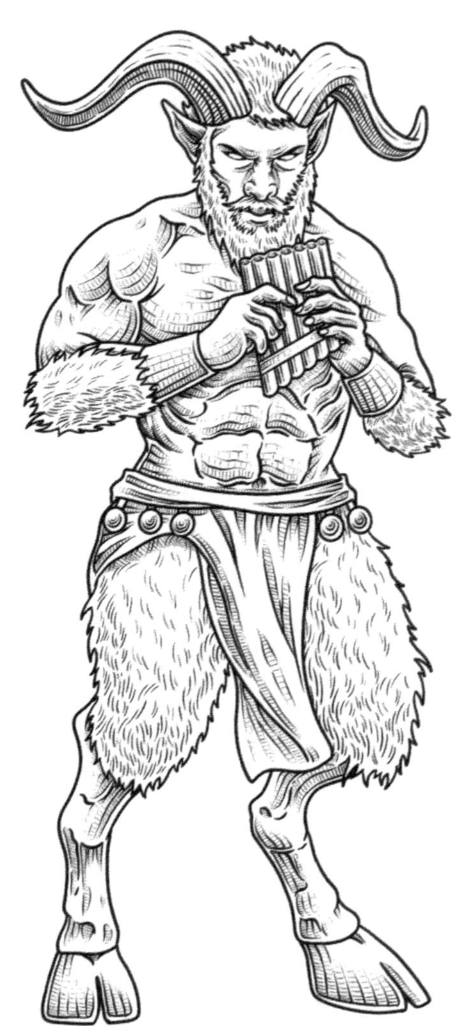

Pro tip: align the horns with the brow line for a natural placement

To make the horns look natural and integrated with the head, use the brow line as your anchor. Start the base of each horn where the brow line meets the sides of the head. This gives the horns a believable anatomical origin, as if they're emerging from the skull rather than sitting on top of it.

01

02

03

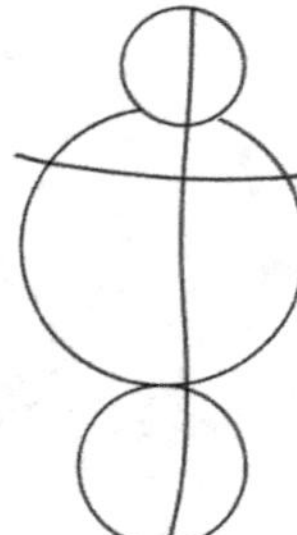

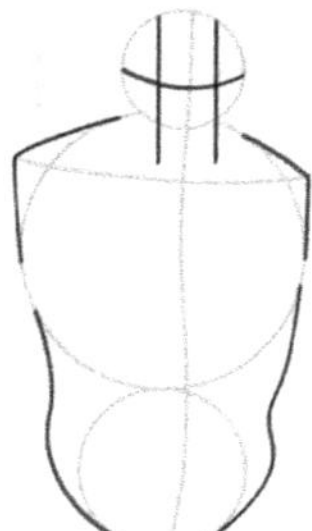

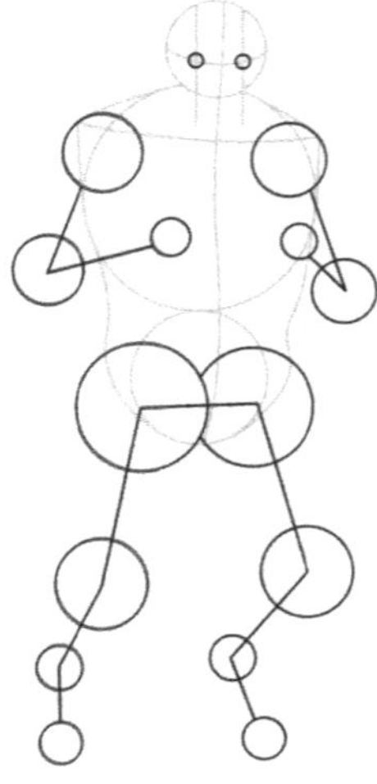

04

05

06
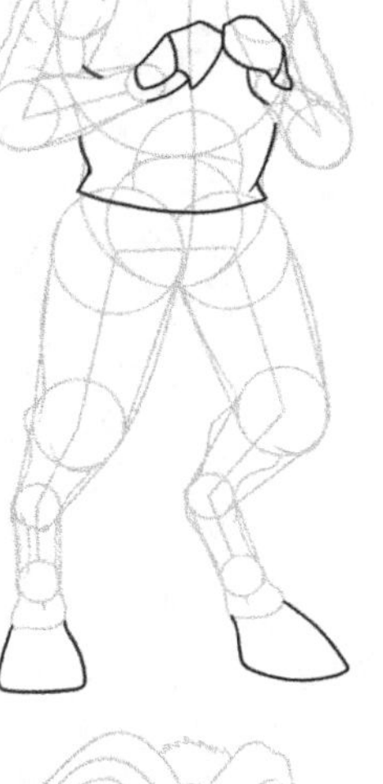

07
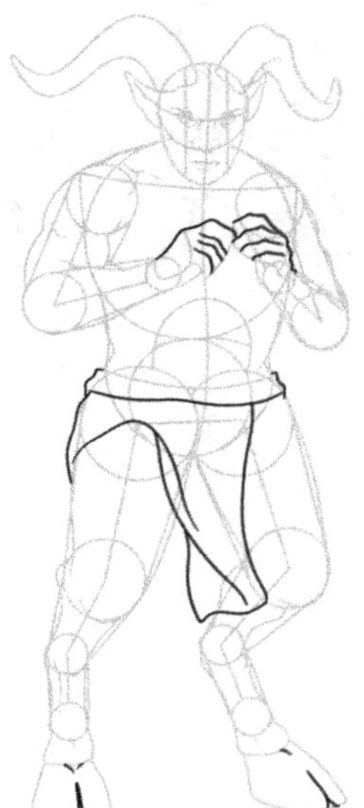

08

09
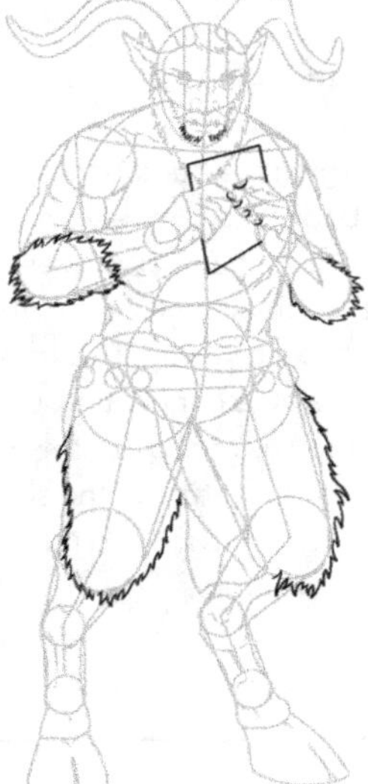

10
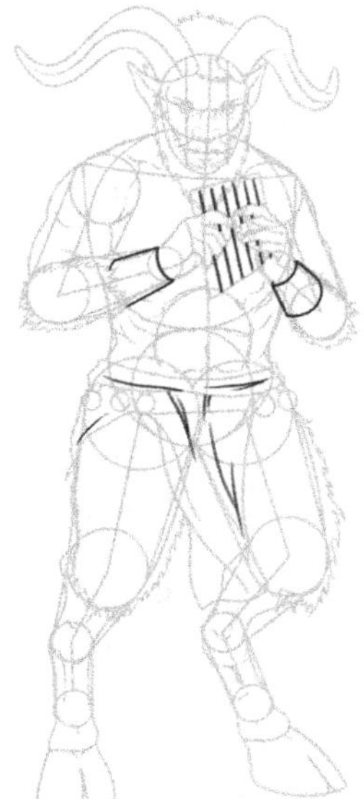

11
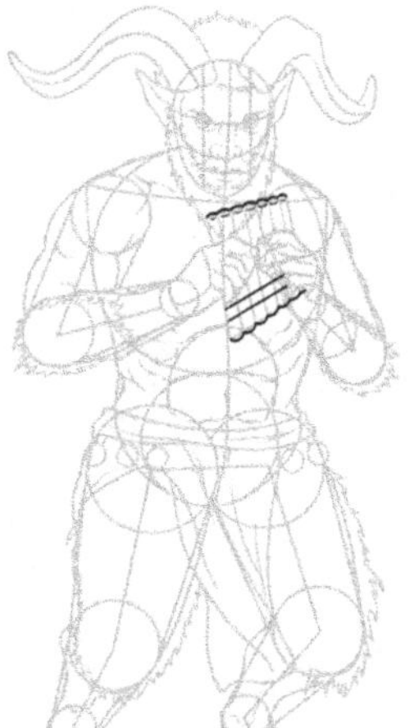

12
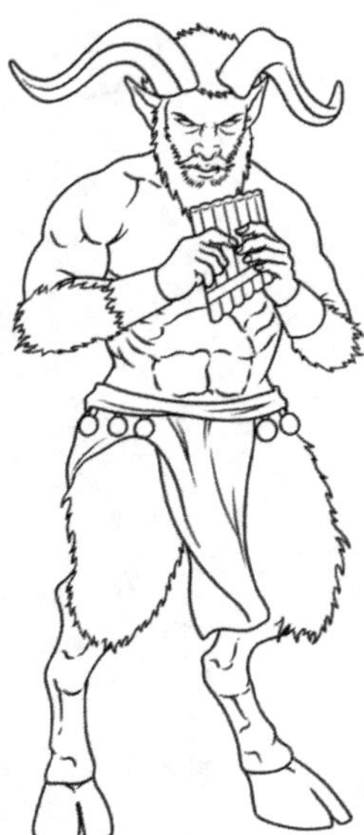

SCORPION CENTAUR

Pro tip: anchor the torso seamlessly

When merging the human torso with the scorpion body, anchor the waist firmly into the front section of the exoskeleton. Think of the torso "slotting into" the upper carapace like a ball joint. This creates a strong, believable connection. Use the central body axis to align both halves, and echo the curvature of the scorpion's shell in the lower ribcage to make the transition feel natural.

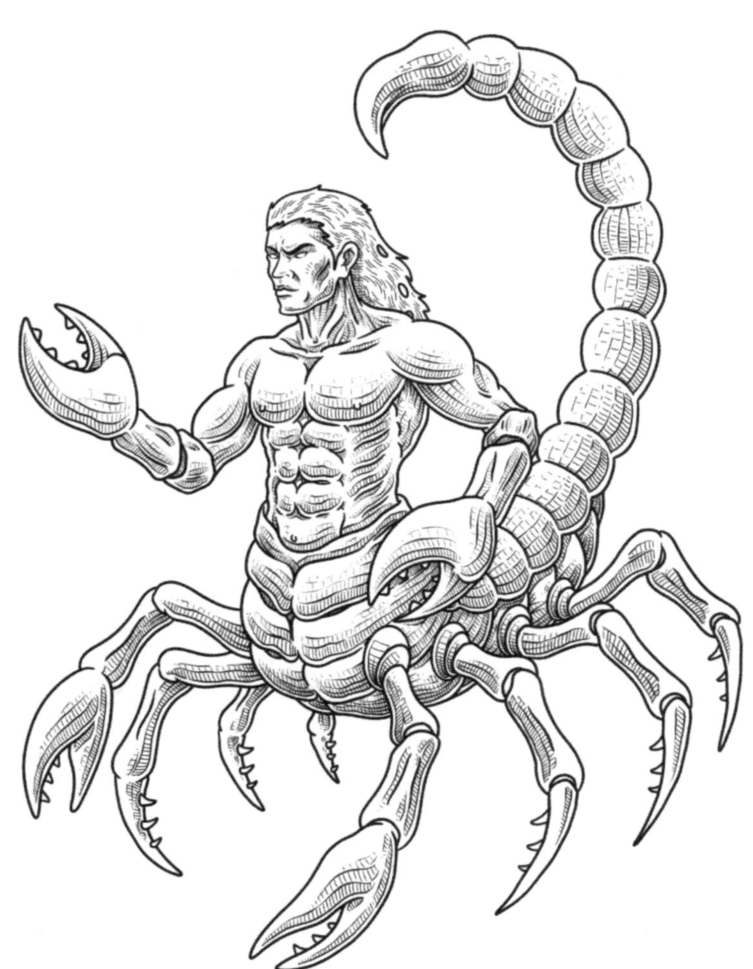

01

02

03

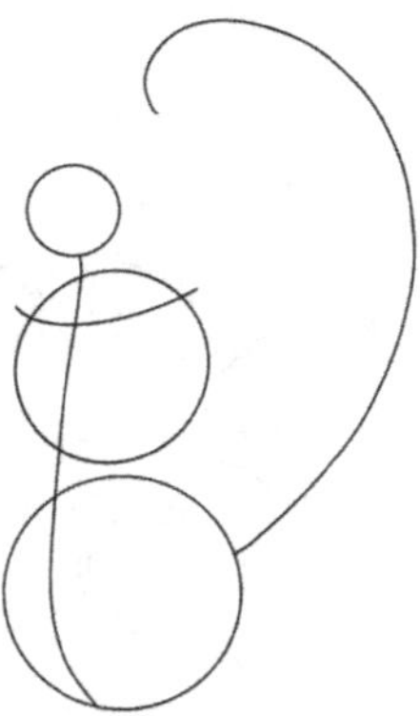

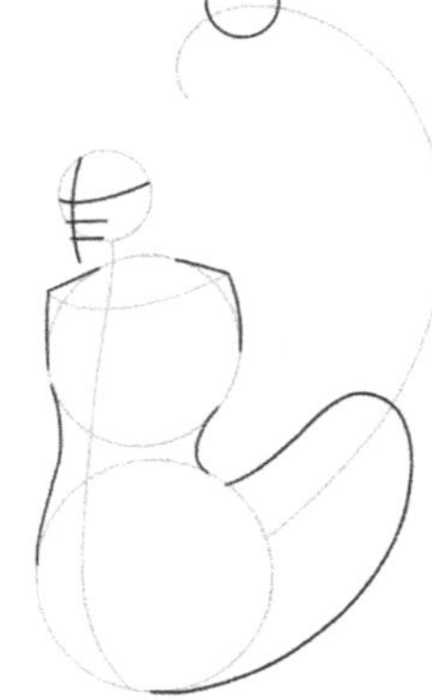

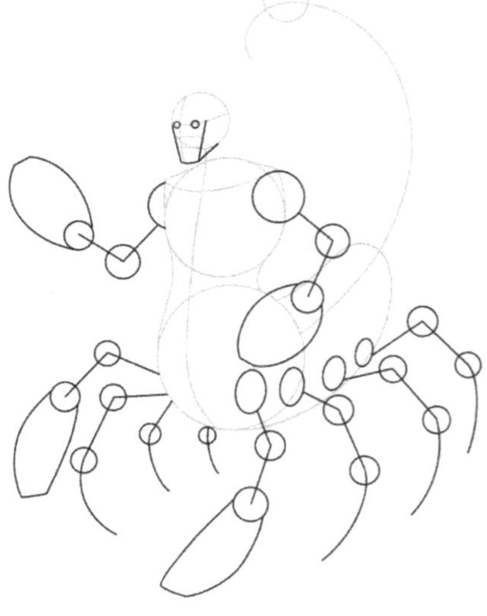

04

05

06

07

08

09

10

11

12

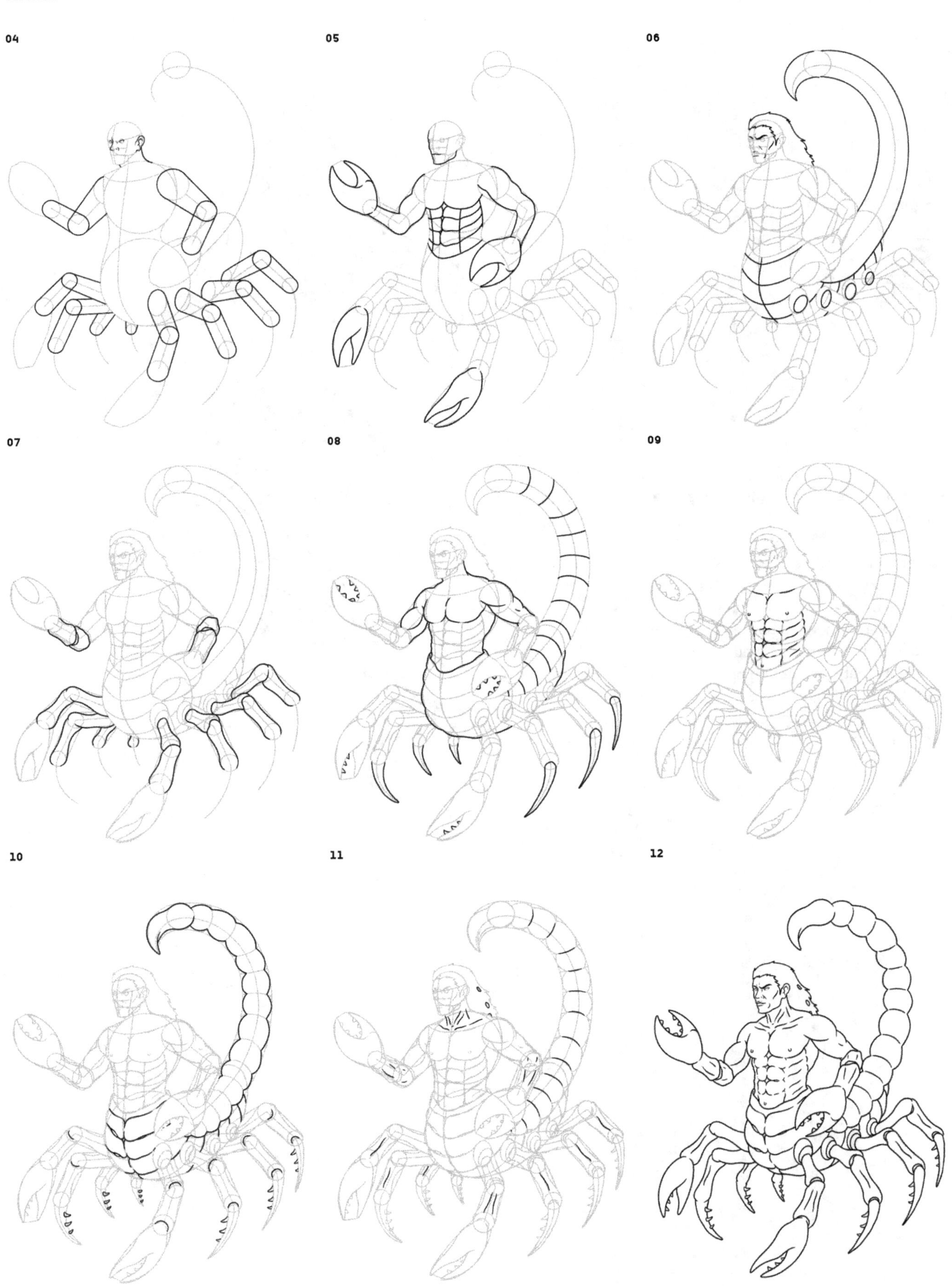

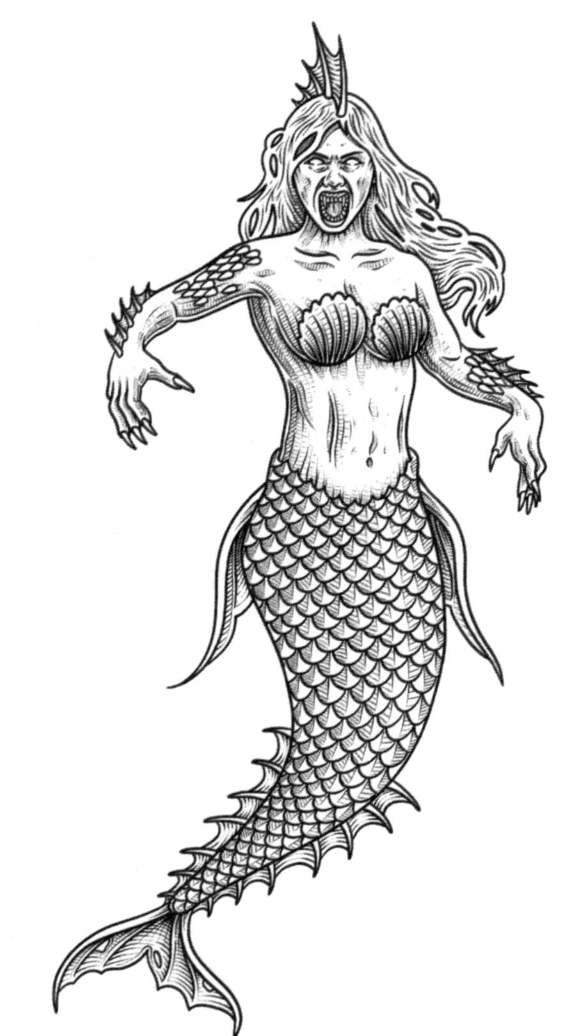

SIREN

Pro tip: use the torso length to measure the tail

To determine the length of the Siren's tail, use the torso as your reference. Measure from the base of the neck to the bottom of the ribcage, then multiply that length by roughly two. This gives you a balanced tail length that feels proportional to the upper body. Using the torso as a unit ensures consistency across different poses and angles.

01

02

03

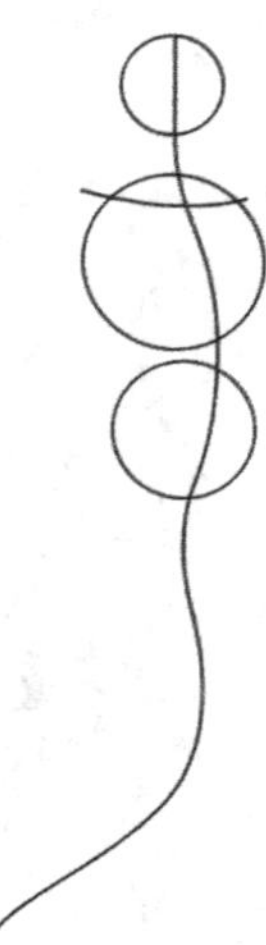

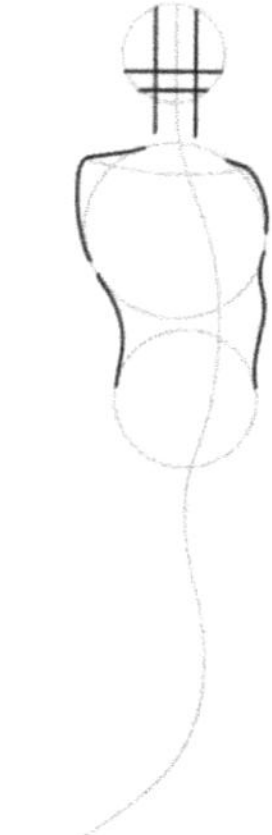

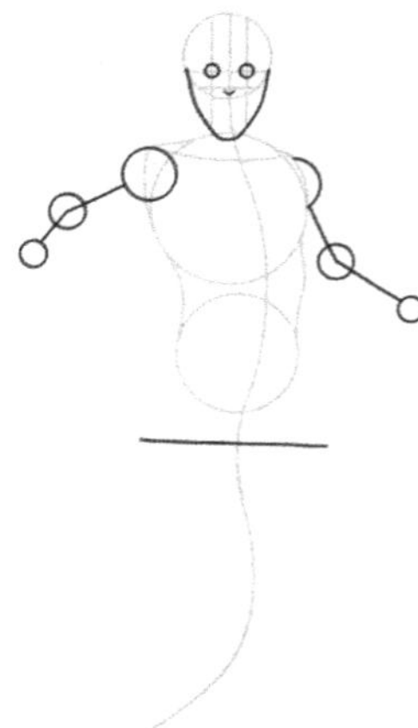

04

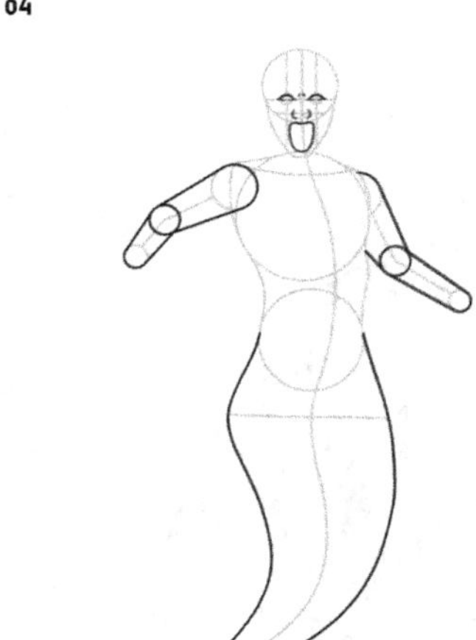

05

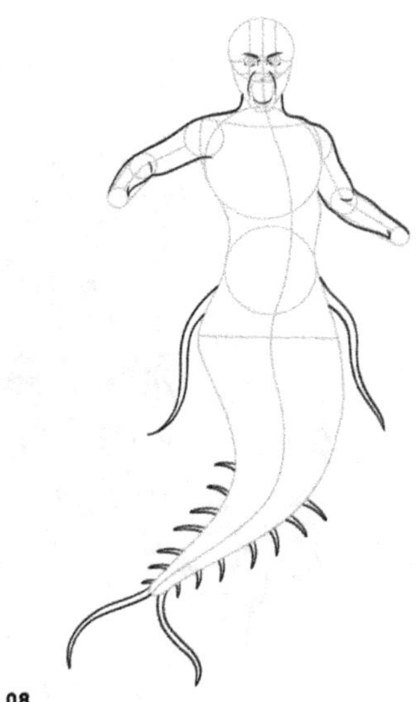

06

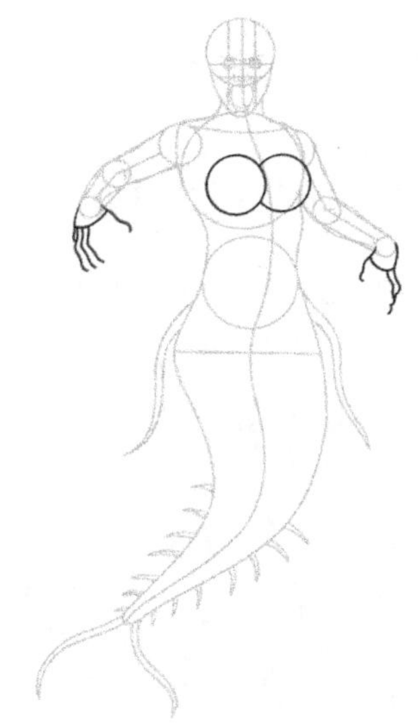

07

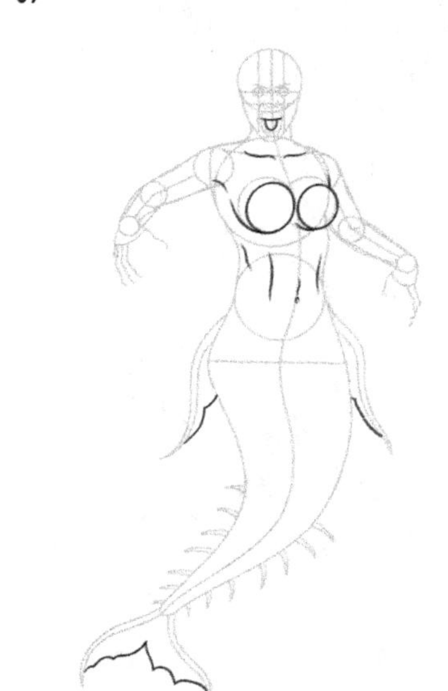

08

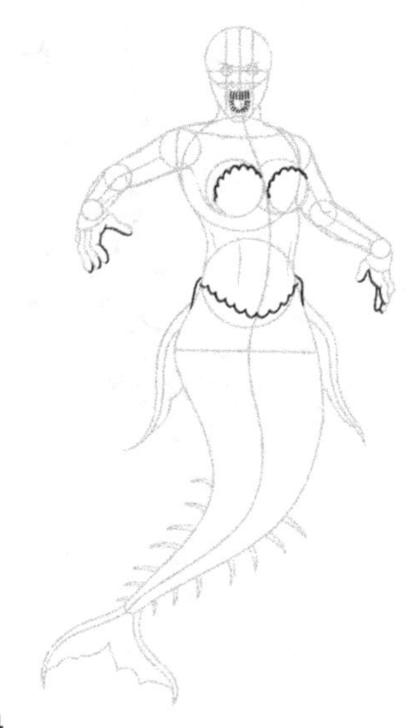

09

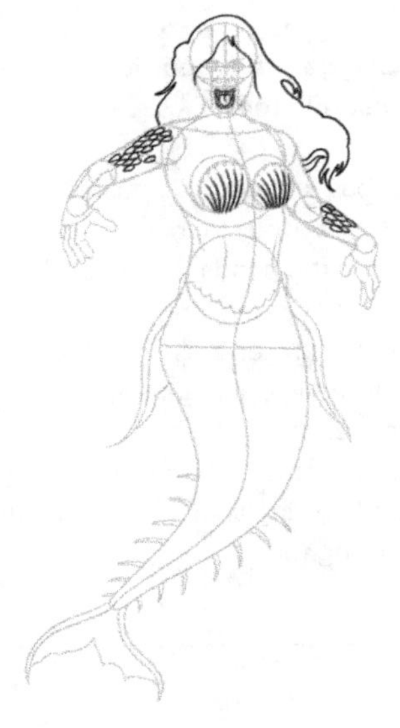

10

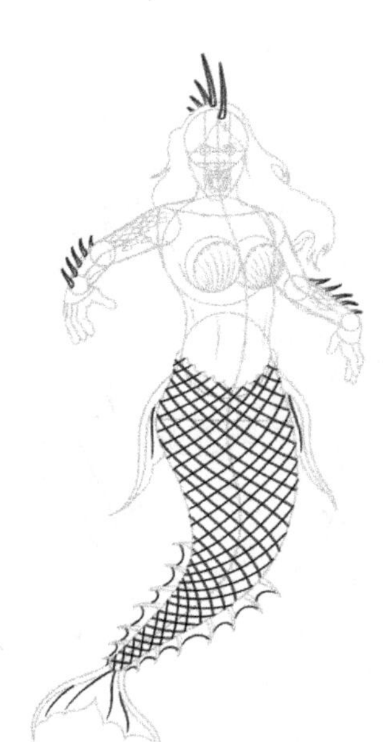

11

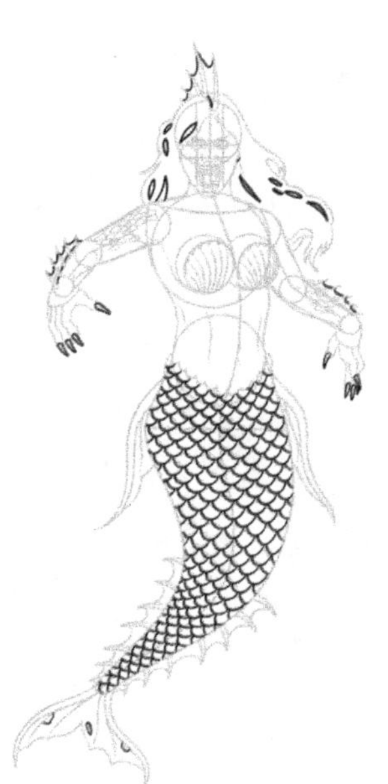

12

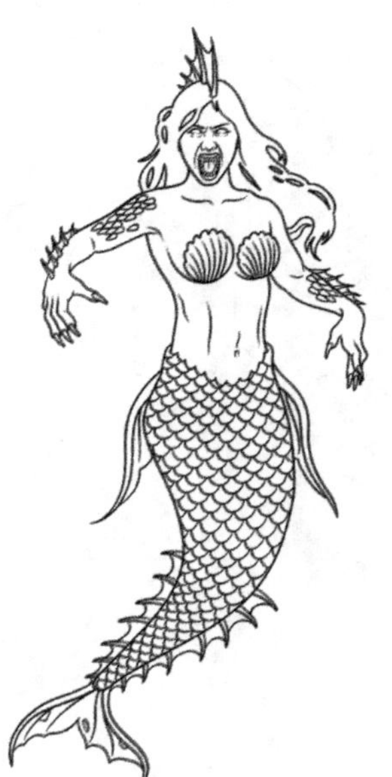

SLIME MONSTER

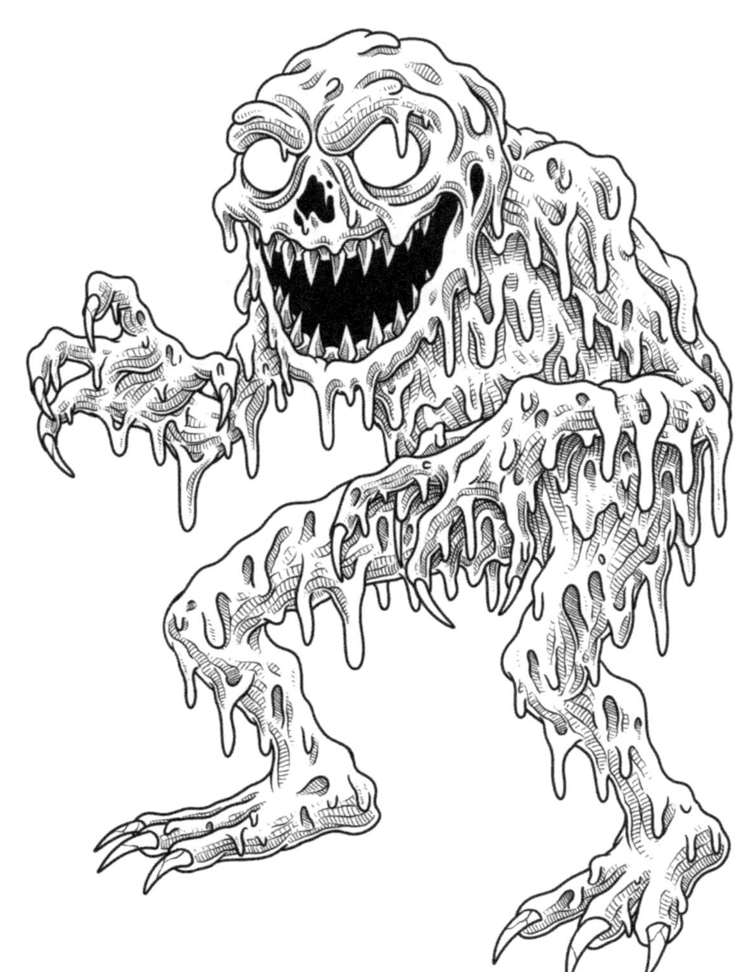

Pro tip: exaggerate proportions for a gooey, unstable feel

For slime-based creatures, push the proportions beyond standard anatomy. Try enlarging the head relative to the torso and keeping the limbs slightly shorter and chunkier. This gives the figure a top-heavy, unbalanced quality that enhances the creature's unsettling, amorphous character. Use rounded shapes and flowing lines to reinforce the gooey, shifting form.

01

02

03

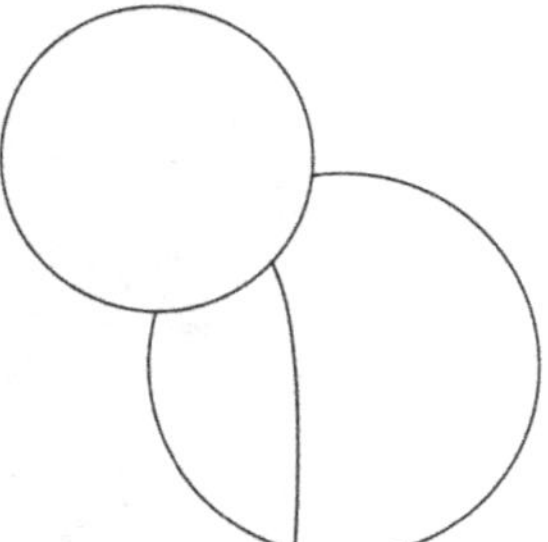

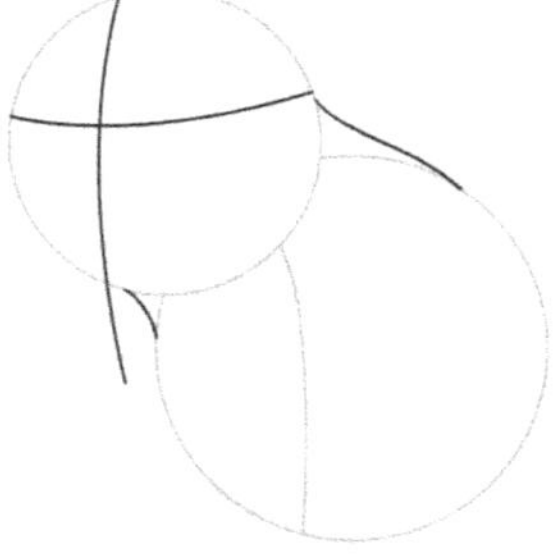

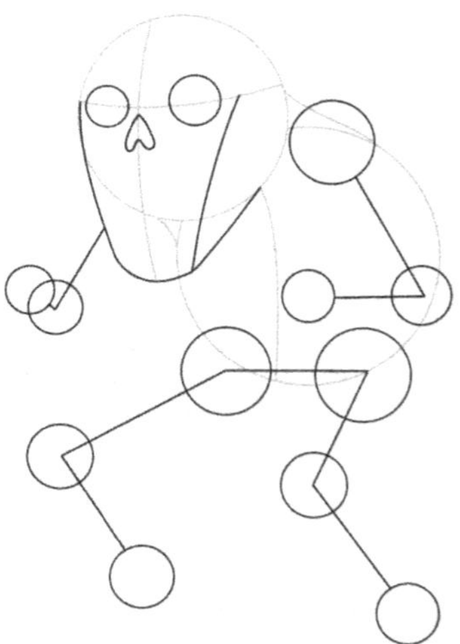

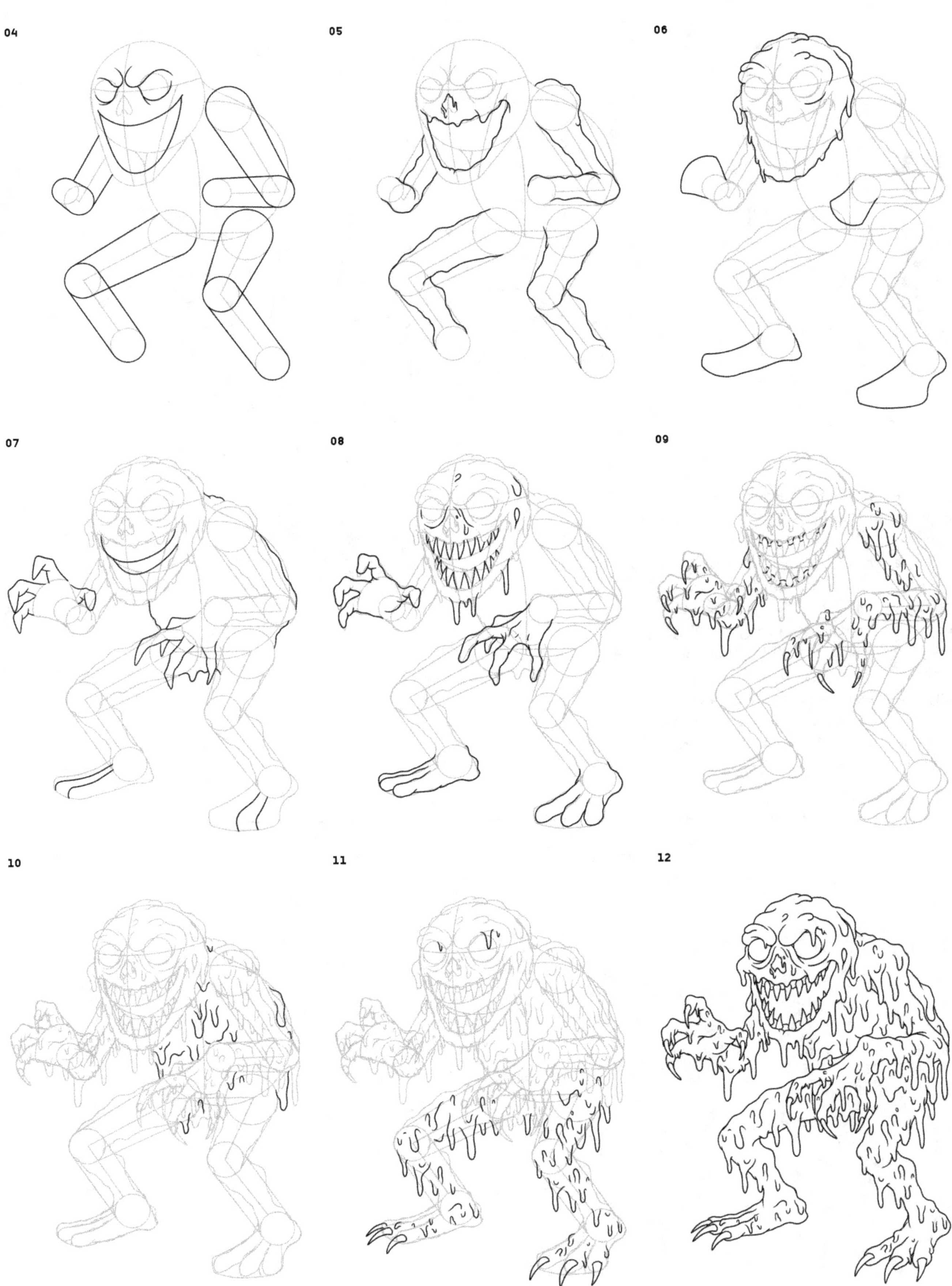

04
05
06
07
08
09
10
11
12
HOW TO DRAW MONSTERS & BEASTS

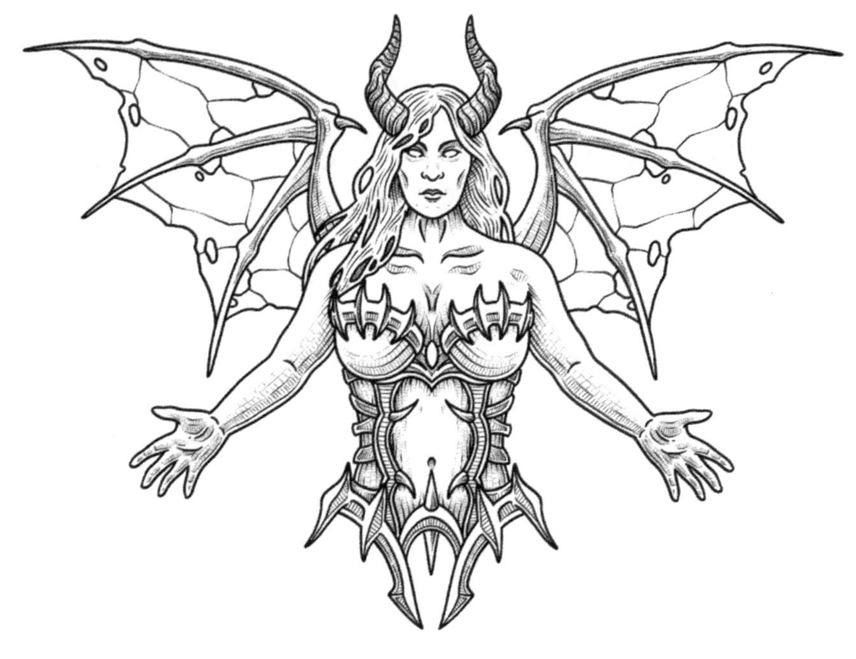

Pro tip: align wing placement with the shoulder line

When attaching the wings, use the shoulder line as your anchor point. The top of each wing should align horizontally with the shoulder joints, giving the wings a believable origin that feels structurally integrated with the upper body. This not only improves balance and symmetry but also reinforces the illusion that the wings are strong enough to support the figure in flight.

01

02

03

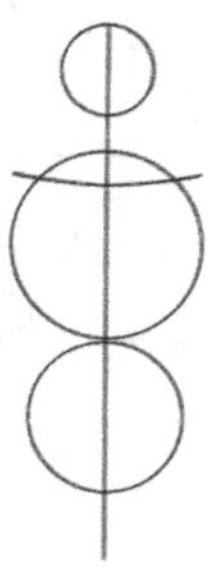

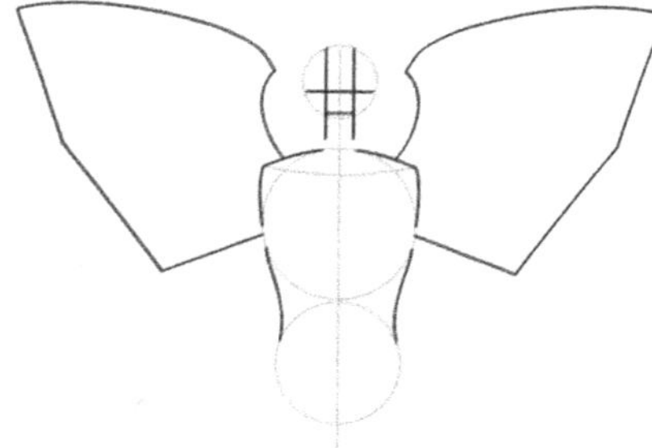

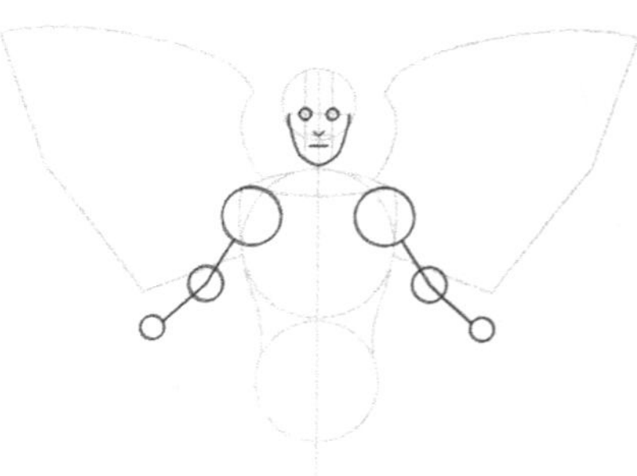

04

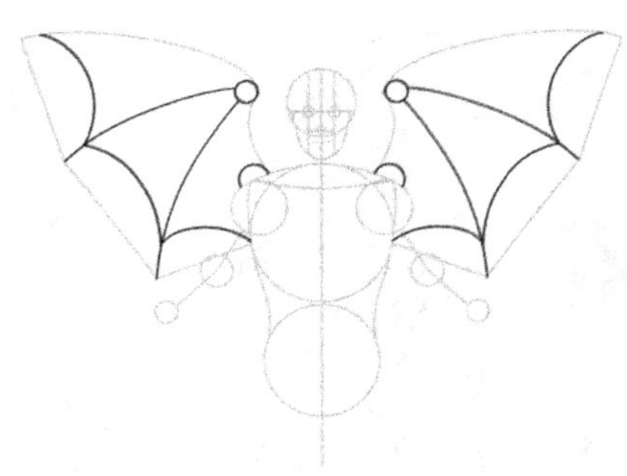

05

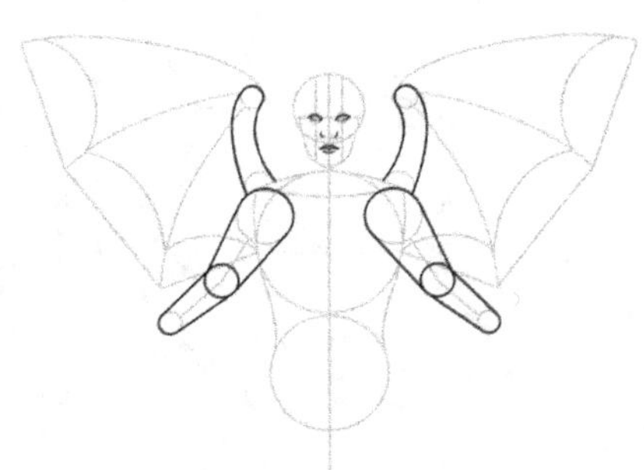

06

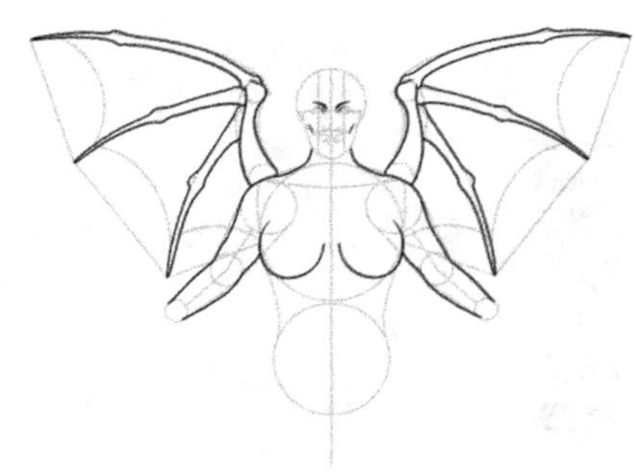

07

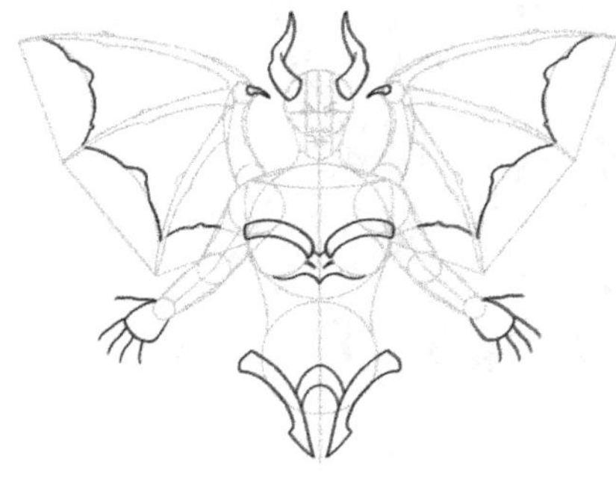

08

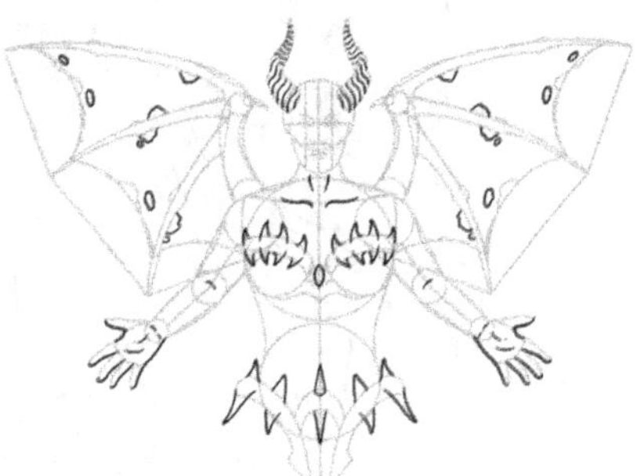

09

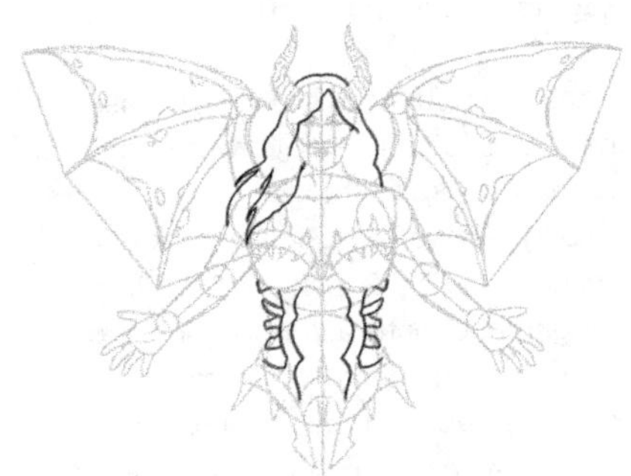

10

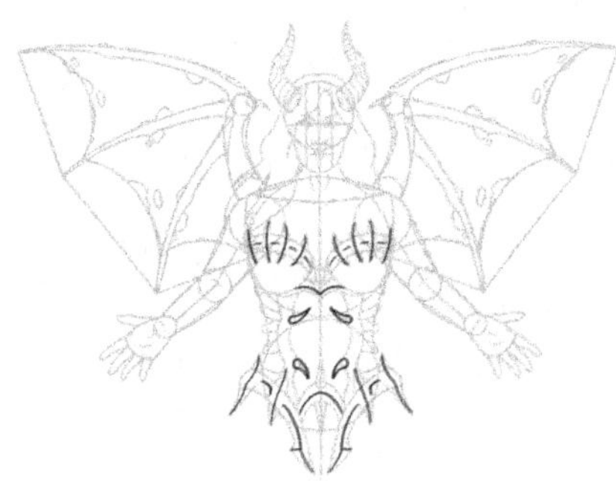

11

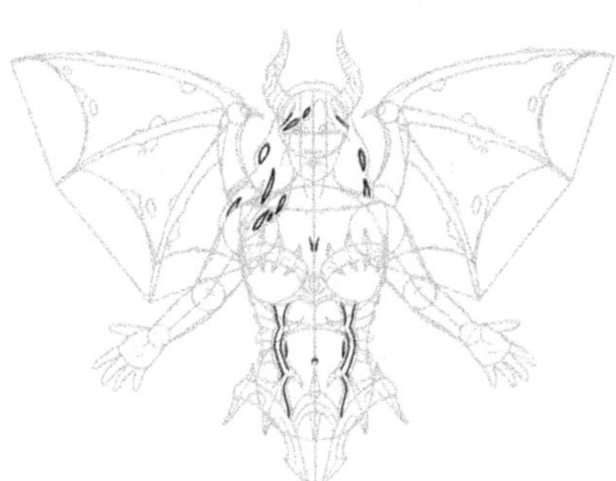

12

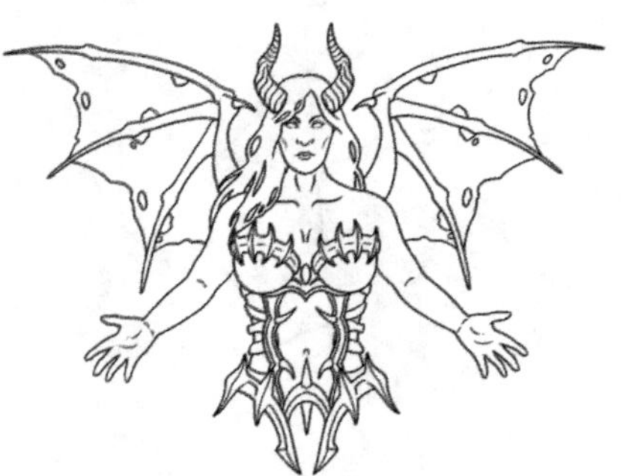

BANSHEE

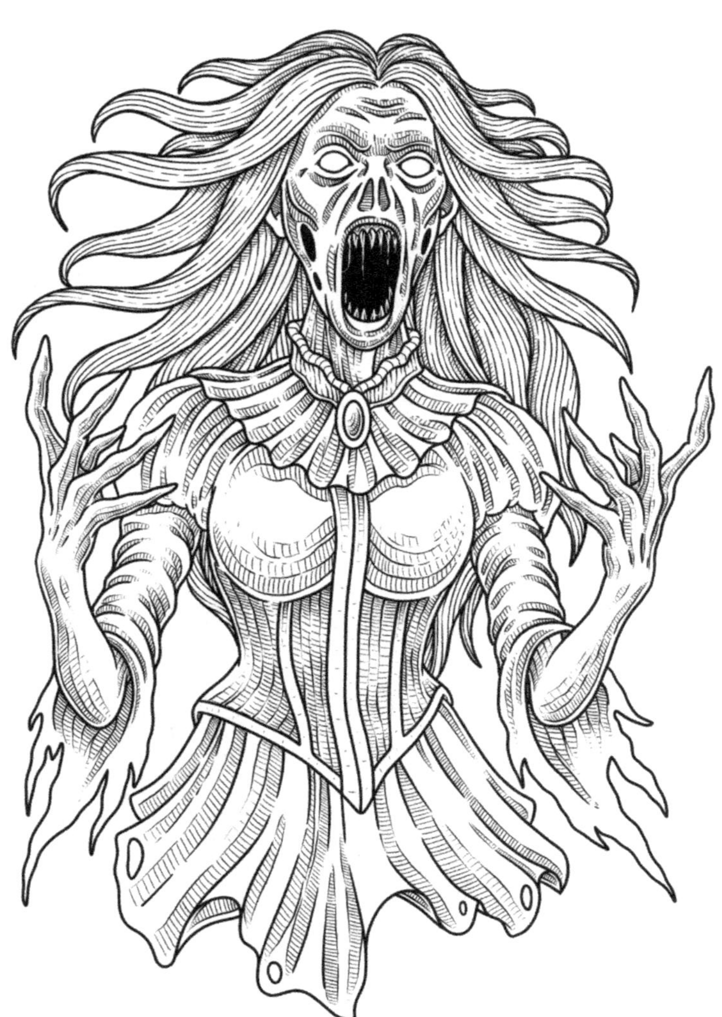

Pro tip: extend the chin for an exaggerated haunting effect

To find the bottom of the chin, measure one full head sphere downward from the base of the skull, effectively doubling the original head height. This extended jawline gives the Banshee's face its elongated, unnatural proportions and emphasises the wide, open-mouthed scream. Keep the jaw sides tapering evenly toward this point to maintain a balanced but eerie silhouette.

01   02   03

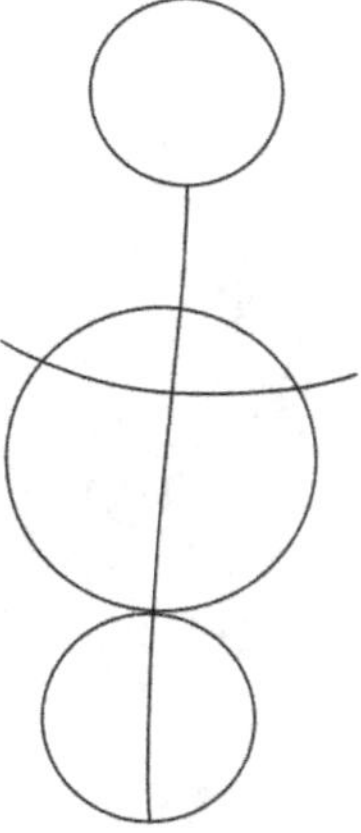 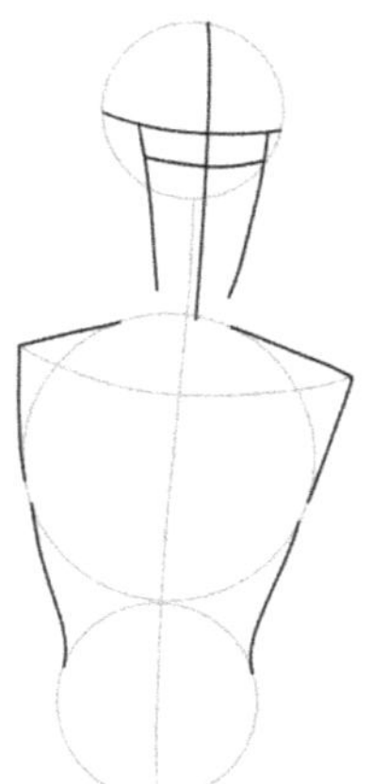 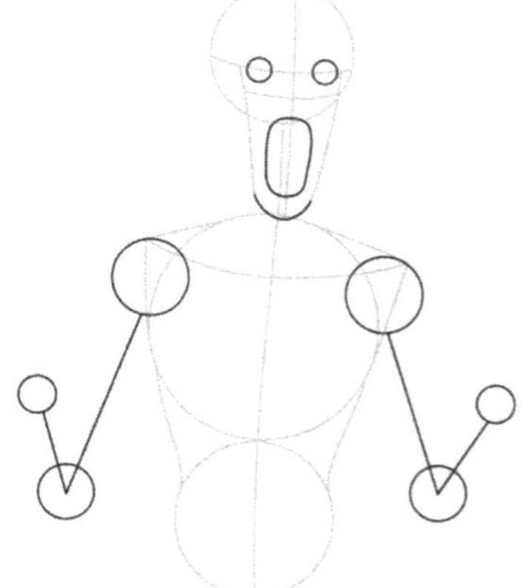

04

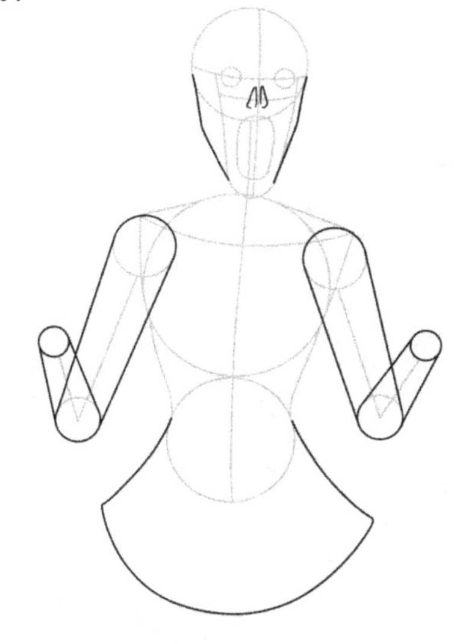

05

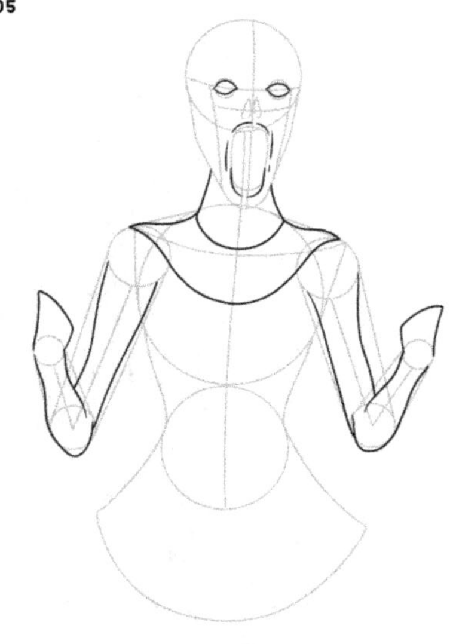

06

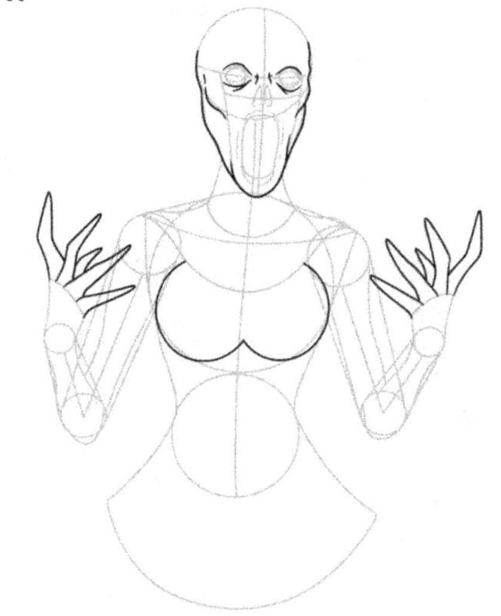

07

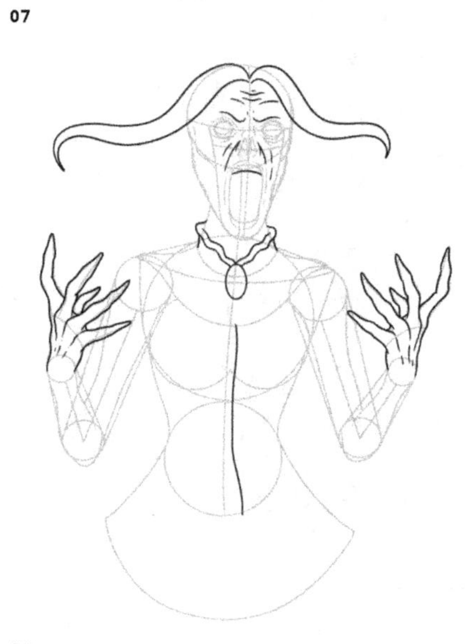

08

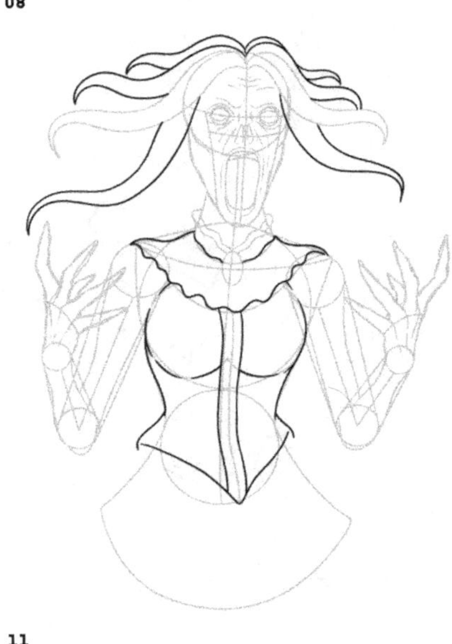

09

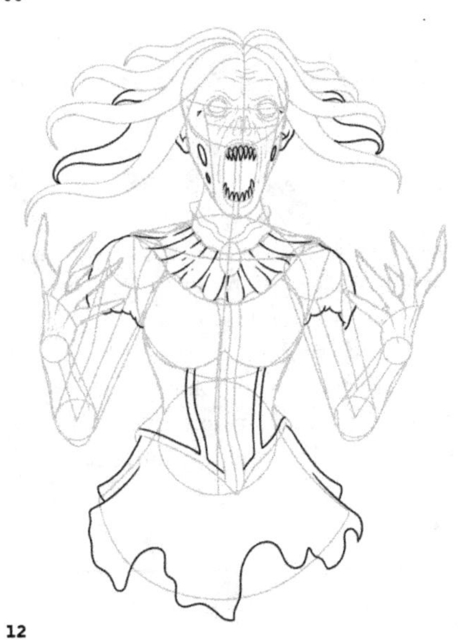

10

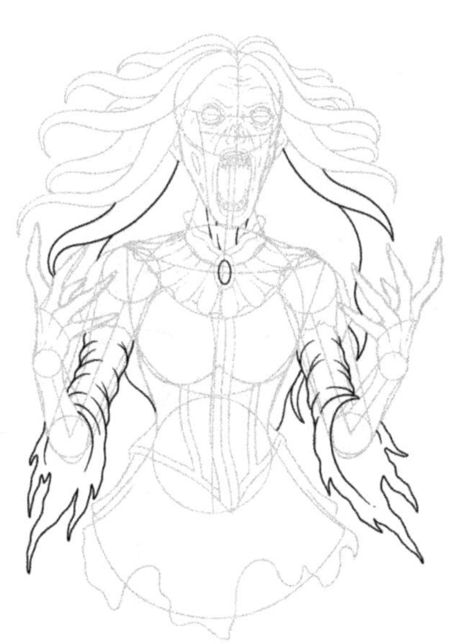

11

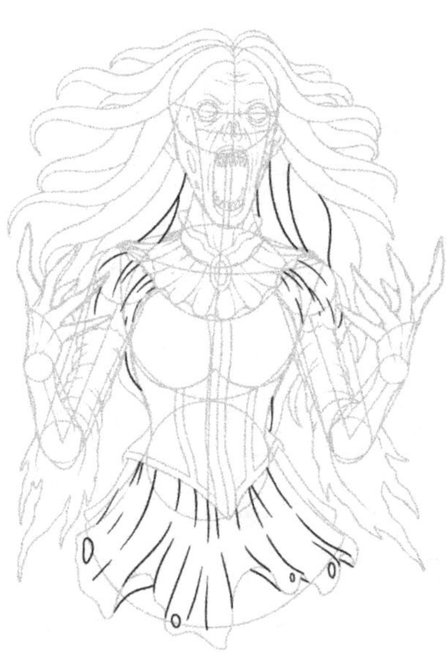

12

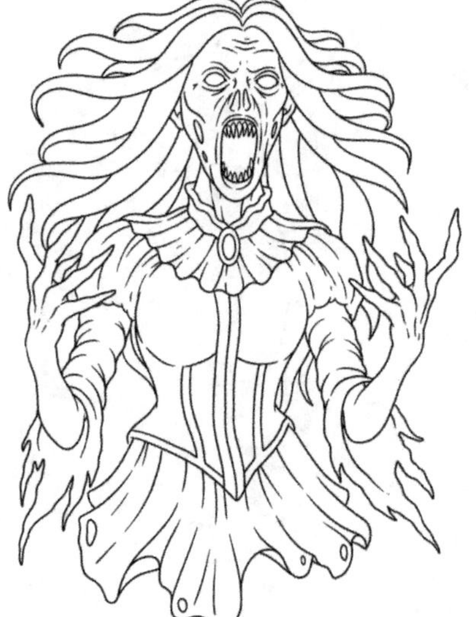

TROLL

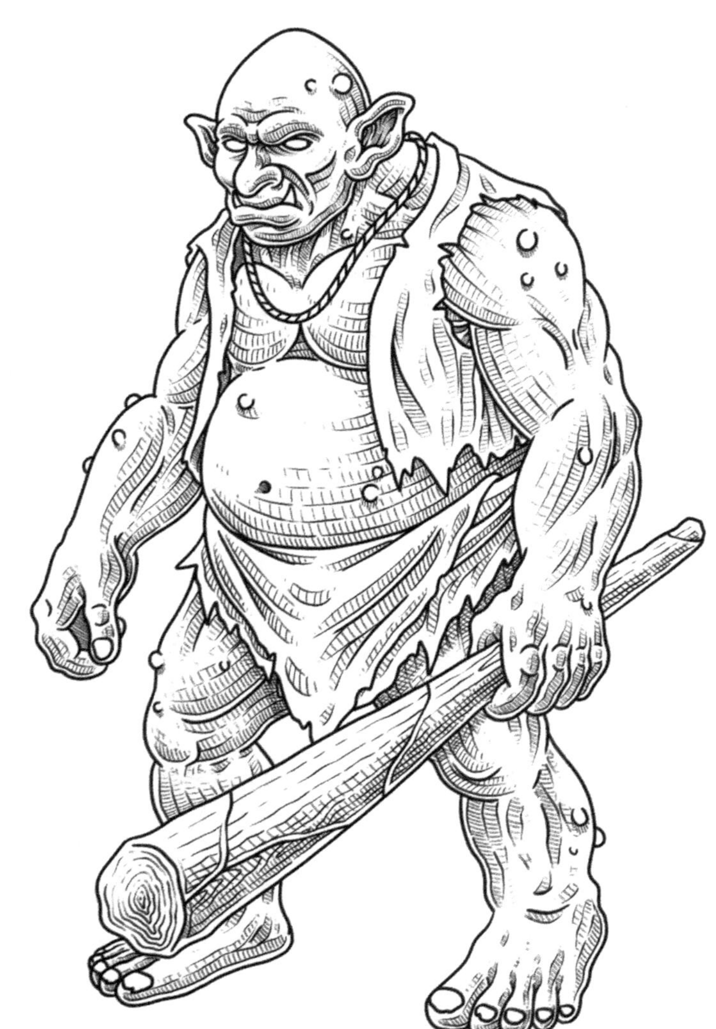

Pro tip: use head heights to determine torso length

For this creature, the torso can be thought of as a tall barrel, roughly 1½ to 2 head heights tall, and slightly wider than the hips. Building it this way gives the figure a heavy, lumbering presence while keeping the proportions believable. Use this barrel form as your anchor, and then layer on limbs and features around it to maintain a solid underlying structure.

01

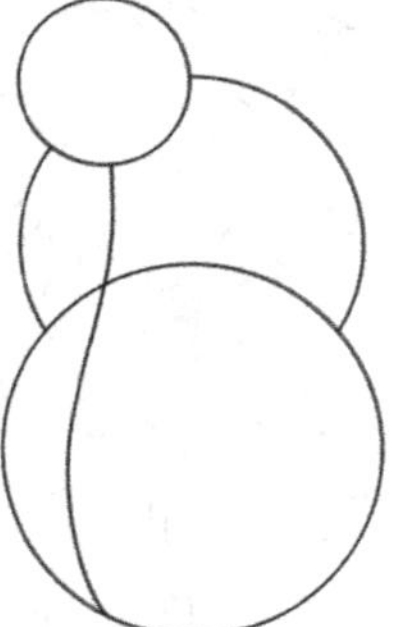

02

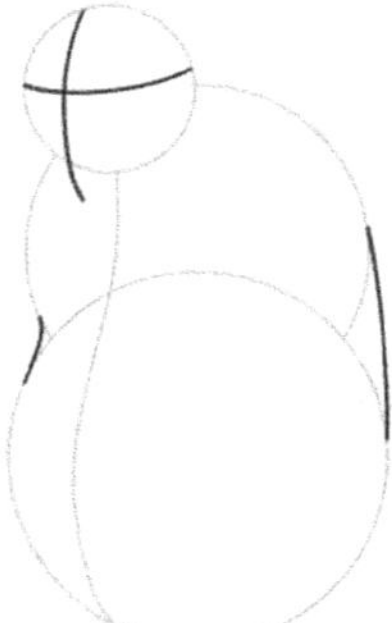

03

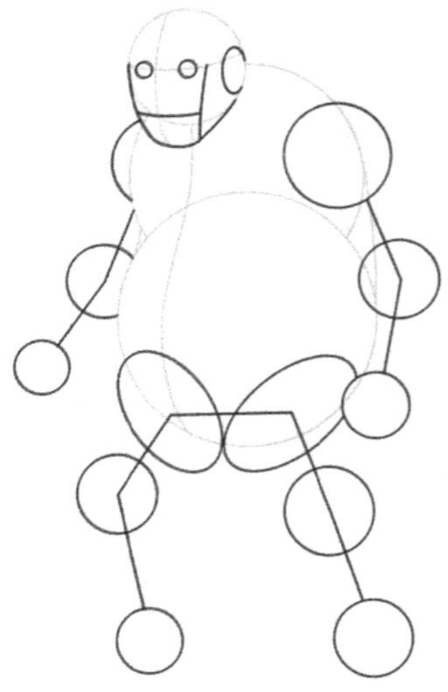

04

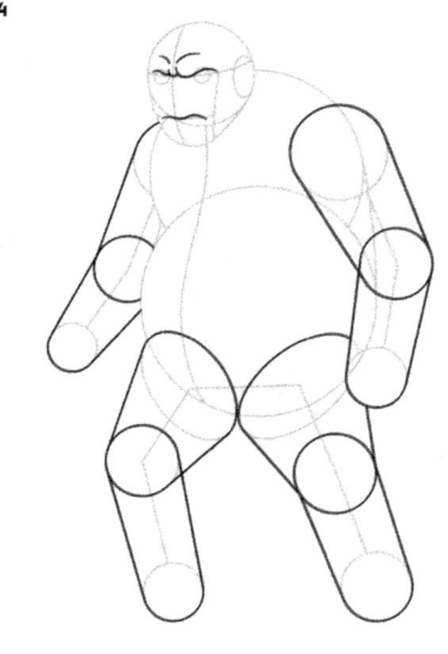

05

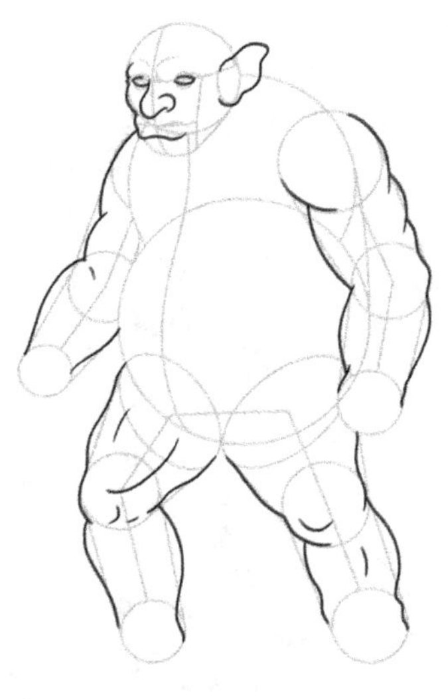

06

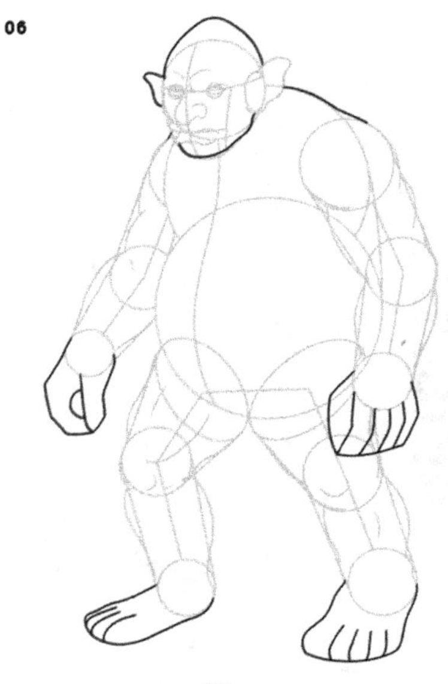

07

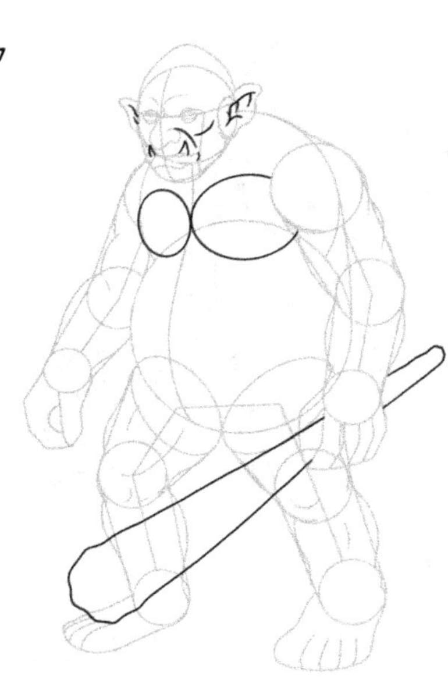

08

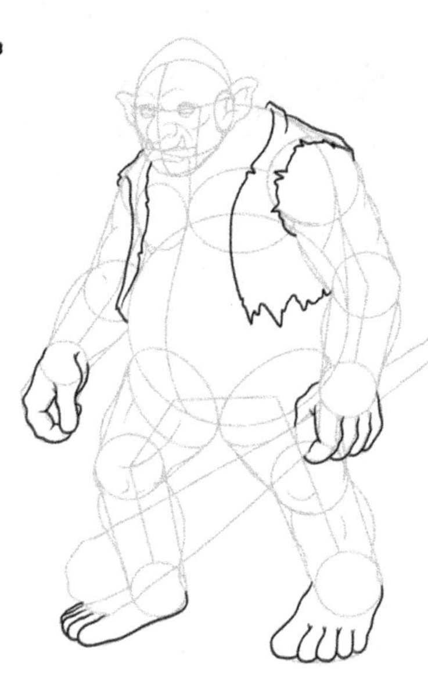

09

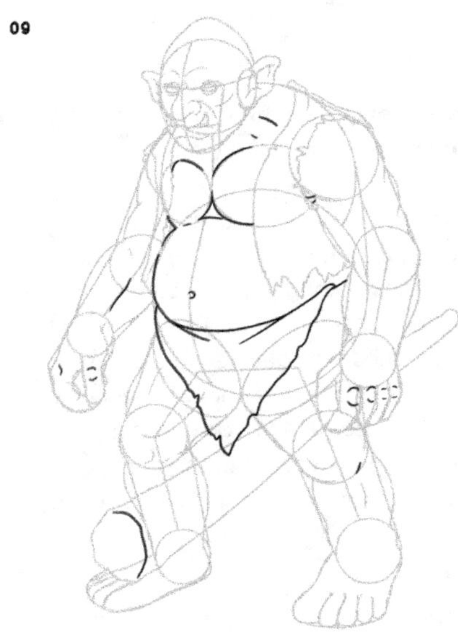

10

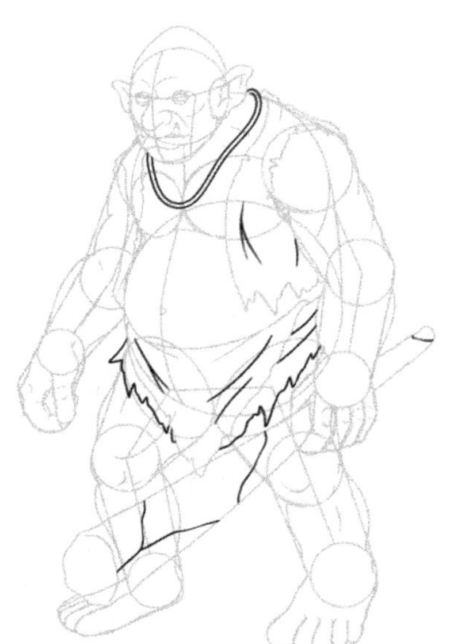

11

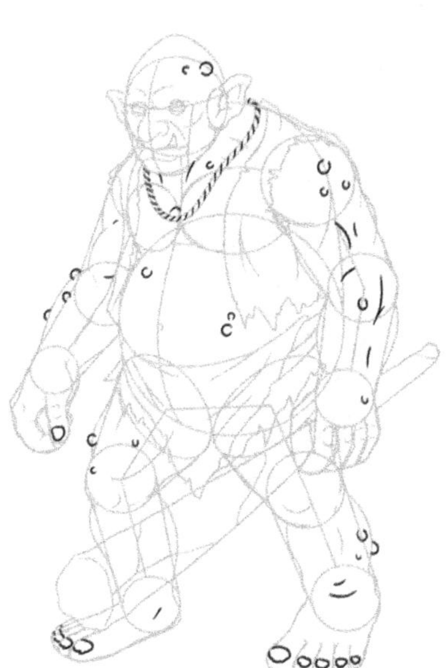

12

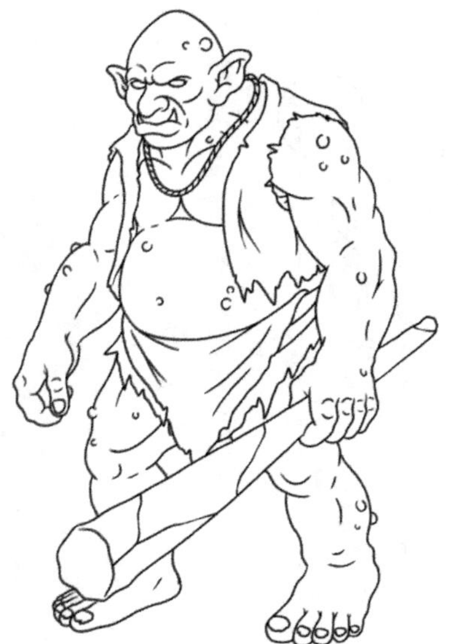

UNICORN

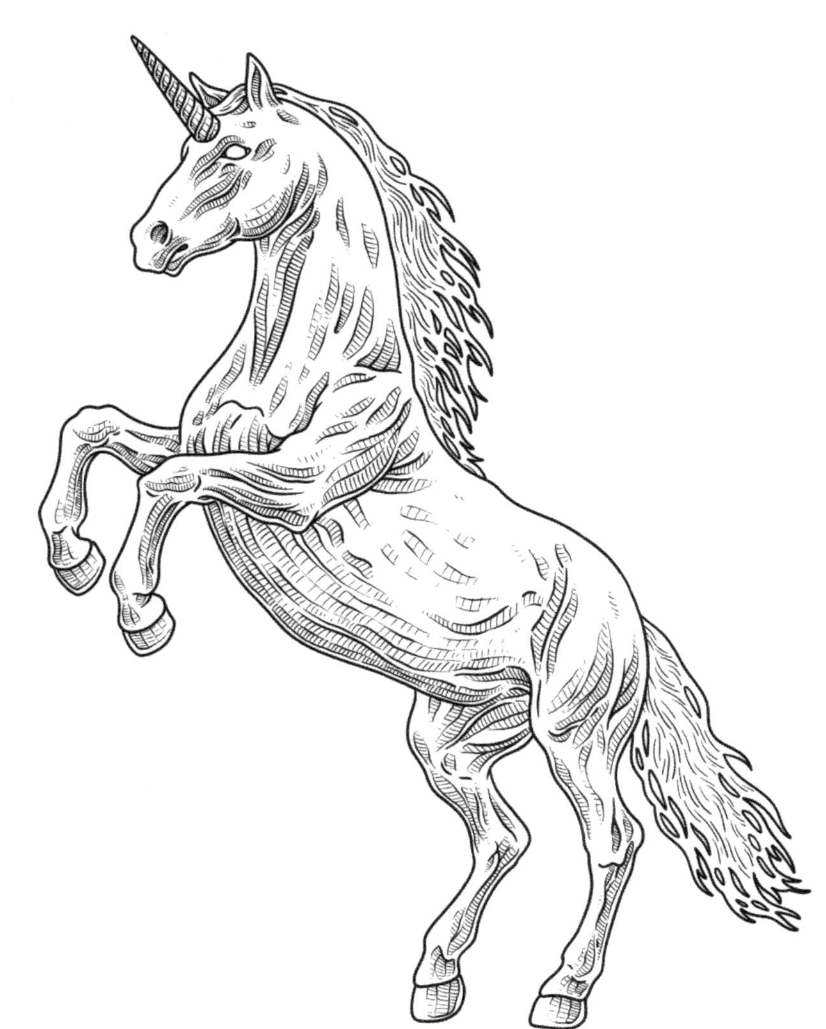

Pro tip: establish the shoulder and hip alignment early

Before refining the unicorn's form, make sure the shoulder and hip circles are aligned along a gentle curve that mirrors the spine's flow. This alignment determines the balance and posture of the creature—especially in dynamic, rearing poses like this one. Getting this curve right early on makes adding legs, musculature, and details far easier and more believable.

01

02

03

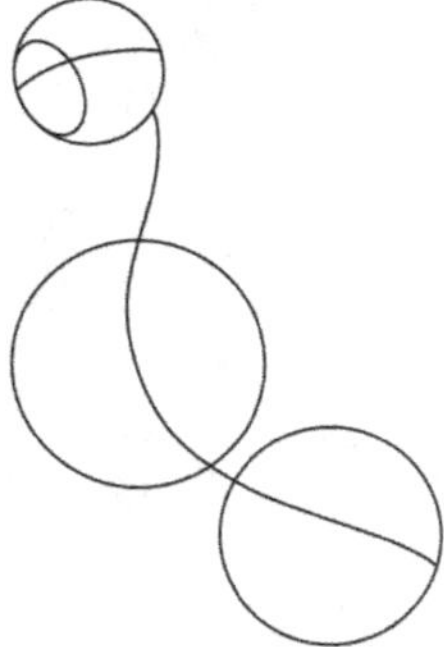

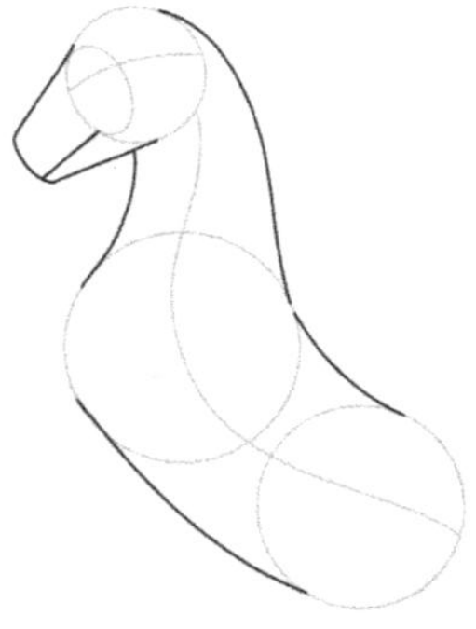

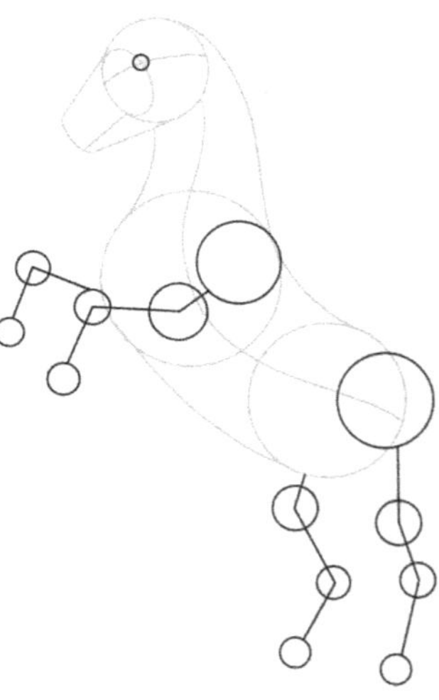

04

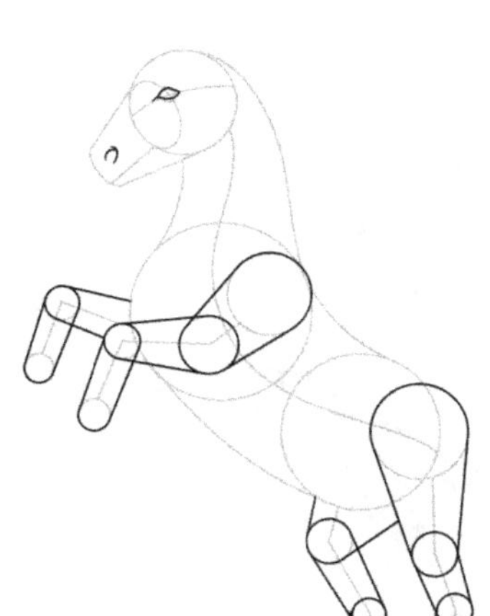

05

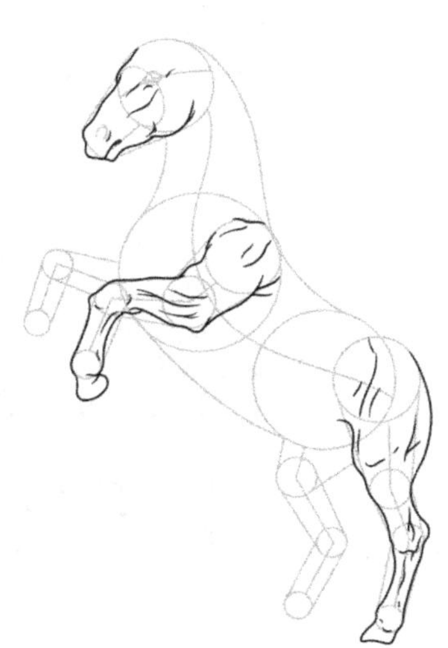

06

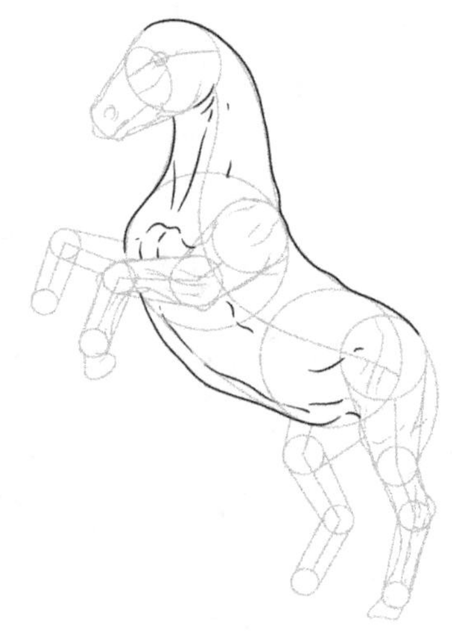

07

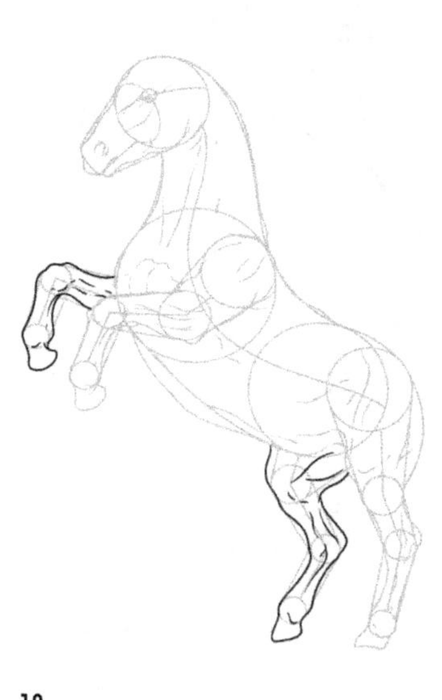

08

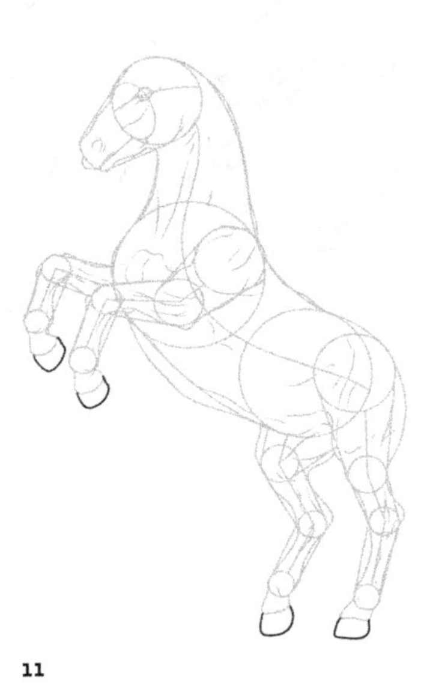

09

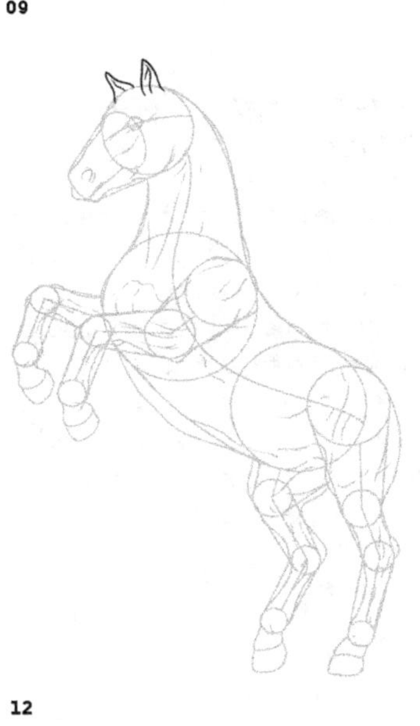

10

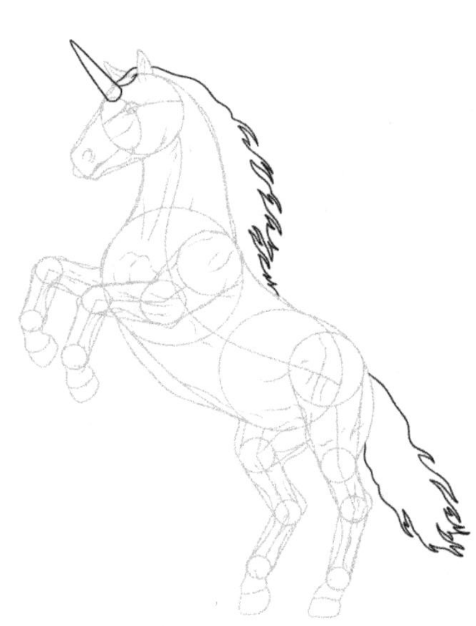

11

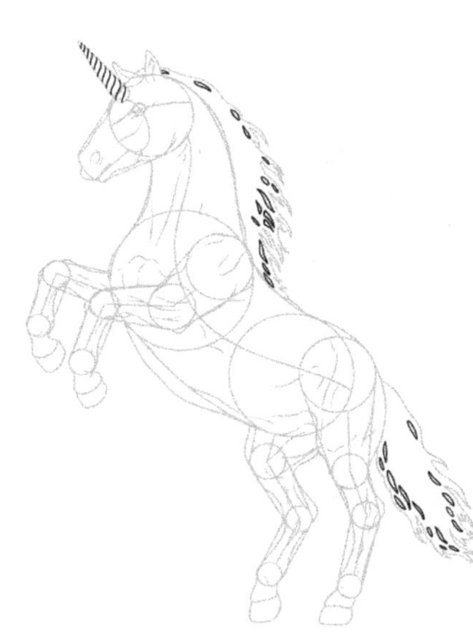

12

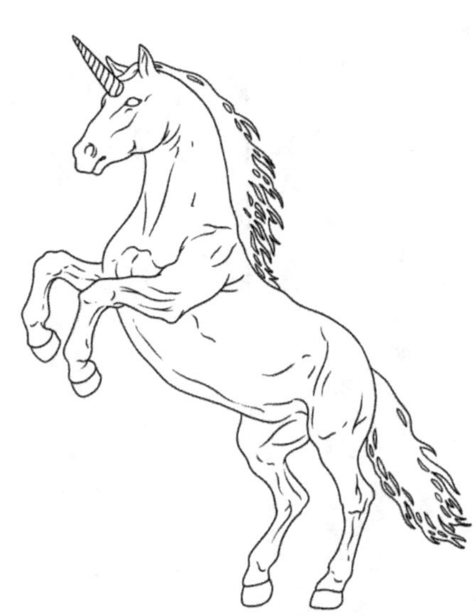

HOW TO DRAW MONSTERS & BEASTS

VAMPIRE

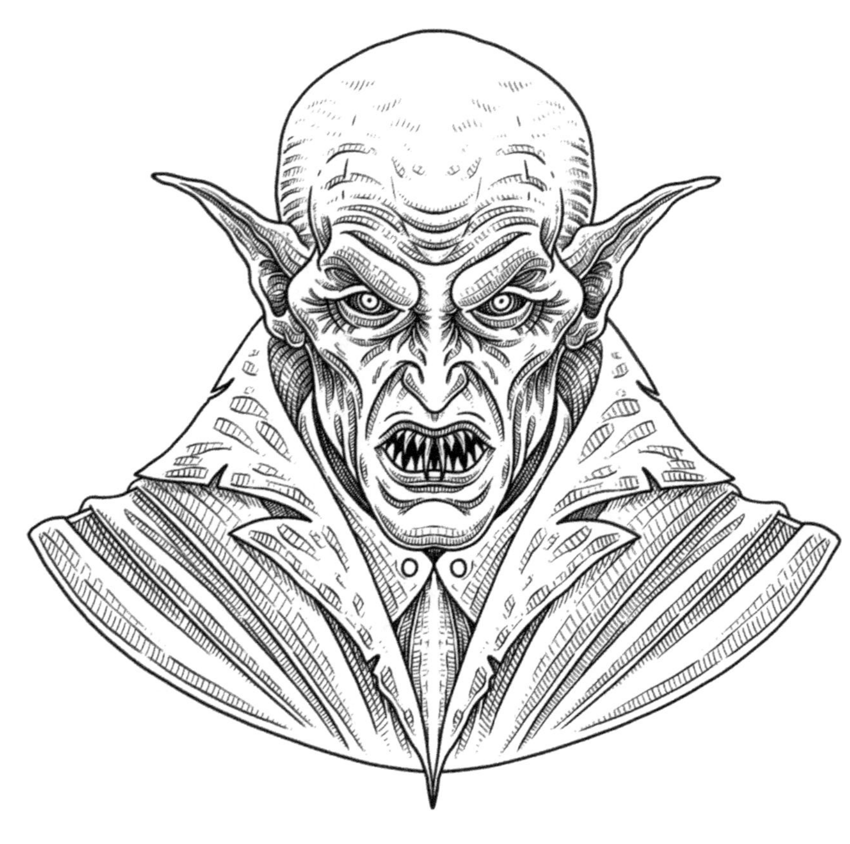

Pro tip: use the five-eye method to place the eyes

The width of the head can be divided into five equal eye widths. To find the correct placement, mark out five equal spaces across the head. The 2nd and 4th spaces indicate where the eyes should sit. This classic proportional guide ensures the eyes are evenly spaced and balanced, even when working with exaggerated or monstrous facial shapes.

01

02

03

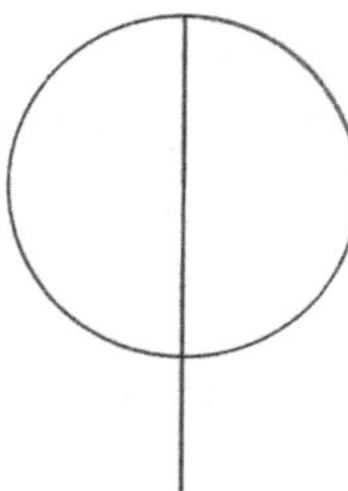

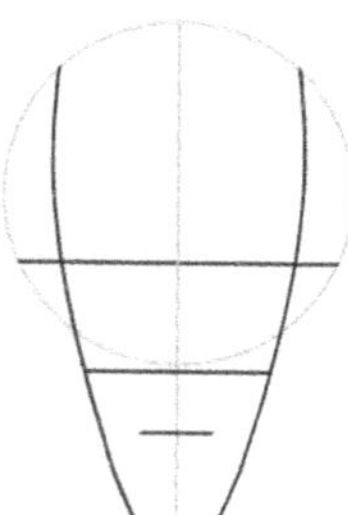

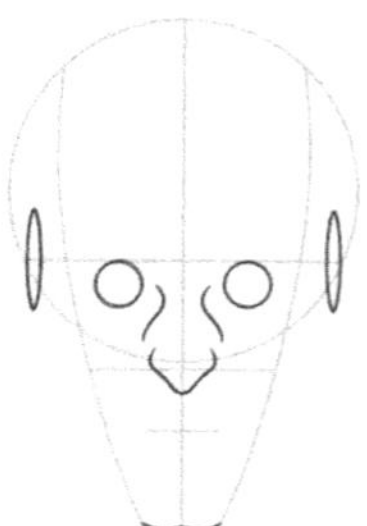

04

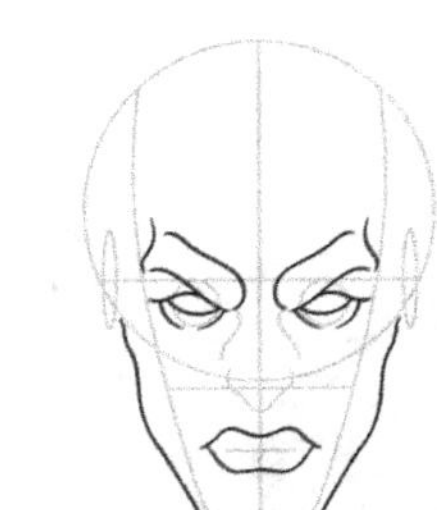

05

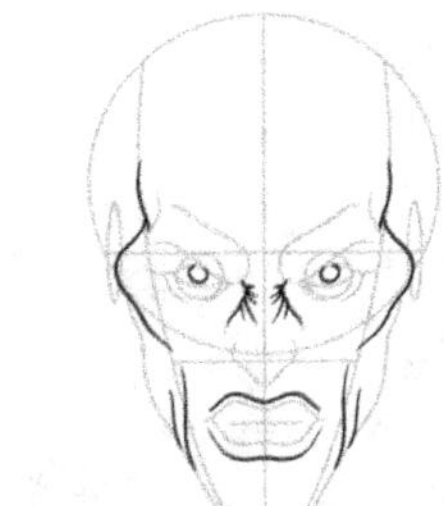

06

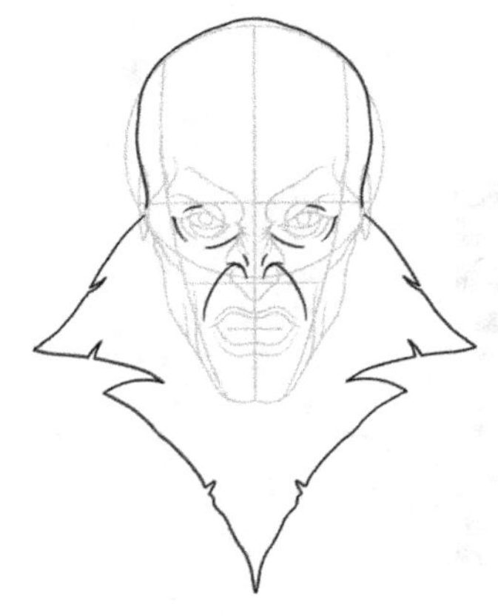

07

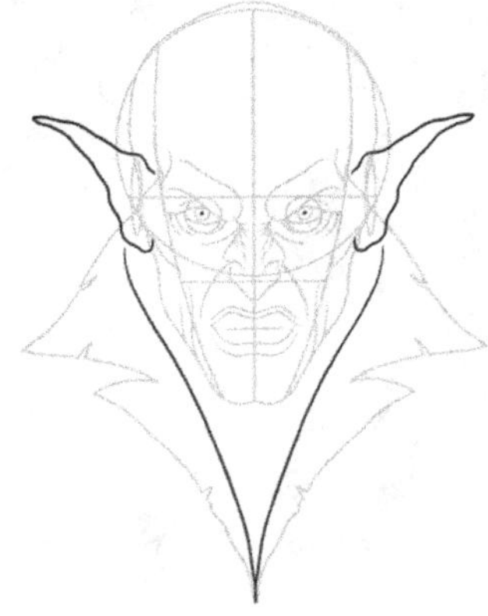

08

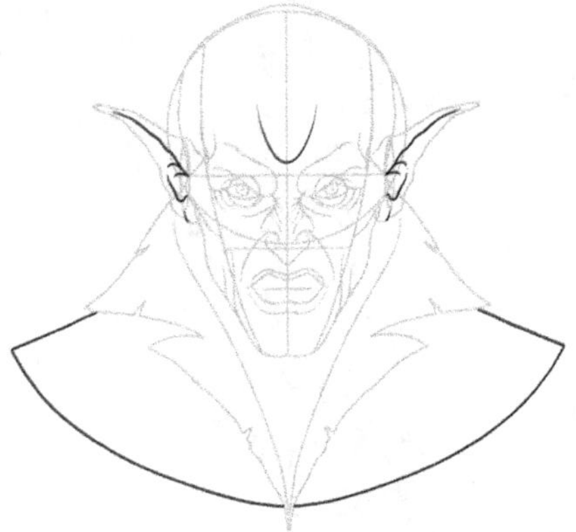

09

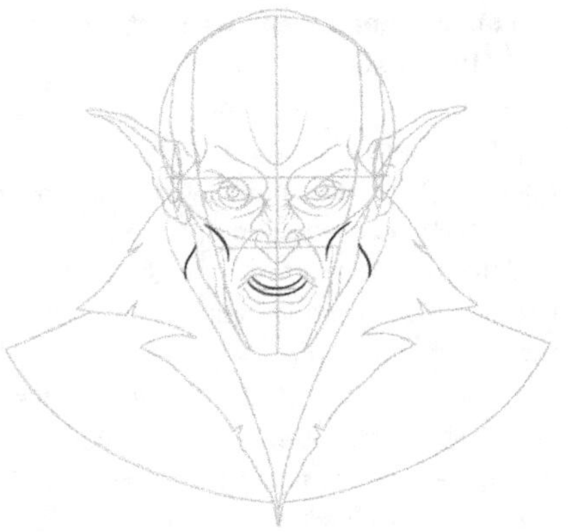

10

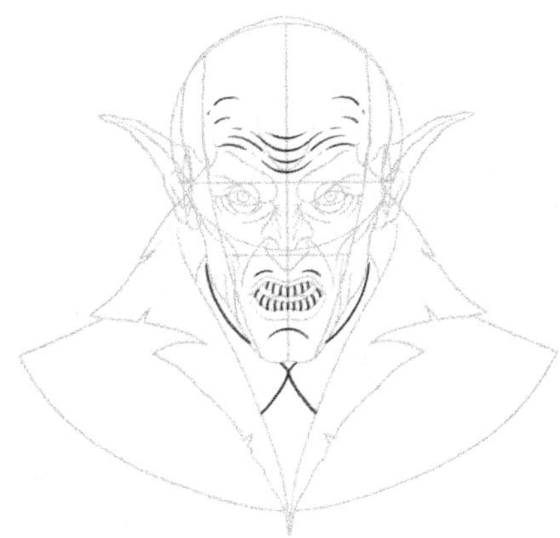

11

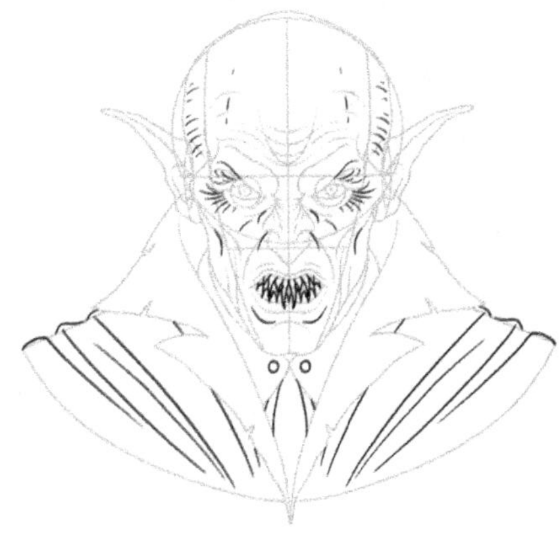

12

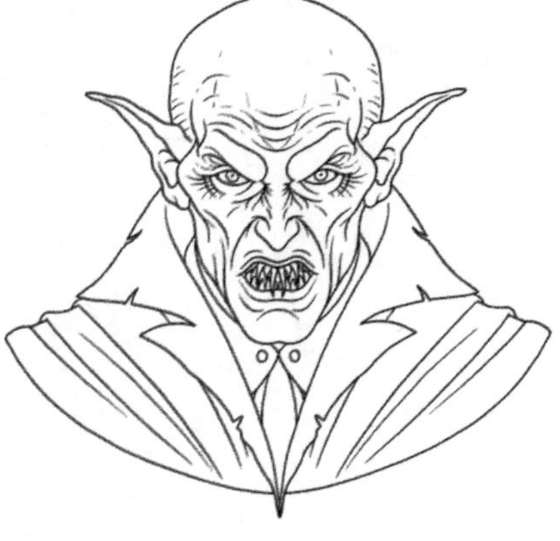

HOW TO DRAW MONSTERS & BEASTS

WEREWOLF

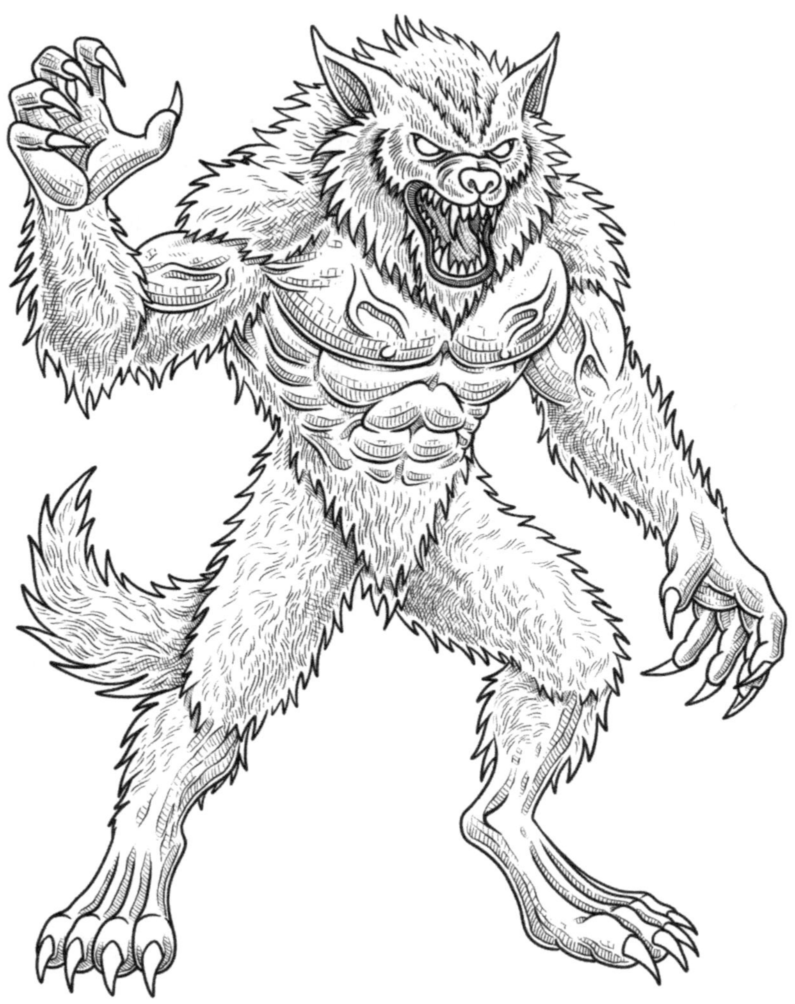

Pro tip: use head measurements to build the torso

The torso should be roughly three heads high and two heads wide. Start by stacking head measurements vertically to determine the torso's overall length. Position the shoulders higher than the top of the head to create a powerful, looming posture that suits the werewolf's aggressive silhouette. This proportional method keeps the figure balanced and helps establish its imposing presence early in the drawing.

01

02

03

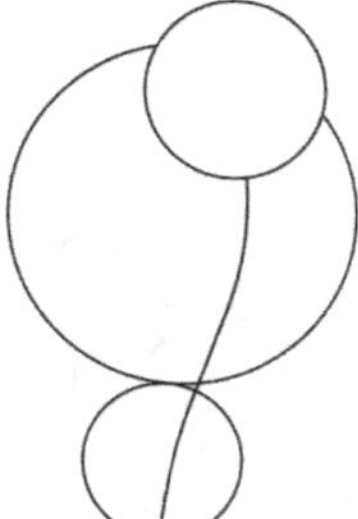

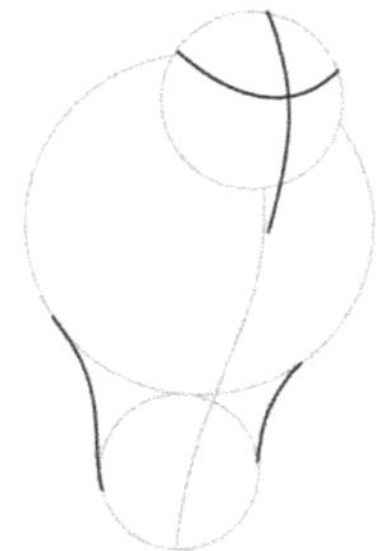

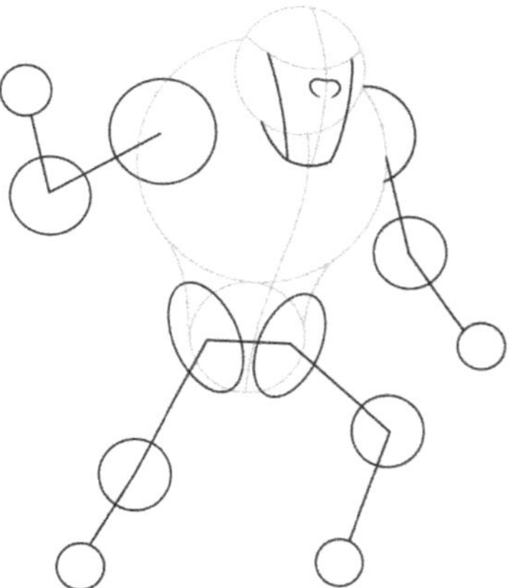

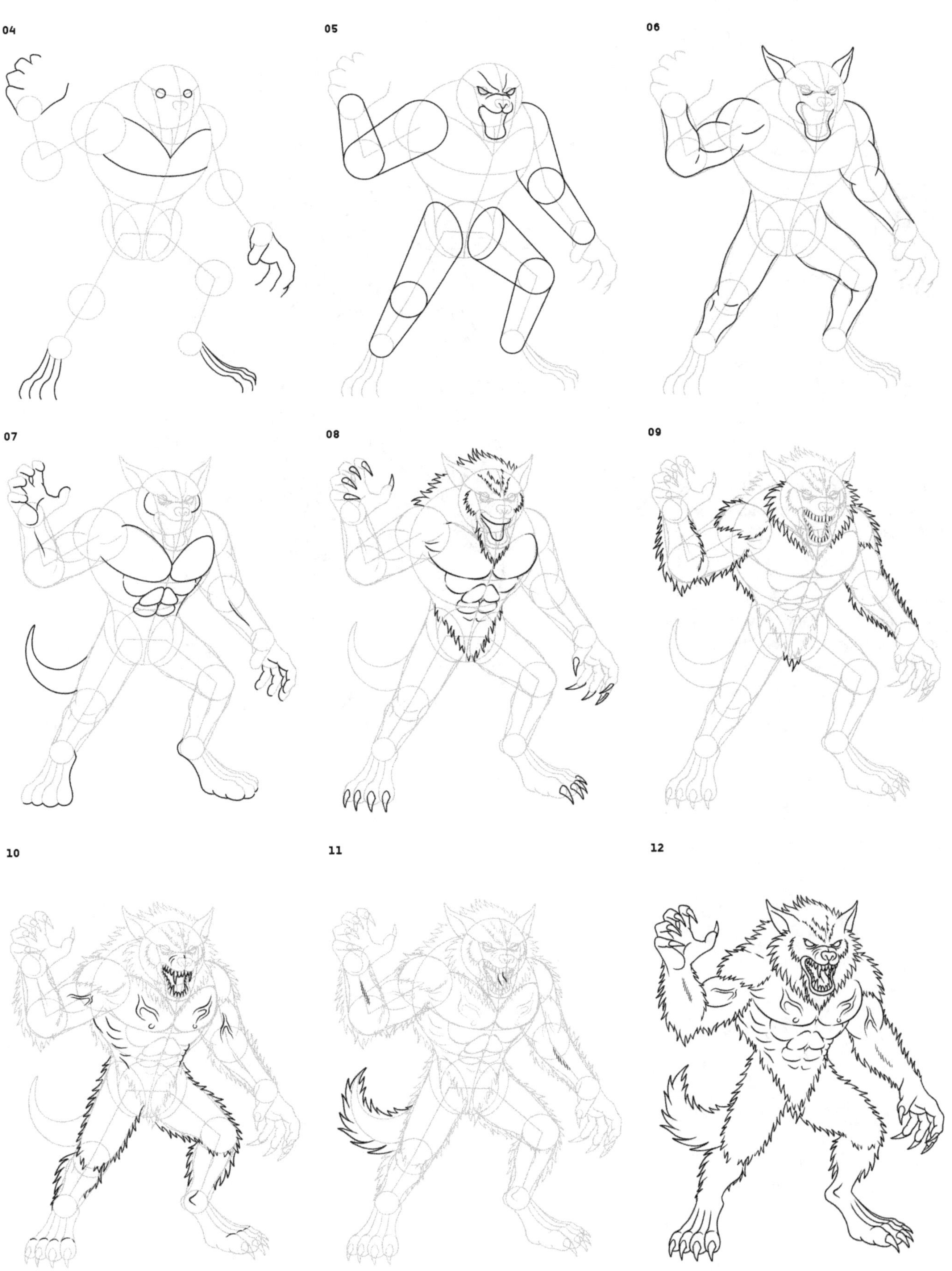

04
05
06
07
08
09
10
11
12
HOW TO DRAW MONSTERS & BEASTS

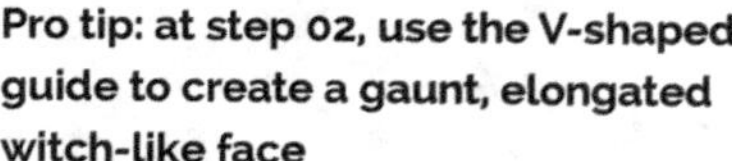

WITCH

Pro tip: at step 02, use the V-shaped guide to create a gaunt, elongated witch-like face

The elongated V-shaped guideline beneath the eye-line (step 02) creates a longer chin and narrow jaw, giving the face a gaunt, angular look. This contrast with the rounded cranium instantly makes the profile more witch-like.

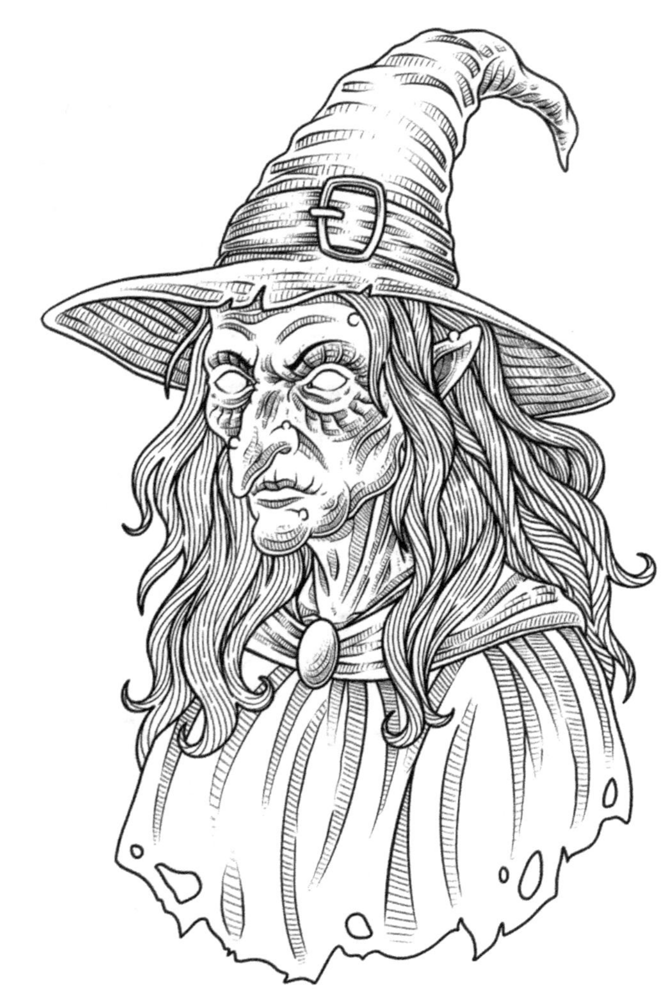

01

02

03

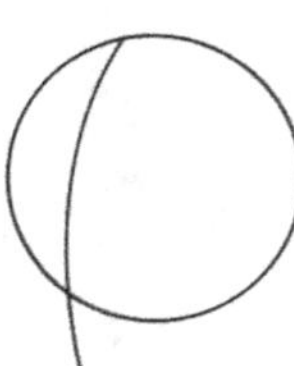

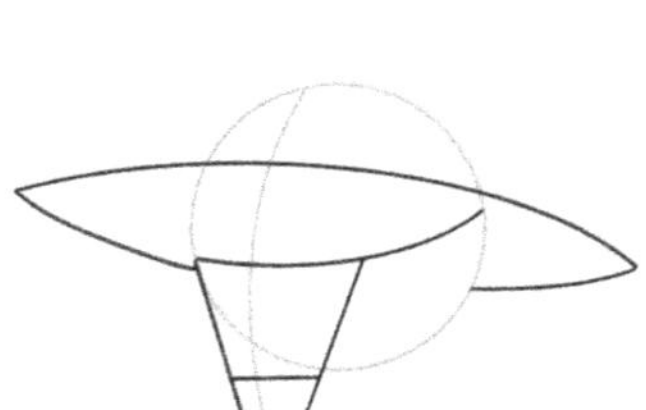

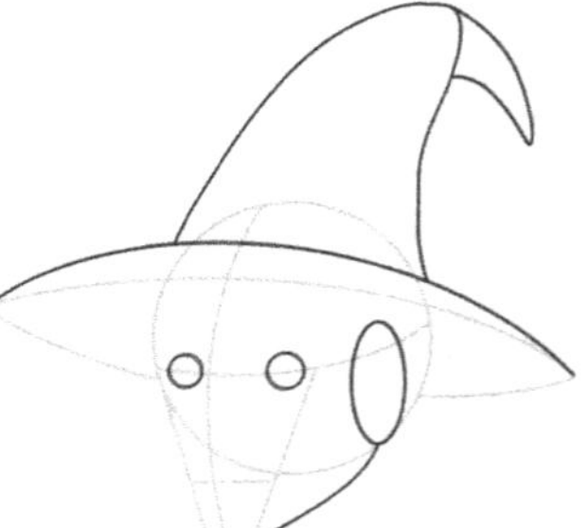

04

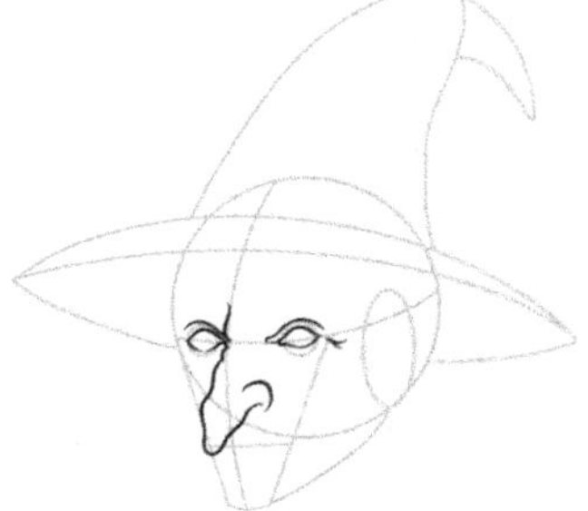

05

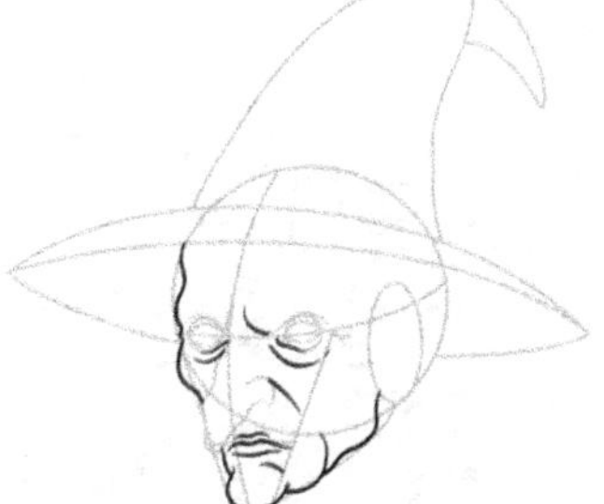

06

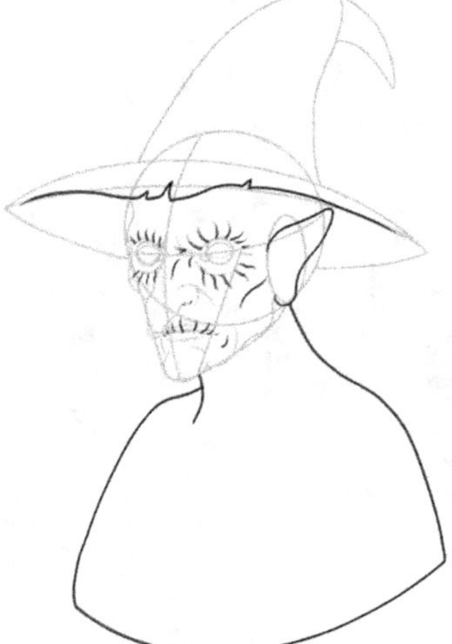

07

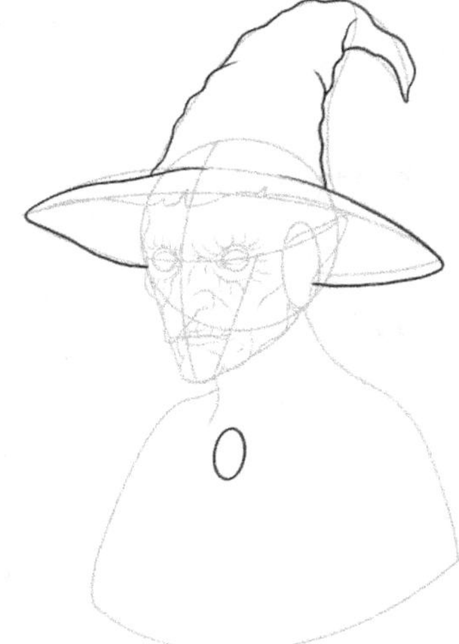

08

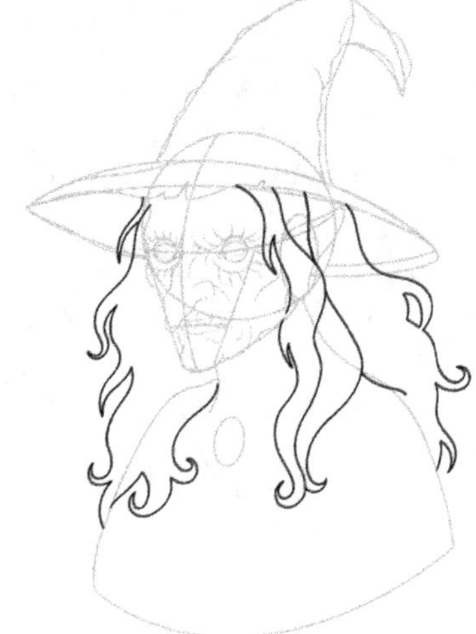

09

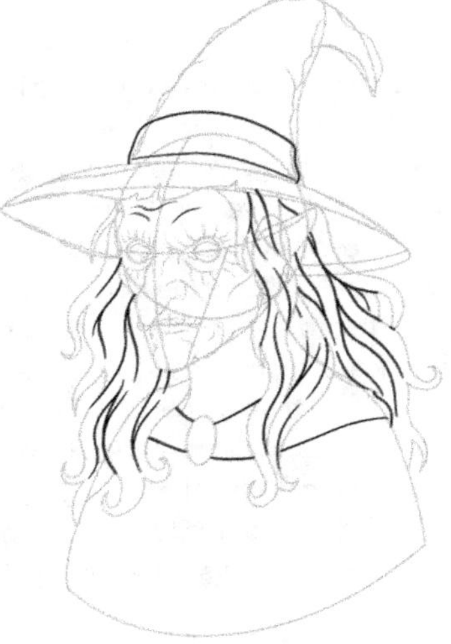

10

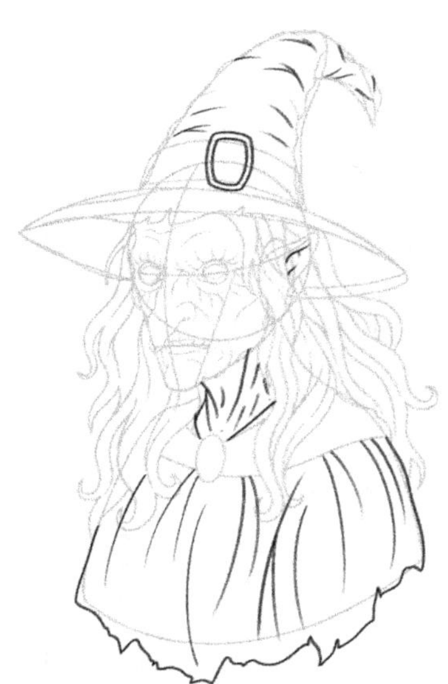

11

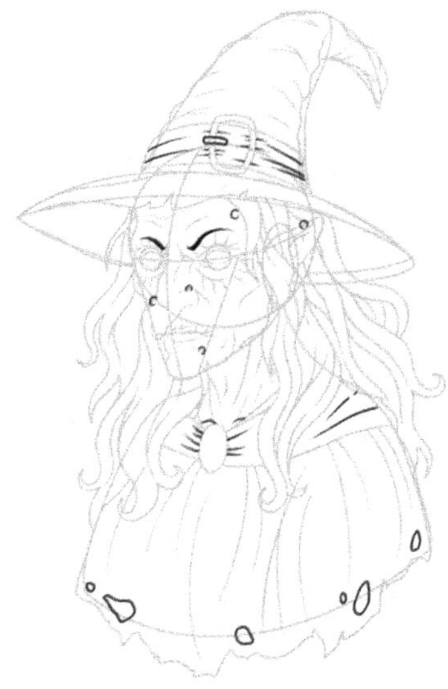

12

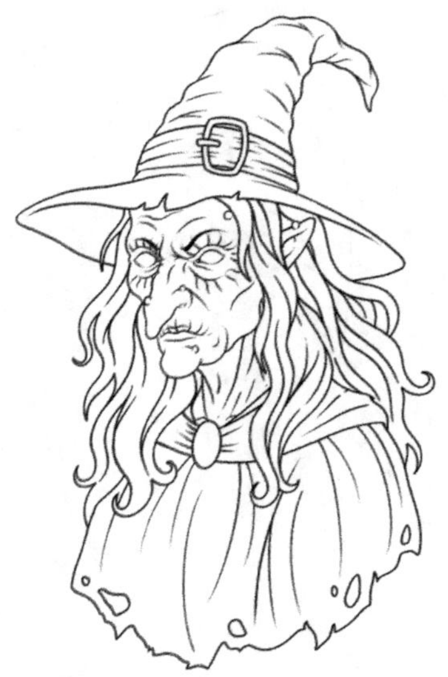

ZOMBIE

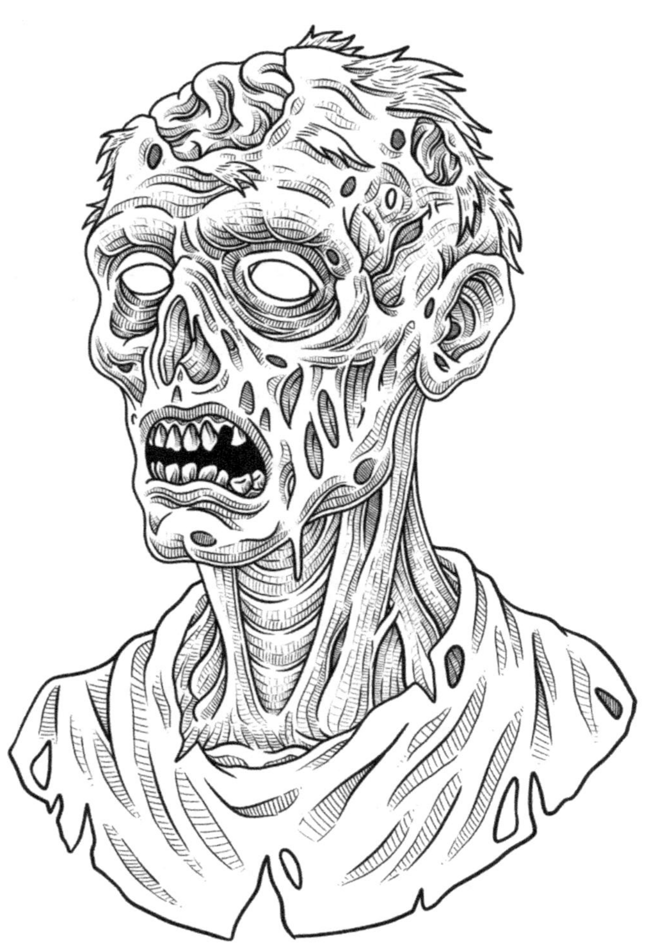

Pro tip: use the eye-line as your anchor

Draw a horizontal guideline across the head to mark the eye-line. On most heads, the eye-line sits halfway between the top of the skull and the bottom of the chin. Use this to align both eye sockets symmetrically, then measure one eye width between them to place the inner corners accurately. Once this spacing is locked in, you can distort or exaggerate the surrounding features for your zombie without losing structural believability.

01

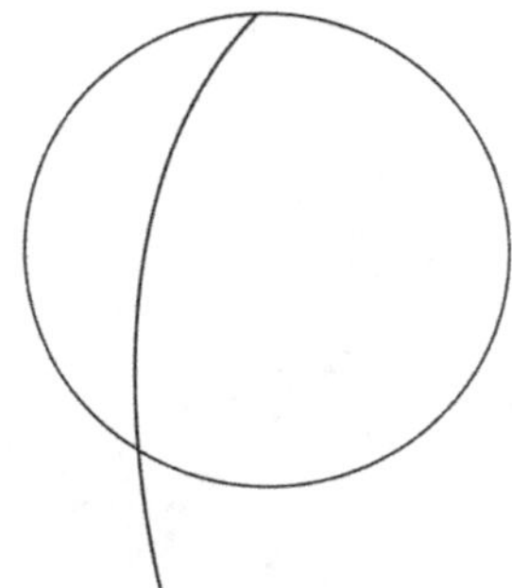

02

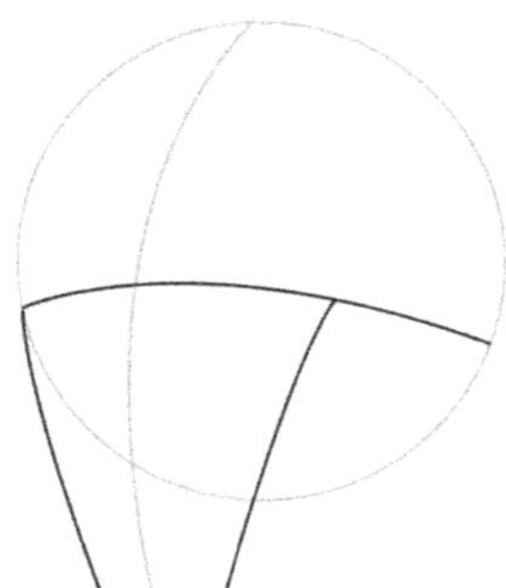

03

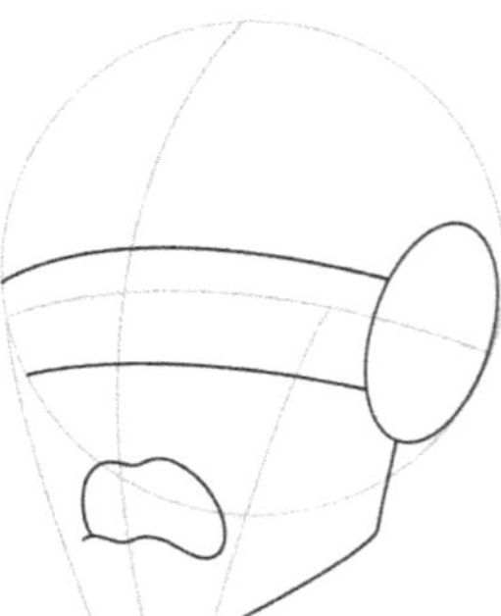

04

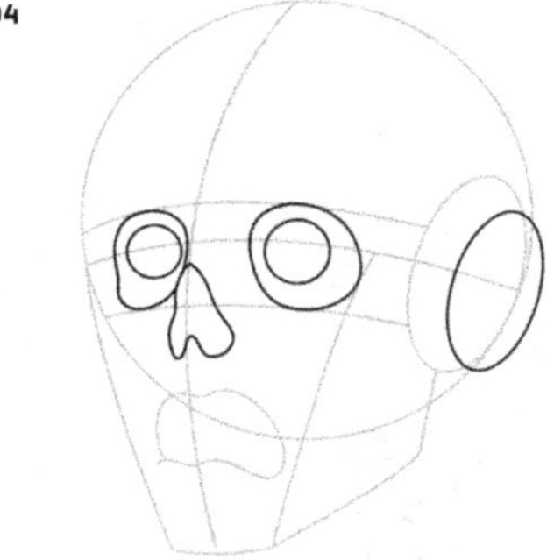

05

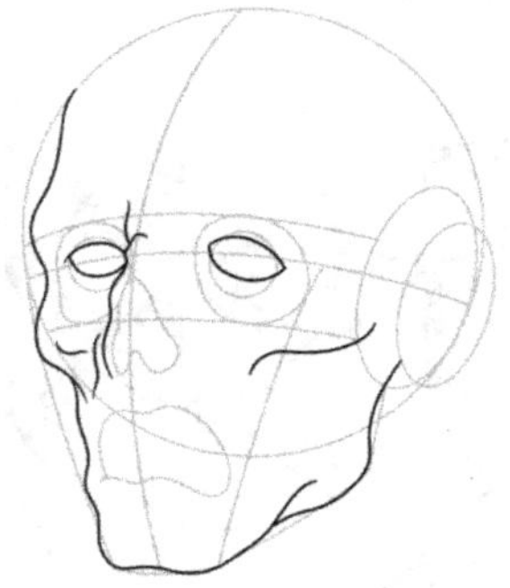

06

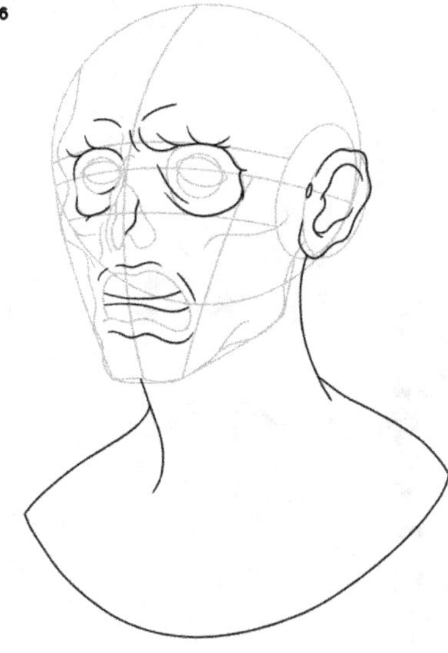

07

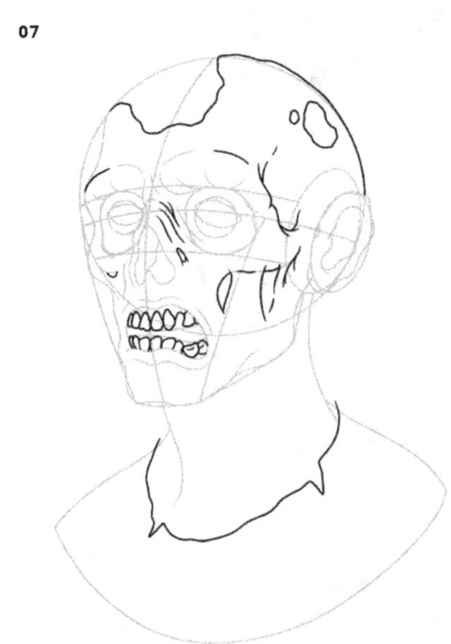

08

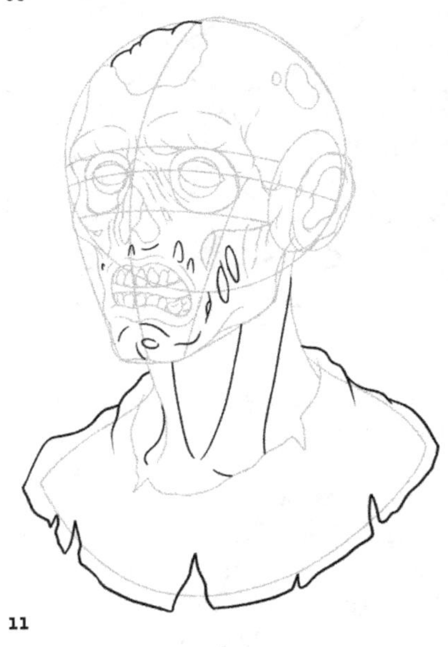

09

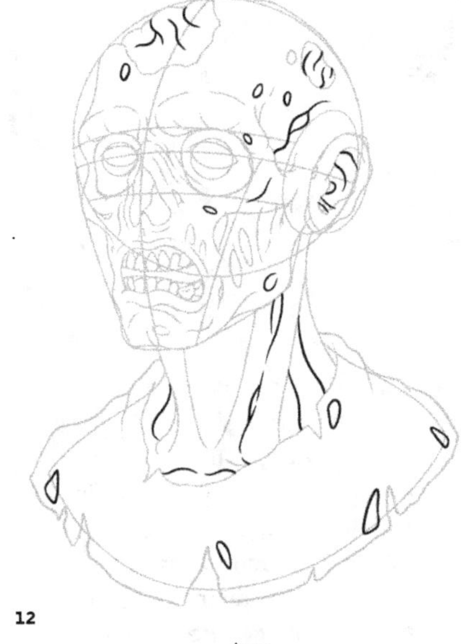

10

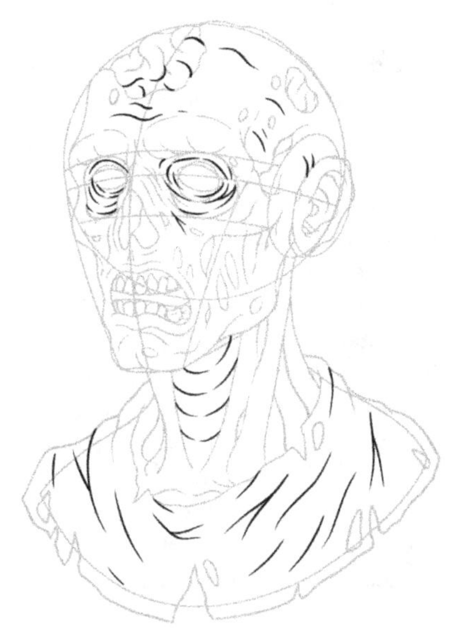

11

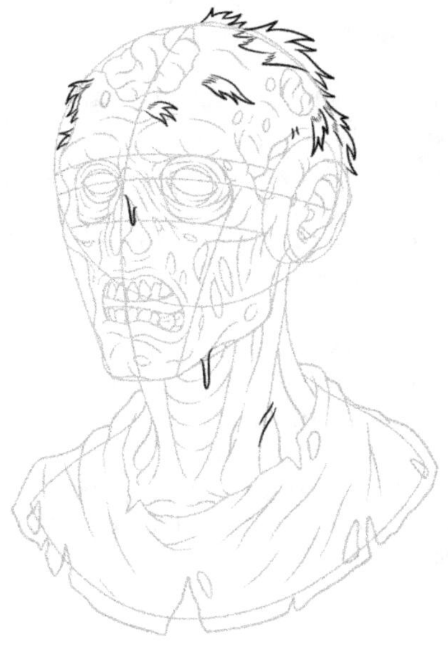

12

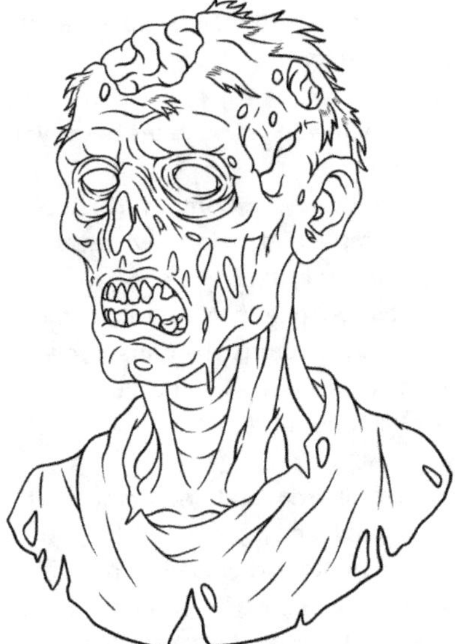

DRAWING SCALES

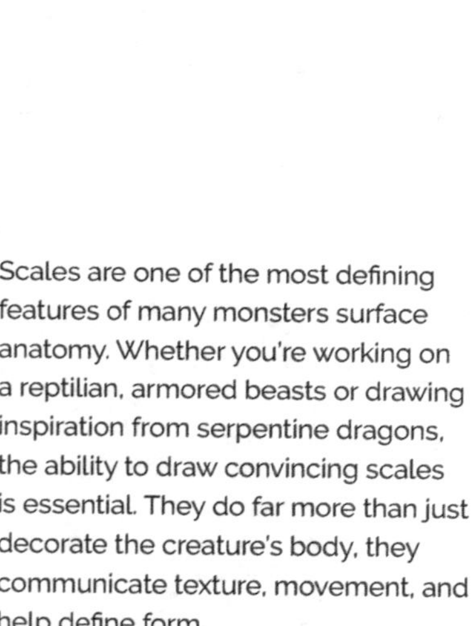

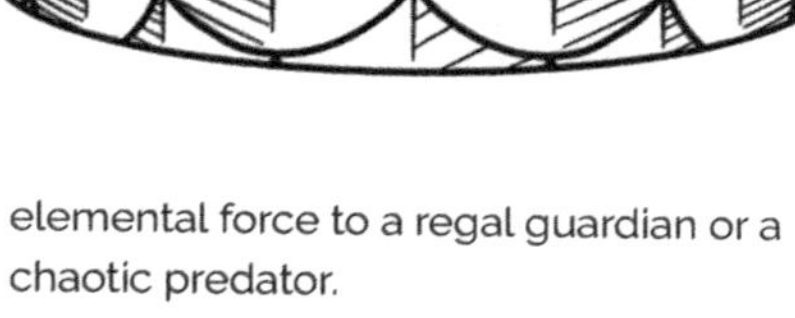

Scales are one of the most defining features of many monsters surface anatomy. Whether you're working on a reptilian, armored beasts or drawing inspiration from serpentine dragons, the ability to draw convincing scales is essential. They do far more than just decorate the creature's body, they communicate texture, movement, and help define form.

Learning how to draw scales helps you:

Define Volume and Contour: The way scales wrap around a form, whether it's a snaking neck, the curve of a haunch, or the twist of a tail helps describe the underlying structure. The pattern follows the anatomy, enhancing the illusion of three-dimensionality.

Suggest Material and Character: Are the scales rough and jagged like chipped stone? Smooth and gleaming like polished armor? Shading and stylisation can shift a monster from an ancient elemental force to a regal guardian or a chaotic predator.

Control Light and Surface Detail: Scales catch light differently across the form. Understanding how to shade them, where to place highlights, shadows, and directional texture adds depth and realism to the creature.

Create Rhythm and Flow: Repeating patterns like scales can guide the viewer's eye along the body, emphasising movement and gesture. Well-placed scale patterns can reinforce the beasts' pose and directionality.

Mastering scales isn't only about decoration, it's also about understanding how surface details interact with anatomy, light, and storytelling. Once you've got the rhythm and structure down, you can break the rules in all the right ways to suit your own design style.

Directional Shading for Depth
In order to enhance the illusion of volume and curvature on the cylindrical form, apply directional shading to each individual scale. Observe how the side of each scale that is shaded shifts depending on its position along the curve of the cylinder:

Left Side: On the left half of the cylinder, the left side of each scale is filled with parallel hatch lines.

Right Side: On the right half of the cylinder, the right side of each scale is shaded instead.

This subtle shift in shadow placement mimics how light would naturally interact with a rounded surface, helping to reinforce the three-dimensionality of the form. It's a simple technique, but when applied consistently, it brings the pattern to life and makes the object appear more convincingly lit and dimensional.

01. Base Cylinder

Begin by drawing a clean, upright cylinder. This serves as your foundational form. Ensure the ellipse at the top and the vertical sides are symmetrical—this will help keep your pattern consistent as it wraps around the form.

02. Flow Lines

Lightly draw a series of curved, diagonal lines running from the top left to the bottom right of the cylinder. These lines follow the natural curvature of the cylindrical form, establishing the first rhythm of the pattern.

03. Crosshatch Grid

Add a second set of curved, diagonal lines that flow in the opposite direction, creating a lattice or crosshatch pattern. This grid will guide the placement of each scale and keep the pattern uniform around the cylinder.

04. Scallop Shapes

Within each diamond-shaped cell of the lattice, draw a curved arc (like a "U" turned upside down) to form the top edge of each scale. Stack them in staggered horizontal rows to mimic a natural fish or reptilian scale pattern.

05. Enhanced Definition

Refine each scale by sharpening the curves and thickening the lines to make them more pronounced. The pattern should now appear more dimensional and unified, following the contour of the cylinder.

06. Final Shading

Apply directional hatching or fill alternate rows with line shading to create contrast and depth. This final touch adds a sense of texture, suggesting form and light— ideal for a more dynamic, visually rich rendering result.

01
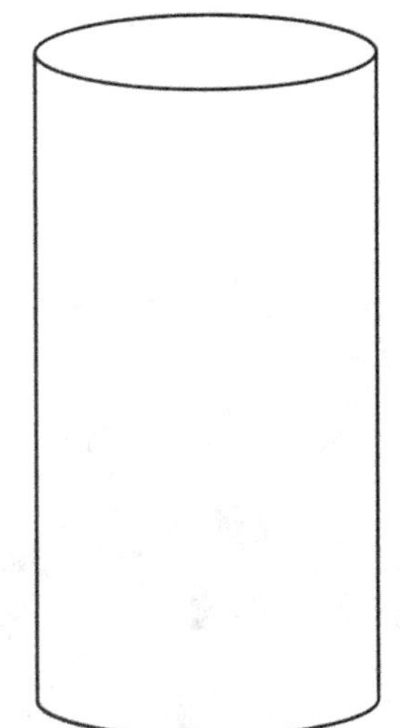

02
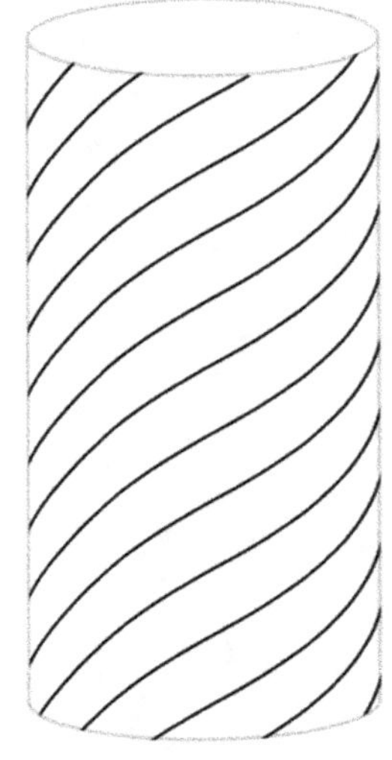

03
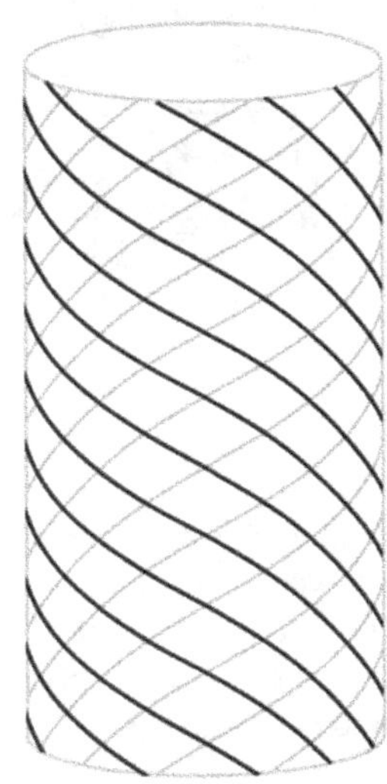

04
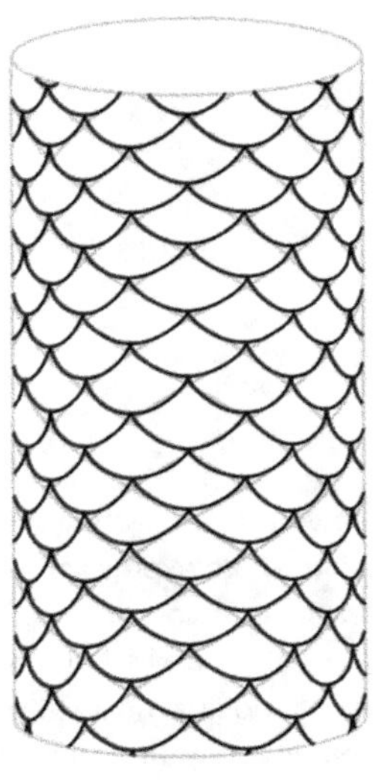

05
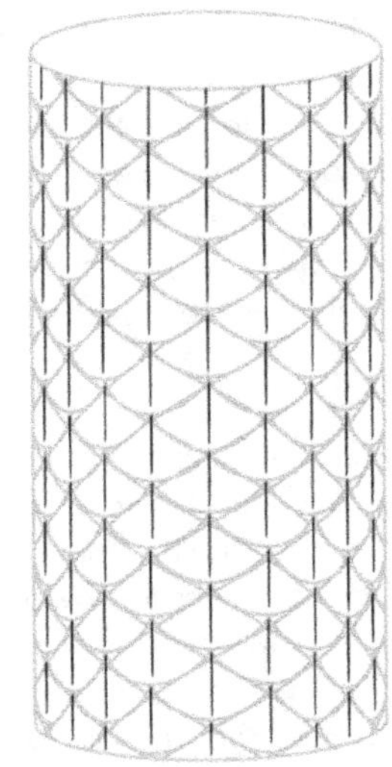

06
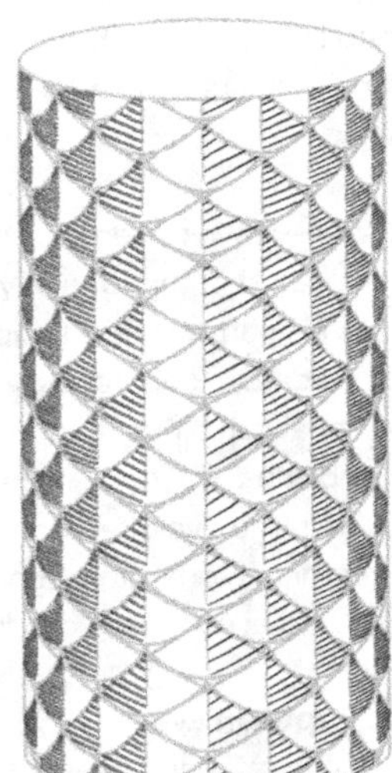

REPTILIAN EYES

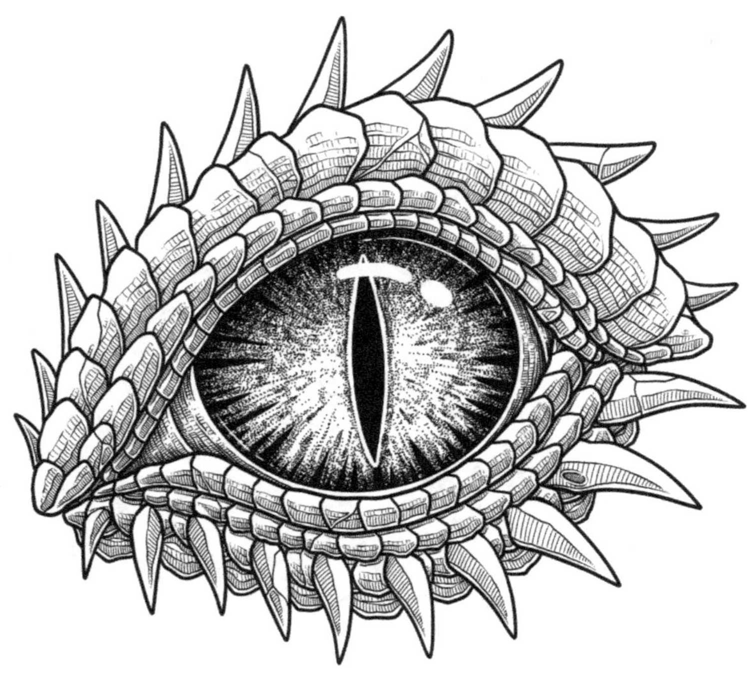

Reptilians eyes are more than windows to the soul; they are expressions of ancient power, emotion, and elemental force. In mythology and art, the eye is often one of a reptiles most striking and defining features, capturing its nature's essence with a single, penetrating gaze. Whether glowing with arcane energy, shimmering like crystal, or burning with molten fury, a reptile's eye tells a story all its own.

As an artist, the way you render a reptile's eye can shift the tone of your entire design. A narrow, slitted pupil may suggest a predator's cold focus, while a glowing spiral can hint at hypnotic or psychic abilities. The colour, shape, and light within the eye offer a window into the creatures elemental alignment, personality, and even its age or wisdom.

01. Slitted Reptilian Eye

A classic feature of many beasts, the slitted reptilian eye suggests heightened awareness and primal intelligence. Its sharp vertical pupil is built for detecting movement, even in low light, and gives the creature an aura of alert menace. Ideal for feral, instinct-driven beasts rooted in the natural world.

02. Glowing Mystic Eye

This ethereal eye glows with an inner light, hinting at arcane knowledge and otherworldly power. Creatures with mystic eyes are often ancient, wise, and connected to magical forces. The intense glow can signify a deep reservoir of magical energy or a beast that serves as a guardian of enchanted realms.

03. Icy or Blind Eye

Pale and misty, this eye can indicate great age, blindness, or a creature's mastery over frost and ice. This eye is often found in creatures that dwell in tundras or mountaintops, their cold-blooded stare can freeze intruders in their tracks. Blind eyes may also suggest heightened senses beyond sight, such as intuition or telepathy.

04. Fiery or Lava Eye

Radiating heat and energy, the lava eye burns with raw, destructive power. Found in fire-breathing creatures or those born from volcanoes, this eye symbolises wrath, dominance, and the untamed fury of nature. Cracks of flame surrounding the iris hint at a volatile temperament.

05. Serpentine Hypnotic Eye

With its swirling pupil and entrancing hue, this eye suggests manipulation, illusion, and psychic control. Beasts bearing hypnotic eyes may be tricksters or spellbinders, luring prey with gaze alone. The spiral pattern adds a mesmerising effect, making it ideal for mysterious or dream-like designs.

06. Nature or Crystal Eye

Gem-like and glowing with natural energy, this eye reflects harmony, vitality, and a deep connection to earth or forest. The green tones and slit pupil hint at reptilian roots and elemental power.

01

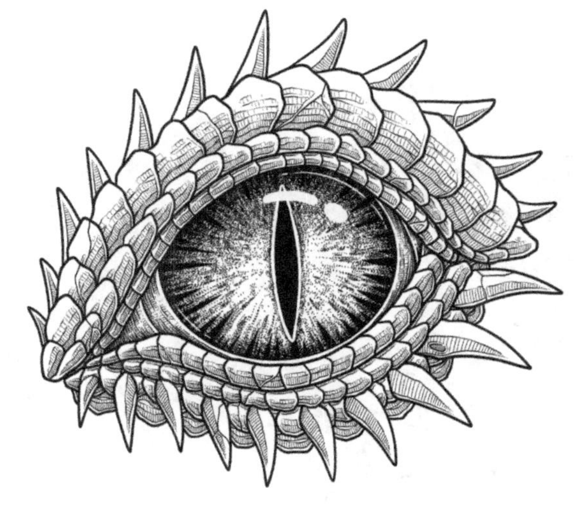

02

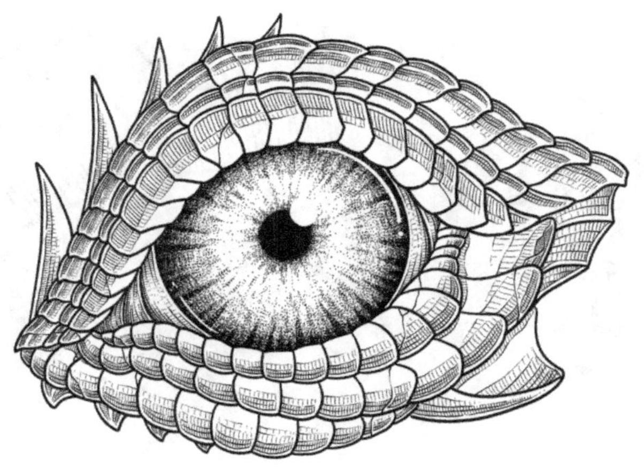

03

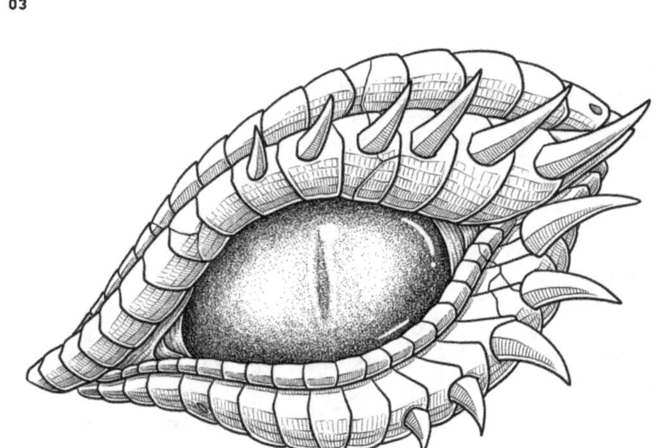

04

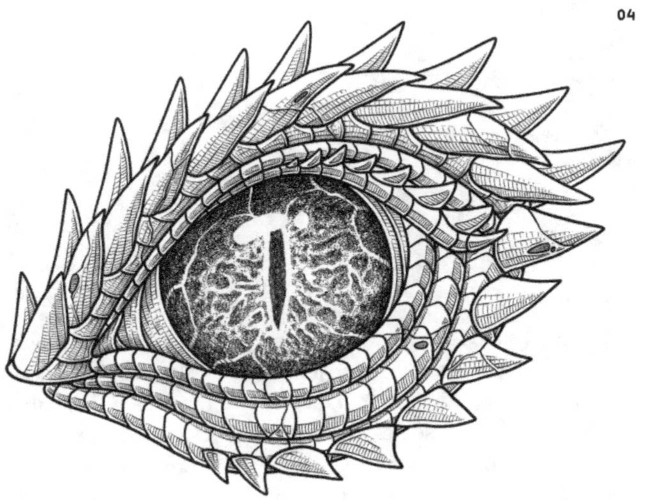

05

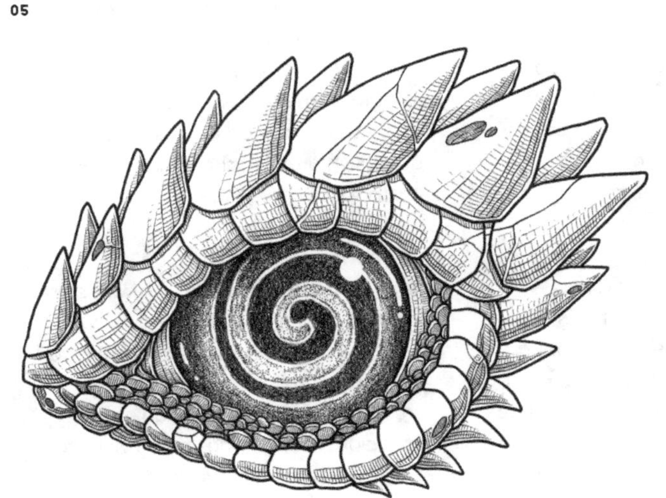

06

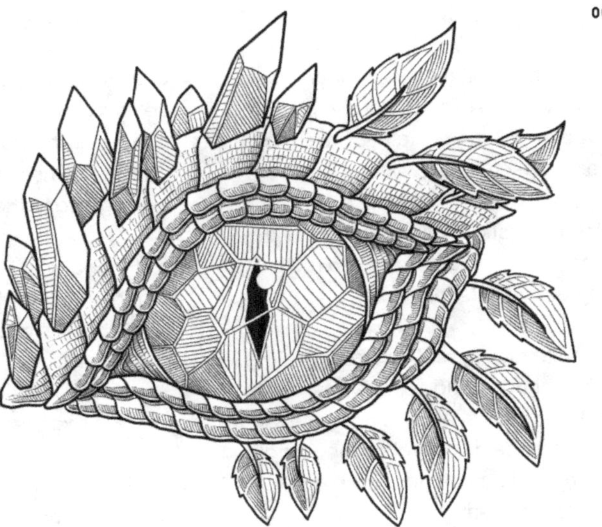

RIDGES, SPINES & CRESTS

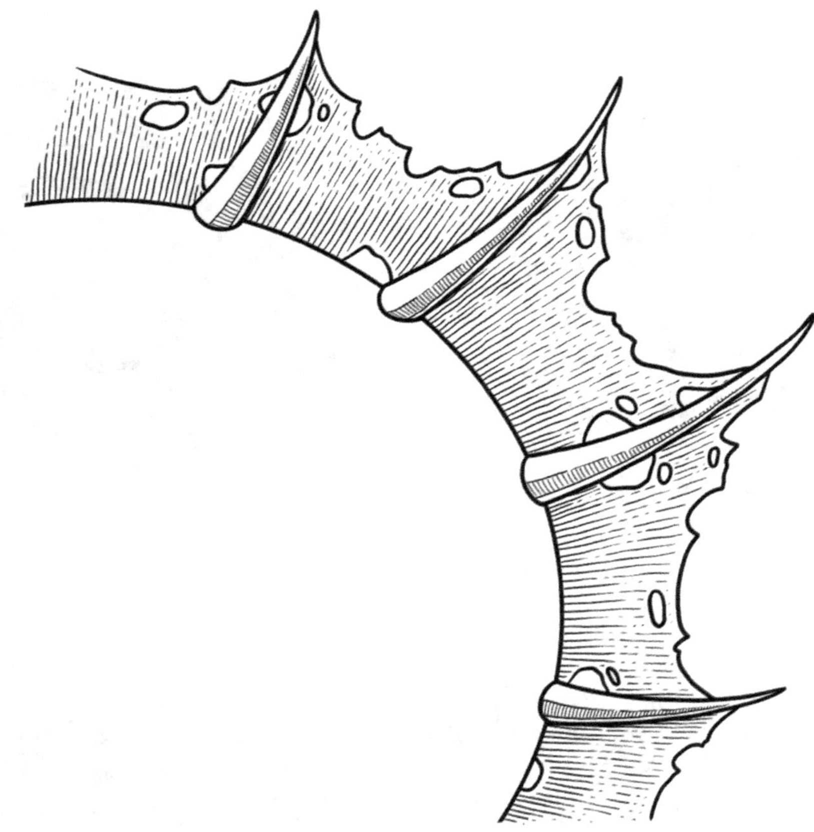

A creature's silhouette is often defined by the structures that run along its spine, from the crown of its head to the tip of its tail. These ridges, spines, or crests are more than decorative; they reveal the creature's origin, environment, and temperament. Whether jagged and weapon-like, soft and feathered, or fluid and finned, these features can transform a beast's character.

Spines may function as armour, display features, or sensory organs. A plated ridge might suggest a heavily armoured, defensive creature, while feathered crests convey lightness and agility. Fins hint at aquatic evolution, whereas barbs, thorns, and needles lean into more aggressive or tactical traits.

In the following section, you'll explore different ridge and spine types, each with its own visual language. Use them as reference or inspiration, and combine elements to create your own distinctive, fantastical creatures.

01. Barbed Spikes

Hooked and jagged, barbed spikes curl backwards like thorns or claws. These aggressive ridges give the beast a dangerous-looking silhouette and are often seen on battle-worn or territorial creatures that rely on intimidation and close combat.

02. Feathered

Soft, layered plumes run along the beasts' back, giving it a majestic or celestial presence. Feathered ridges are commonly found on air or sky beasts, adding a sense of lightness, speed, and avian grace to their design.

03.Finned

Smooth and flowing, finned ridges resemble the crests of exotic fish or marine reptiles. These soft, webbed structures are common among water and sea monsters, helping them glide effortlessly through ocean currents. Their streamlined shape suggests speed, agility, and an affinity with the deep.

04.Needle

Thin, rigid, and tightly spaced, needle spines stand upright like rows of metallic quills. These sharp features give the monster a tense, high-strung look—ideal for fast-moving, defensive creatures that lash out when threatened.

05.Plated

Broad and overlapping like armour plates, these ridges reinforce the spine with thick, protective segments. Plated spines, often seen on earthbound or heavily armoured beasts suggest durability, brute strength, and a slow but unstoppable presence.

06.Thorn

Long, curved, and hook-like thorn spines resemble sharpened talons growing along a beast's ridge. Their shape gives the impression of a sleek yet dangerous creature built for intimidation and precision. These spines add a vicious elegance to the silhouette, ideal for cunning or predatory beasts.

01

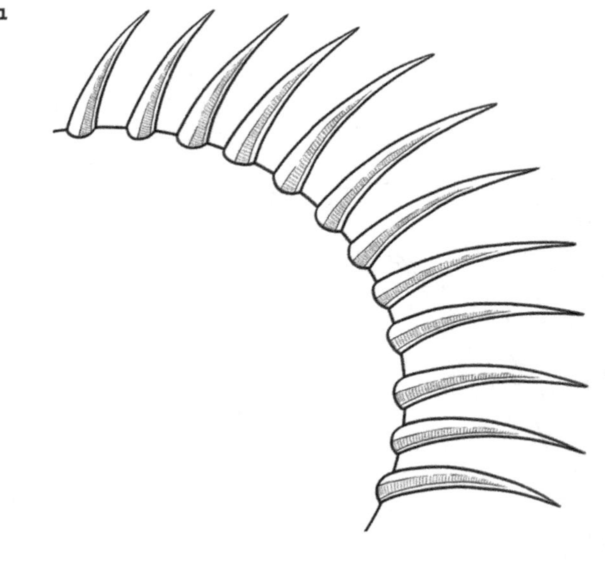

02

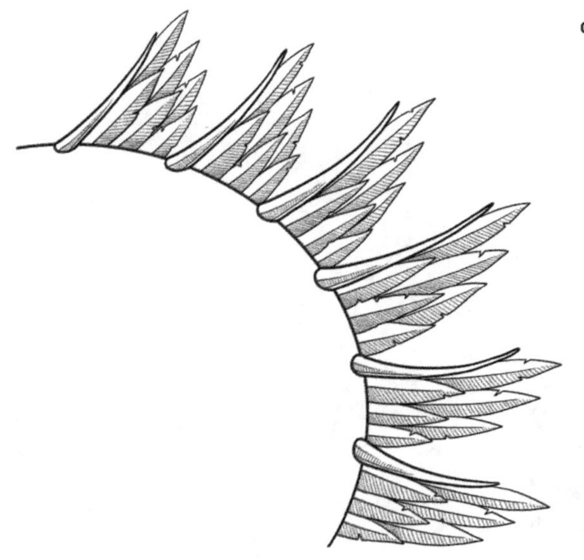

03

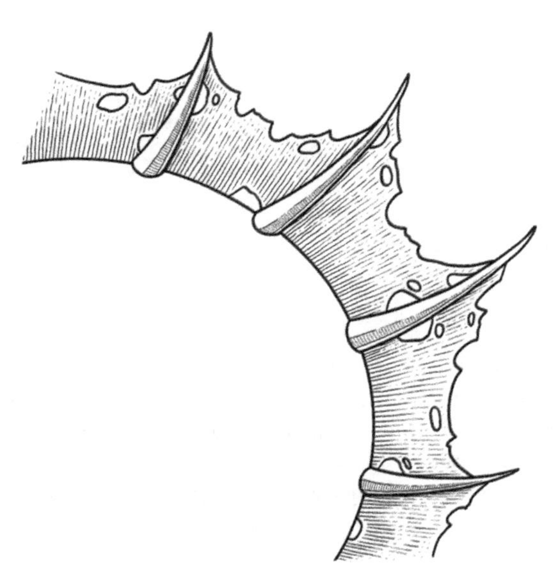

04

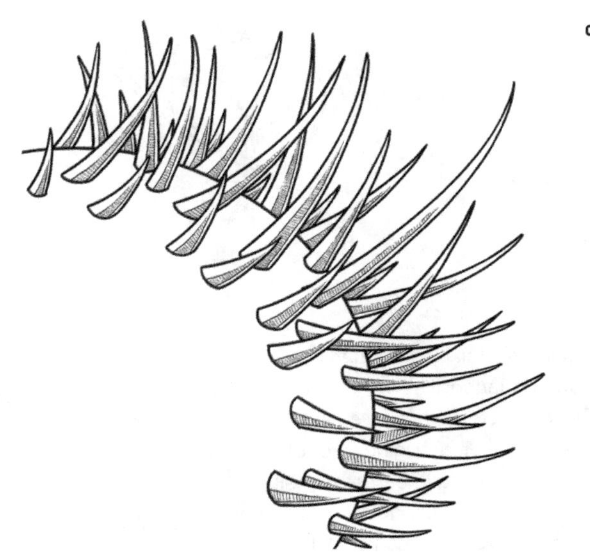

05

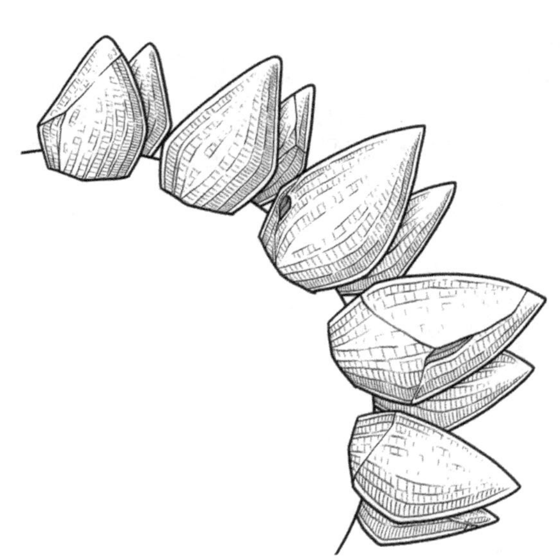

06

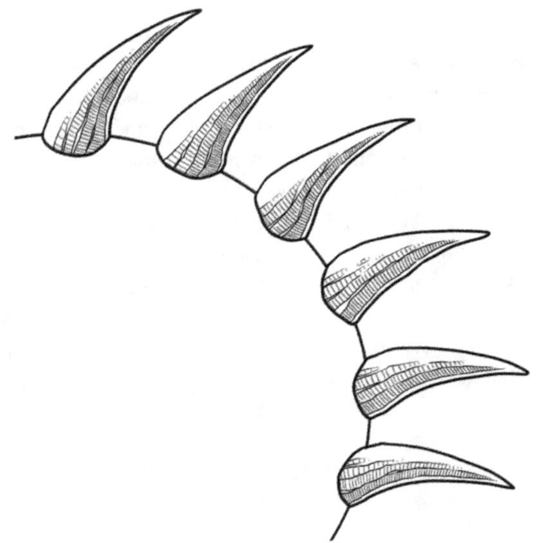

TAILS

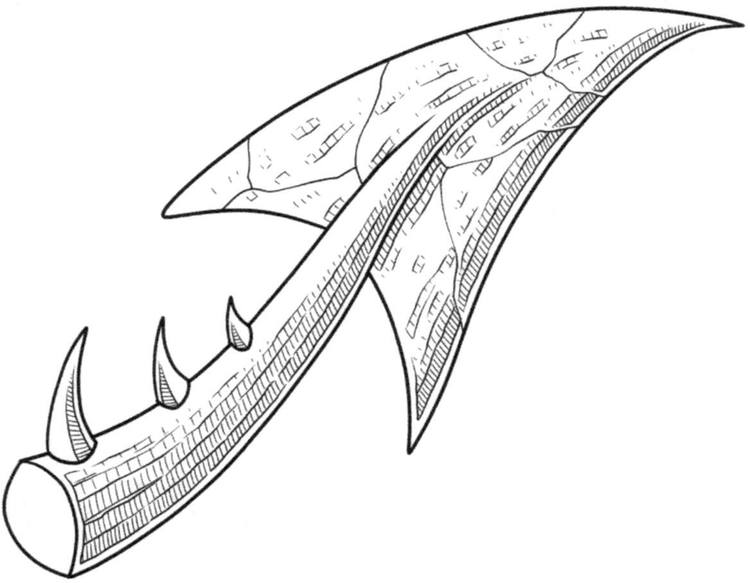

A creature's tail is more than a counterbalance; it's a powerful extension of its character. Whether sweeping through the air, dragging through ancient dust, or whipping in battle, the tail helps define a beast's silhouette, movement, and fighting style. It can signal mood, emphasise posture, or deliver devastating force in a single blow.

Tail types vary widely across species and environments. Some end in heavy clubs or razor-like spines, while others feature elegant fins, feathers, or fantastical elements like magical flames. These endings can function as weapons, display features, or clues to the creature's habitat and temperament.

In the following section, you'll explore a range of tail designs. Use them to inspire your creature's physicality, personality, and story, or mix and match details, forms, and textures to create monsters and beasts that feel unique, powerful and expressive.

01. Spade Tail

Long, slender, and flexible, the spade tail ends in a flat, pointed shape. Common in agile or airborne beasts, it helps with balance, manoeuvrability, and swift directional shifts in flight.

02. Clubbed Tail

Thick and heavy, this tail ends in a rounded or spiked club, ideal for delivering crushing blows. Often seen in land-dwelling beasts or battle-hardened monsters, it adds mass and menace to the design.

03. Spiked Tail Tip

Tapering to a point and lined with sharp spines or bony ridges, this tail doubles as a weapon. It adds a brutal, defensive edge to your monster and is perfect for creatures that lash out from behind.

04. Finned Tail Tip

This tail suggests speed and fluid motion and consists of decorative or aquatic-style fins. Common in sea or river beasts,

05. Fire Tip

Ending in a dramatic burst of flame, the fire tip of this tail glows with raw energy. It is ideal for elemental or magical monsters as a weapon and a striking visual centrepiece.

06. Feathered Tip

This tail conveys elegance and mystique. It is covered in soft feathers or ornamental plumage. Often seen on sky, spirit, or celestial beasts, it softens the creature's profile while adding movement and flair.

01

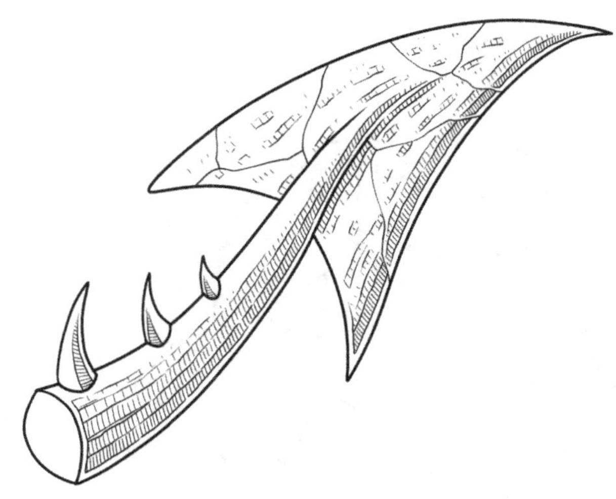

02

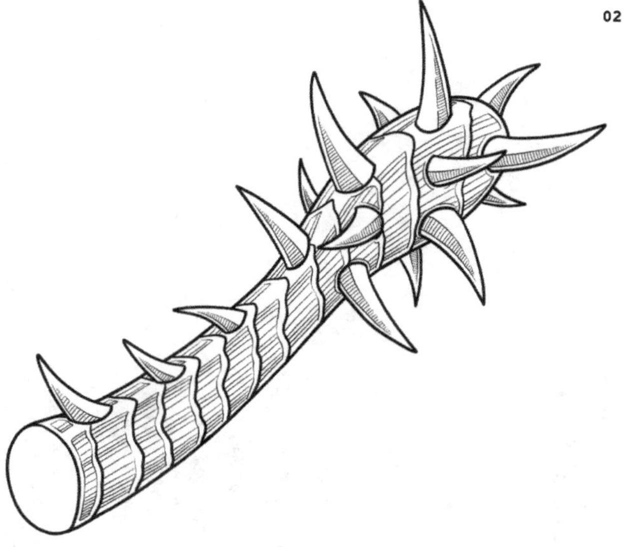

03

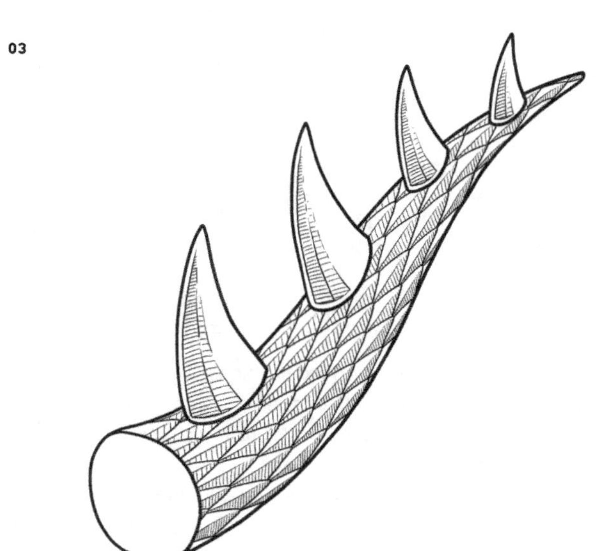

04

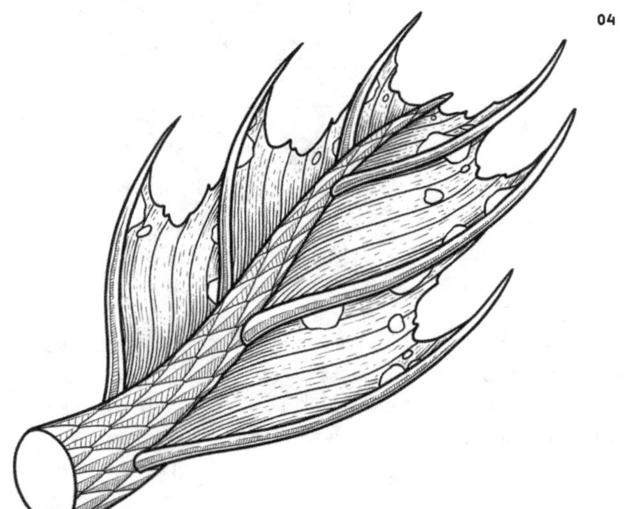

05

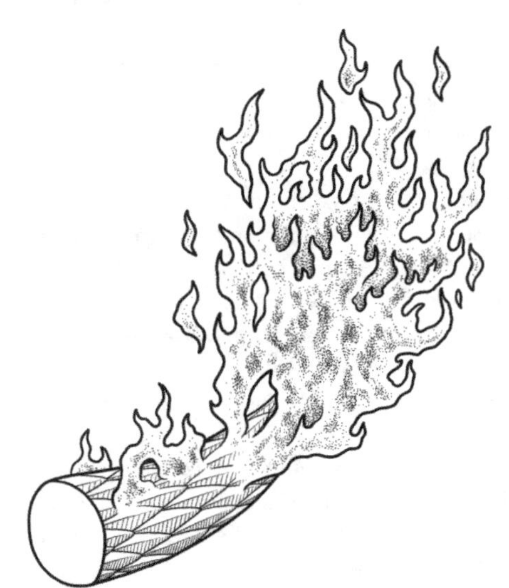

06

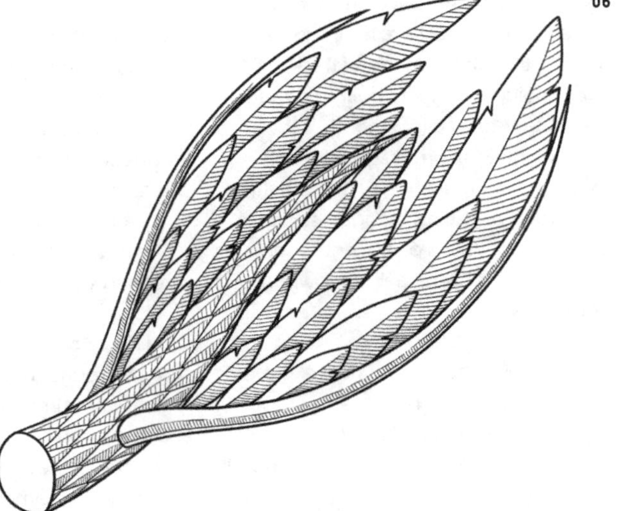

SCALES

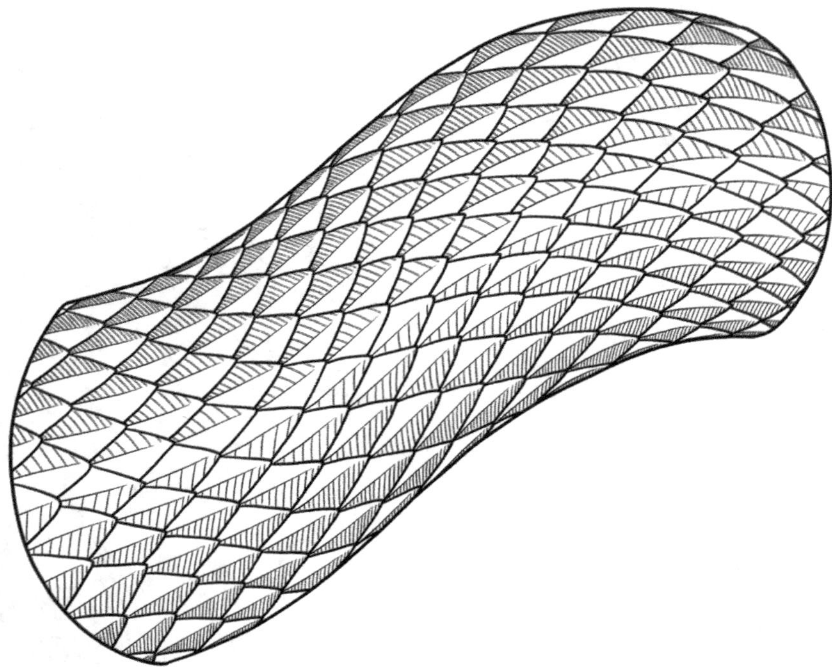

The surface of a creature tells its story. Every ridge, pattern, and plate contains clues about the being beneath, its strength, nature, and the world it was shaped by.

Skin and scale types vary widely across species and environments. Some creatures are covered in tightly knit diamond patterns that shimmer like metal or crystal. Others bear rugged, armour-like plates made of thick, overlapping segments built to deflect steel, claw, or magic. Smooth, serpentine textures glide effortlessly with each movement, suggesting agility, stealth, and precision. Rough, jagged surfaces evoke the rawness of ancient mountains or fractured rock, hinting at power drawn from primal forces.

In the following section, you'll explore a range of surface formations, each with its own character and visual rhythm. Use them to help shape the spirit and identity of your monster or beast.

01. Serpent Scales

Thin, overlapping, and slightly raised, serpent-like scales move smoothly with the body. They evoke agility and stealth, perfect for creatures that slither, coil, or creep through tight spaces. This scale type often belongs to leaner, faster beasts, subtle in appearance but deadly in motion.

02. Diamond Scales

Angular and tightly interlocked, diamond scales create a sharp, geometric pattern that reflects light like cut crystal. These surfaces suggest precision and durability, making them ideal for creatures with crystalline, elemental, or magical traits. Their sleek symmetry gives the beast a refined yet formidable presence.

03.Fish Scales

Small, rounded, and highly reflective, fish scales shimmer like armour in motion. Common in aquatic or sea-dwelling creatures, they create an impression of fluidity and camouflage beneath the water. These surfaces suggest a beast adapted for speed, grace, and survival in wet, shifting environments.

04.Plated (Armour-like) Scales

Large, segmented, and shield-like, plated scales resemble slabs of armour forged for battle. Often layered or ridged, they add bulk and toughness to a creature's form, making them ideal for earthbound or warlike beasts. These surfaces may reduce agility slightly but provide exceptional protection.

05.Circular Scales

Rounded and uniform, circular scales form a soft, organic pattern along the body. This type gives a balanced, neutral appearance, well-suited to creatures of land, air, or spirit. They suggest adaptability and versatility.

06.Rocky Scales

Jagged and uneven, rocky scales appear carved from stone. They suggest weight, age, and elemental power.

01

02

03

04

05

06

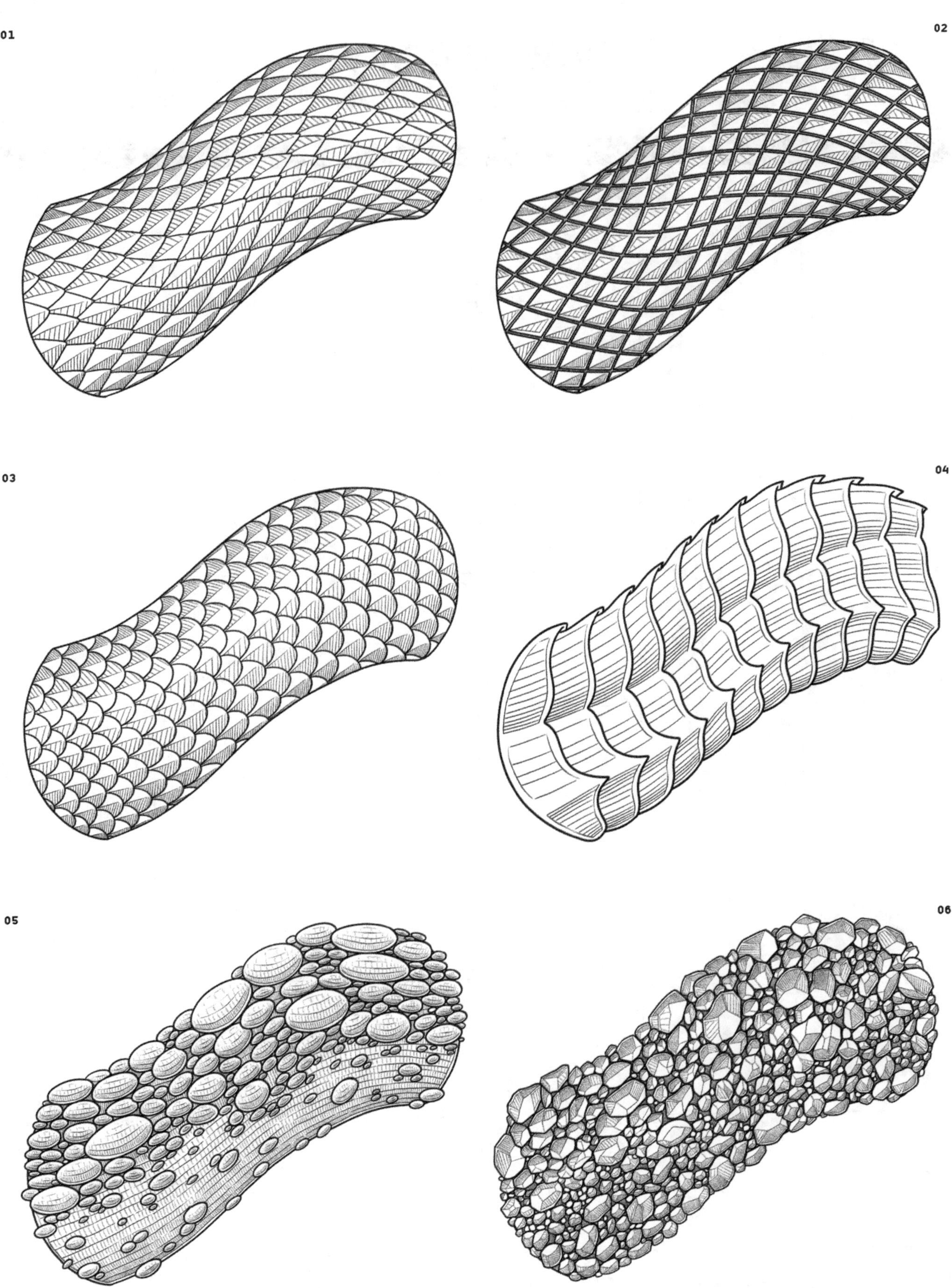

HOW TO DRAW
PRACTICE BOOK

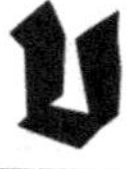
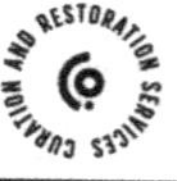

LEARN MORE

VAULTEDITIONS.COM

PRACTICE MAKES PERFECT
T R D — M R K

HOW TO DRAW
PRACTICE BOOK

PRACTICE MAKES PERFECT
T R D — M R K

Vault Editions Ltd

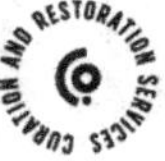

LEARN MORE

VAULTEDITIONS.COM

PRACTICE
MAKES
PERFECT
TRD MRK

HOW TO DRAW
PRACTICE BOOK

PRACTICE
MAKES
PERFECT
TRD MRK

Vault Editions Ltd

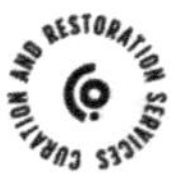

LEARN MORE

VAULTEDITIONS.COM

PRACTICE
MAKES
PERFECT
TRD MRK

HOW TO DRAW
PRACTICE BOOK

PRACTICE
MAKES
PERFECT
TRD MRK

CONCLUSION

Monsters and beasts take endless forms. From the myths and legends of ancient worlds to the stories we tell today, these beings can be grotesque or beautiful, terrifying or mesmerising. In this book, you've explored a diverse range of them — from familiar figures like zombies and vampires, to mythic icons such as Medusa and the centaur, and original creations born from pure imagination, like the alien and mutant rat. You've studied anatomy, movement, and character, and learned how features like eyes, scales, fins, and spikes can deepen the lore of your designs.

One of the most important lessons to remember is that monsters and beasts are never fixed. They can be reshaped, merged, and reinvented to tell entirely new stories. As you continue to develop your skills, treat every creature you draw as an experiment in creativity. Mix styles, push proportions, invent your own hybrids, and embrace the unexpected. Keep drawing, let your imagination evolve, and build a world that's entirely your own — alive with unique and extraordinary creatures.

ABOUT THE ARTIST

Syadat Baihaqi, known as Blasphemy Ink, is an illustrator specialising in dark, intricate artwork that draws on themes of death, mythology, and the occult. His black-and-white compositions often feature skeletal figures, decayed forms, and surreal, otherworldly imagery inspired by gothic art, metal music, and symbolic ideologies.

Blasphemy Ink's work is defined by its fine linework, rich textures, and a strong sense of atmosphere. Each illustration invites the viewer into a world where the grotesque meets the beautiful, where decay is rendered with precision and reverence. His style balances classical drawing techniques with a contemporary edge, resulting in pieces that feel both timeless and raw.

Syadat's art has been used across various creative projects, including album covers, apparel, and personal commissions. His illustrations are visually bold, emotionally charged, and deeply rooted in storytelling—offering a distinctive voice in the world of dark art.

LEARN MORE

At Vault Editions, our mission is to provide the highest-quality reference materials for artists and designers, offering meticulously curated resources that inspire and empower creativity. If you've found value in this book, we invite you to explore more of our expertly crafted titles at vaulteditions.com, where you'll discover a world of visual inspiration and practical tools designed to elevate your creative work.

REVIEW THIS BOOK

As a family-owned and operated independent publisher, reviews are essential to the success of our business. Please leave an honest review of this book wherever you purchased it.

JOIN OUR COMMUNITY

Are you the creative and curious type? If so, you will love our community on Instagram. Every day, we share bizarre and beautiful artwork ranging from 17th and 18th-century natural history and scientific illustrations to mythical beasts, ornamental designs, anatomical drawings and more; join our community of 300K+ people today by searching @vault_editions on Instagram.

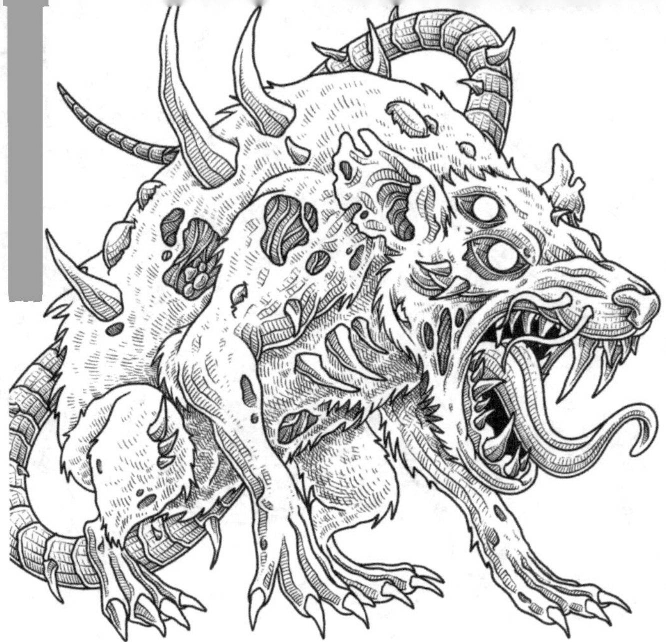

DOWNLOAD YOUR FILES

To enhance your creative journey, *How-to Monsters & Beasts* comes with a digital PDF version of the book and a specially designed set of Procreate brushes. These resources are tailored to help you refine your skills and streamline your workflow, whether working traditionally or digitally.

The digital PDF provides easy access to the book's contents on any device, so you can reference the designs anytime, anywhere. It's perfect for artists on the go, allowing you to study and practice whenever inspiration strikes.

The custom Procreate brushes are designed to support the Monsters and Beasts drawing process by helping you improve your draftsmanship and build stronger technical skills. They offer precision and flexibility as you sketch, refine, and finalise your artwork, making it easier to develop clean, confident lines and consistent forms.

Download yours now and get creating!

STEP ONE

Enter the following web address on a desktop or laptop computer in your web browser.

vaulteditions.com/pages/htm

STEP TWO

Enter the following password to access the download page:

htm837262sxda

STEP THREE

Follow the prompts to access your high-resolution files.

CONTACT

For technical support, please email:
info@vaulteditions.com

Copyright © 2025
Vault Editions Ltd

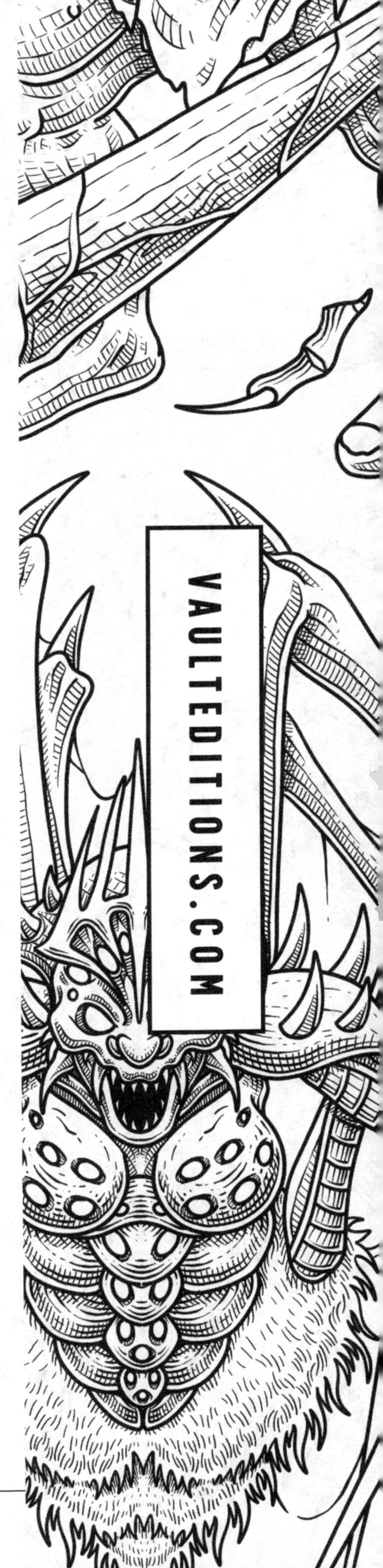

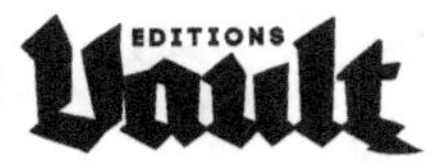

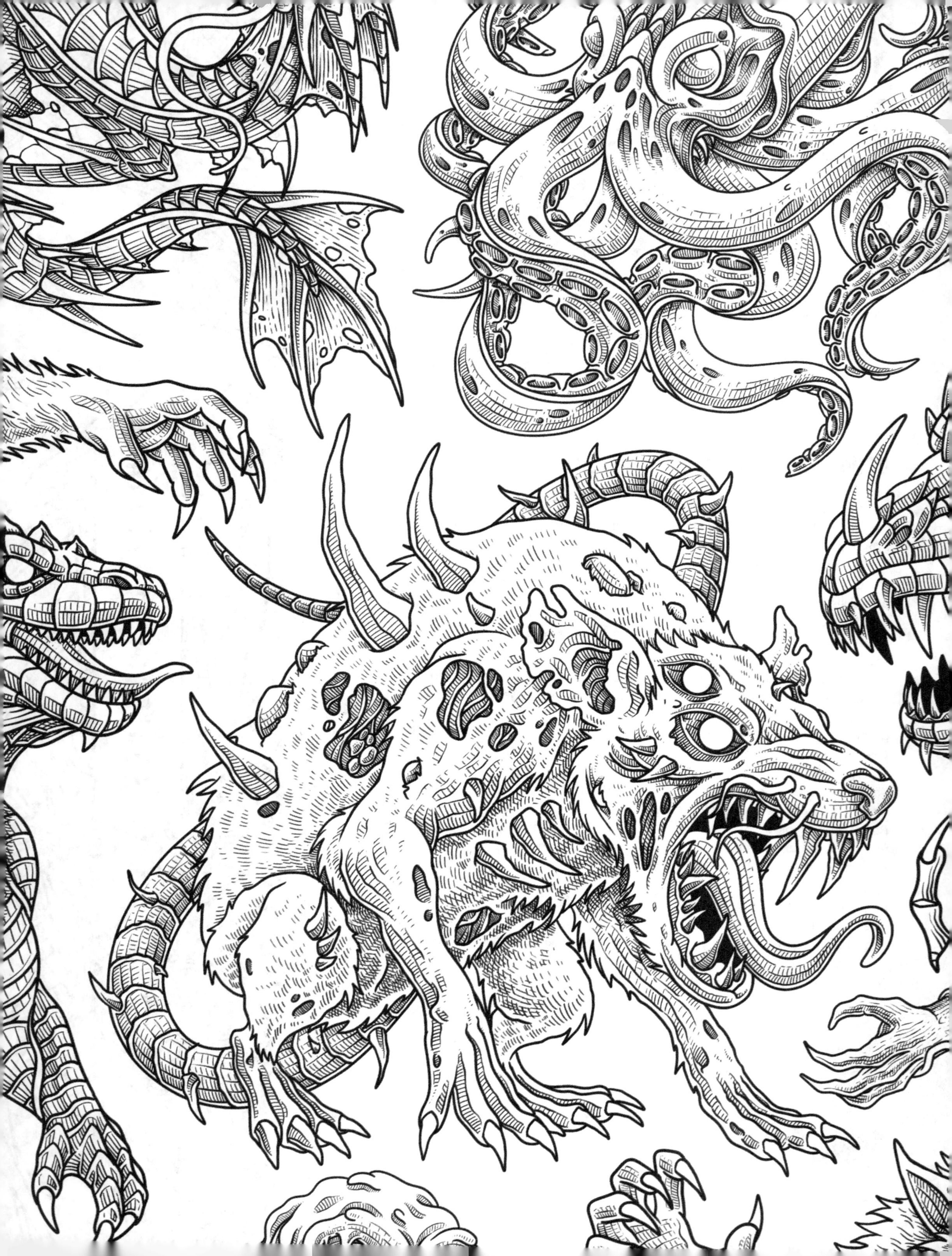